Cognitive Behavioral Therapy for Beginners

Cognitive Behavioral Therapy for Beginners lays out an experiential learning program replete with exercises to guide new clinicians, as well as more experienced therapists re-specializing in CBT, through the process of systematically implementing successful CBT interventions both for themselves and their clients. Each chapter examines a key construct in understandable terms, presenting an overarching view of how clinicians put these concepts and techniques into practice in typical as well as in difficult or unexpected scenarios. Readers will come away with a deep understanding, not just of the standard principles of CBT, but also of the real decisions and strategies that allow seasoned therapists to implement these principles in a way that maximizes the benefit to clients.

Amy Wenzel, PhD, ABPP is owner and president of Wenzel Consulting, LLC, and a clinical assistant professor of psychology in psychiatry at the University of Pennsylvania. She has authored or edited 21 previous books, many of which are on cognitive behavioral therapy (CBT).

Clinical Topics in Psychology and Psychiatry

Much of the available information relevant to mental health clinicians is buried in large and disjointed academic textbooks and expensive and obscure scientific journals. Consequently, it can be challenging for the clinician and student to access the most useful information related to practice. **Clinical Topics in Psychology and Psychiatry** includes authored and edited books that identify and distill the most relevant information for practitioners and presents the material in an easily accessible format that appeals to the psychology and psychiatry student, intern or resident, early career psychologist or psychiatrist, and the busy clinician.

Series Editor: Bret A. Moore, PsyD, Boulder Crest Retreat, Virginia, USA

Trial-Based Cognitive Therapy
A Handbook for Clinicians
Irismar Reis de Oliveira

Cognitive Behavioral Therapy for Preventing Suicide Attempts
A Guide to Brief Treatments Across Clinical Settings
Edited by Craig J. Bryan

Treating Disruptive Disorders
A Guide to Psychological, Pharmacological, and Combined Therapies
Edited by George M. Kapalka

Women's Mental Health Across the Lifespan
Challenges, Vulnerabilities, and Strengths
Edited by Kathleen A. Kendall-Tackett and Lesia M. Ruglass

Practical Psychopharmacology
Basic to Advanced Principles
Thomas L. Schwartz

Integrating Psychological and Pharmacological Treatments for Addictive Disorders
An Evidence-Based Guide
Edited by James Mackillop, George A. Kenna, Lorenzo Leggio, and Lara Ray

Neurodevelopmental Disorders in Children and Adolescents
A Guide to Evaluation and Treatment
Christopher J. Nicholls

Cognitive Behavioral Therapy for Beginners
An Experiential Learning Approach
Amy Wenzel

For more information about this series, please visit: www.routledge.com/Clinical-Topics-in-Psychology-and-Psychiatry/book-series/TFSE00310

Cognitive Behavioral Therapy for Beginners

An Experiential Learning Approach

Amy Wenzel

Routledge
Taylor & Francis Group
NEW YORK AND LONDON

First published 2019
by Routledge
52 Vanderbilt Avenue, New York, NY 10017

and by Routledge
2 Park Square, Milton Park, Abingdon, Oxon, OX14 4RN

Routledge is an imprint of the Taylor & Francis Group, an informa business

Library of Congress Cataloging-in-Publication Data
A catalog record for this title has been requested

ISBN: 978-1-138-96056-5 (hbk)
ISBN: 978-1-138-96058-9 (pbk)
ISBN: 978-1-315-65195-8 (ebk)

Typeset in Univers
by Swales & Willis Ltd, Exeter, Devon, UK

Contents

Series Editor's Foreword

Cognitive Behavioral Therapy for Beginners: An Experiential Learning Approach is the latest volume in one of Routledge's most popular series, Clinical Topics in Psychology and Psychiatry (CTPP). The overarching goal of CTPP is to provide mental health practitioners with practical information on psychological and psychopharmacological topics. Each volume is comprehensive but easy to digest and integrate into day-to-day clinical practice. It is multidisciplinary, covering topics relevant to the fields of psychology and psychiatry, and appeals to the student, novice, and senior clinician. Books chosen for the series are authored or edited by national and international experts in their respective areas, and contributors are also highly respected clinicians. The current volume exemplifies the intent, scope, and aims of the CTPP series.

Over the past several decades, cognitive and behavioral models of psychological care have grown at a breakneck pace. Previous surveys have revealed that approximately eight out of ten behavioral health professionals list these approaches as primary with regard to patient care. Considering the popularity of these models, it is reasonable to assume that a variety of training aides have come into existence. This is in fact the case. There are a number of cognitive behavioral therapy (CBT) "how to" books, videos, and websites dedicated to teaching the theoretical framework of CBT as well as its techniques. Although many therapists find these teaching aides useful in the development of their psychotherapeutic skills, a number of limitations are noted. For example, as discussed in the present volume, some therapists new to CBT find existing books and videos lacking with regard to managing patient's issues in the "moment". Although these sources of training are informative, for some, they do not capture the "spirit" of CBT. They provide little opportunity for reflection and contemplation, particularly when it comes to more complex and challenging patients.

In *Cognitive Behavioral Therapy for Beginners: An Experiential Learning Approach,* Dr. Amy Wenzel provides a superb overview of not only the "how" of CBT, but the "why" as well. Dr. Wenzel draws on her nineteen years of experience as a supervisor for hundreds of therapists, and her work at the Beck Institute for Cognitive Behavior Therapy, to help the new CBT therapist understand the key elements of CBT in easy-to-understand terms and provides relevant examples throughout the volume. In addition, she provides a number of reflective exercises that help the therapist develop a deeper understanding of the model. This book goes well beyond teaching terms and techniques. It is a book that teaches one how to be an effective CBT therapist.

I am convinced that *Cognitive-Behavioral Therapy for Beginners* will become one of the lead textbooks in training future psychotherapists in cognitive behavioral therapy. It will also function as an excellent review for experienced practitioners looking for an easily digestible presentation of basic but crucial components of effective delivery of this evidence-based approach.

Bret A. Moore, PsyD, ABPP
Series Editor
Clinical Topics in Psychology and Psychiatry

CHAPTER 1 BACKGROUND AND RATIONALE

Background and Rationale

CHAPTER 1

When psychotherapists hear the term, *cognitive behavioral therapy* (or CBT for short), they usually have a noticeable reaction. After all, CBT was quite a change from the traditional approaches to psychotherapy—psychodynamic psychotherapy and client-centered therapy—that were the dominant psychotherapeutic approaches in the 1950s and 1960s. Beginning in the 1970s, behavioral and cognitive psychotherapeutic approaches began to make a "splash" (or perhaps, I should say that they created more of a "tsumani") in the empirical research literature, when they were demonstrated to be efficacious in the treatment of a wide, wide range of emotional, adjustment, and behavioral problems. Landmark studies demonstrated that CBT is just as efficacious as psychotropic medications for moderate to severe instances of mental health disorders (e.g., Barlow, Gorman, Shear, & Woods, 2000; DeRubeis et al., 2005)—a notion that went against conventional thinking, which was that psychotherapies such as CBT are efficacious for mild clinical presentations but that psychotropic medications are essential when clinical presentations go beyond the mild. Moreover, data from naturalistic follow-up studies provided even more interesting and compelling evidence supporting CBT's impressive effects, as these studies found that relapse rates were lower for people who received CBT than people who took psychotropic medication for emotional disturbances (Barlow et al., 2000; Hollon et al., 2005).

If you are reading this book, then it is likely that you are about to embark on a journey in which you hope to develop competence in CBT. Of course, I hope that you are excited about this notion and that there is something about CBT that inherently draws you to it. However, it is entirely possible that you are reading this book for a course, or that the agency that employs you is requiring you to develop competence in CBT, and that you are not particularly keen on being told that you must learn (and presumably deliver) CBT. Before we move on further, I would like you to provide a reflection on what you think of when you hear the term, *CBT*. This will be one of many, many reflections in which you will engage as you work through this program. When responding to the questions below, please indicate the first things that come to mind when you think about CBT.

BOX 1 **INITIAL REFLECTION ON CBT**

What do you know about CBT that you find attractive?

What do you know about CBT that concerns you?

In the next several pages, allow me to describe the fundamental tenets of what I call *contemporary CBT*, or CBT that is practiced in a way that is informed by up-to-date theory, practice, empirical research, and scholarship. I outline stereotypes about CBT that I have encountered over the course of years of practice, training, supervision, and scholarship, and I share my view of the truths and misconceptions associated with these stereotypes. I describe some examples that I have witnessed first-hand in my clients, supervisees, trainees, and even in myself that illustrate the power that can be harnessed from CBT. Then, I will invite you to revisit the "first impressions" that you just described above and reconsider them in light of the information that I have presented.

Pre-test: Self-assessment of CBT Skills

Before proceeding, I would like you to first collect "baseline" information about your knowledge of, and skill in, CBT. The rationale underlying my request is that cognitive behavioral therapists conduct themselves as *practitioner-scientists*, meaning that they incorporate a scientific approach into their clinical work. Being a practitioner-scientist means two things: (a) that you use the scientific literature to inform your practice, and (b) that you collect data in session to evaluate the degree to which your interventions are achieving their desired aims. Those data could be scores on questionnaires, dimensional ratings (e.g., 0–10 Likert-type ratings) on constructs such as depression or anxiety, or observations of clients' behavior. Practitioner-scientists adjust their clinical work on the basis of these data, and in addition, the data inform clinicians of the degree to which clients are meeting their treatment goals and can move toward the completion of treatment.

We can apply the same framework to the acquisition of learning how to deliver a system of psychotherapy. That is, you can see where you stand in your knowledge of, and skill in, the psychotherapy to be learned before you begin the experiential learning program in earnest. When you have completed the experiential learning program, you can again see where you stand in these

Table 1.1 Pre-test: Self-assessment of CBT Skills

Please use the following scale to rate your perceived ability to deliver aspects of CBT.
0 = Not At All (0%)
1 = A Little (25%)
2 = Somewhat (50%)
3 = A Good Deal (75%)
4 = Extremely (100%)

1.	I have a sound understanding of the fundamental tenets of CBT.	0 1 2 3 4
2.	I have a sound understanding of cognitive behavioral theory.	0 1 2 3 4
3.	I am confident in my ability to develop a case formulation and treatment plan with clients.	0 1 2 3 4
4.	I have a sound understanding of the fundamentals of the therapeutic relationship in CBT.	0 1 2 3 4
5.	I am confident that I can cultivate a strong therapeutic relationship while simultaneously implementing CBT structure and strategy.	0 1 2 3 4
6.	I have a sound understanding of CBT session structure.	0 1 2 3 4
7.	I am confident in my ability to implement CBT session structure.	0 1 2 3 4
8.	I have a sound understanding of ways to implement cognitive restructuring with clients.	0 1 2 3 4
9.	I am confident in my ability to implement cognitive restructuring with clients.	0 1 2 3 4
10.	I have a sound understanding of ways to implement behavioral activation with clients.	0 1 2 3 4
11.	I am confident in my ability to implement behavioral activation with clients.	0 1 2 3 4
12.	I have a sound understanding of ways to implement problem solving with clients.	0 1 2 3 4
13.	I am confident in my ability to implement problem solving with clients.	0 1 2 3 4
14.	I have a sound understanding of ways to implement exposure with clients.	0 1 2 3 4
15.	I am confident in my ability to implement exposure with clients.	0 1 2 3 4
16.	I have a sound understanding of ways to implement mindfulness and acceptance skills with clients.	0 1 2 3 4
17.	I am confident in my ability to implement mindfulness and acceptance skills with clients.	0 1 2 3 4
18.	I have a sound understanding of ways to implement relapse prevention with clients.	0 1 2 3 4
19.	I am confident that I can implement relapse prevention with clients.	0 1 2 3 4

domains and evaluate the degree to which you have changed. In this spirit, I encourage you to take this self-assessment of your CBT skills as a "pre-test." I will ask you to take this test again in the final chapter of the book, so that you can evaluate the ways in which this experiential learning program allowed you to grow as a cognitive behavioral therapist.

What did you notice about your responses? Did you tend to score differently on the questions assessing understanding than the questions assessing your confidence in delivering aspects of CBT? Don't worry if you gave yourself low ratings (or even if you did not fully understand some of the terminology included in the questions). The purpose of this book is to guide you through, step-by-step, so that you can learn core CBT strategies to use with your clients, and along the way, gain some practice in applying them to your own life in an experiential manner. This pre-test is just a starting point. My hypothesis is that you will be pleasantly surprised to observe the change in your ratings when you retake this test at the end of the book. In fact, low scores on many of these items can be viewed in a positive light, as they allow for tremendous growth to be achieved throughout out the course of this experiential learning program.

CBT's Fundamental Tenets

Let's begin with some of the most basic, fundamental tenets of CBT. These general principles serve almost as "meta-guidelines" that will help you to steer the overall course of your practice with clients. Read through these tenets and my commentary about them.

CBT is Active, Problem-focused, and Time-sensitive

CBT emerged in a time in which it was common for clients to attend psychotherapy for years, often scheduling more than one appointment per week. The idea underlying many psychotherapeutic approaches of the time was that clients needed space in a safe environment to develop insight into their emotional distress, unhealthy relationships, poor decision making, and so on, and once insight was achieved, they would be able to readily translate it into meaningful change. The activities that were pursued in these sessions included exploration of childhood relationships and events, discussion of emotional experiences, analysis of dreams, and examination of clients' reactions to their therapist (i.e., transference) and their therapists' reactions to them (i.e., countertransference).

This is not at all to say that the exploration of childhood relationships and events, discussion of emotional experiences, analysis of dreams, and examination of clients' reactions to their therapist and their therapists' reactions to them are *unimportant* in psychotherapy. In many instances in this book, I provide examples of ways in which some of these activities are pursued within a CBT framework. Instead, cognitive behavioral therapists believe that therapeutic work focused *solely* on developing insight, exploring the past, and cultivating the therapeutic relationship is insufficient and inefficient, and that the aims of psychotherapy could be achieved more directly with a more active, problem-focused approach.

What does an active, problem-focused approach look like? In the research literature, many CBT protocols that are 10, 12, 16, or 20 sessions in length have been evaluated (e.g., Elkin et al., 1989; Safren et al., 2009). This is not to say that these are "magic numbers." When I explain this point to my clients, I say that it was a necessity for researchers to define a specific number of sessions as comprising a CBT protocol, so that they could be sure that each research participant was given the same amount of therapy. In reality, in "real life" clinical practice with "real life" clients, therapists are not limited to an exact number of sessions (unless an insurance company indicates that it will only reimburse a maximum number of sessions, but that is a different story). I have seen some clients for only four or five sessions, but they left satisfied with the "product" that they received, and they gave me the feedback that, not only did they view the problems that they brought to treatment as being resolved, but they also had confidence that they would be able to continue implementing what they had learned into their lives even if we were no longer meeting regularly. In contrast, I have other clients on my caseload who I have seen for more than 100 sessions. Usually, these are clients who have relatively complicated clinical presentations, such as a history of trauma, a personality disorder, chronic depression, or "bad luck" that results in them facing recurrent stressors that are out of their control. Am I still doing quality CBT with these longer-term cases? Absolutely, because I am implementing an active, problem-focused approach no matter how many sessions I have worked with them.

In Chapter 4 of this volume, you will learn more about CBT's session structure. Session structure is one aspect of CBT that makes it active and problem-focused. Rather than allowing their clients to meander into a session of "unloading" or providing endless detail about their life problems (unless clients specifically express a desire to do so), cognitive behavioral therapists gracefully and sensitively structure the session, so that clients think carefully about what they would like to accomplish in session, and so that there is space for something to be done to address their life problems. My motto, then, is for each of my clients to leave each session with something more than they came with, whether that "something more" is a solution to a problem, a new way of viewing a problem, acceptance, a skill or a tool to implement between sessions, and so on. Psychotherapy requires a large investment of time, energy, and (often) money, so it is my belief that the efficient delivery of services shows sensitivity and respect for this investment.

The "Heart" of CBT is the Case Formulation

CBT's *case formulation* is the application of cognitive behavioral theory to the individual client's clinical presentation. You will learn much more about cognitive behavioral case formulation when you read the next chapter, Chapter 2 of this volume. Although case formulation is important in any therapeutic approach (Eells, 2007), the role it plays in CBT cannot be underestimated. In fact, in a 2016 lunch meeting I had with Dr. Aaron T. Beck, who is regarded by most as the "father" of CBT, we concluded that the CBT case formulation is the "heart" of CBT. The reason case formulation plays such a central role in CBT is because (a) it provides a coherent framework for understanding the development, maintenance, and exacerbation of a client's mental health problems; (b) it provides a template for integrating disparate pieces of information about a client's history; (c) this understanding, in turn, provides clear pathways for intervention; and (d) it makes events that transpire throughout the course of therapy, especially those that impact the therapeutic relationship, understandable.

Thus, cognitive behavioral therapists do not simply "jump" into psychotherapy and see what direction it takes. Rather, they are mindful of cognitive behavioral theory, and in the early sessions when they are getting to know their client, they are assimilating what they are learning about the client into their formulation, while simultaneously developing hypotheses about how the client got to where he or she is and where to go from here. They are thinking critically about the most salient aspects of the client's clinical presentation (in light of cognitive behavioral theory) and formulating a plan for intervention. All the while, they are cognizant of the fact that this formulation will evolve over the course of treatment, as they continue to get to know their client, observe the way in which their client responds to positive and stressful events in his or her life, and develop a felt sense of what it is like to form a relationship with the client.

CBT is Collaborative and Transparent

When I first meet with my clients and educate them about CBT, I say the following: "I want you to know that by initiating a course of CBT, we are embarking on a collaboration. I have knowledge and expertise about psychology, psychotherapy, and CBT, specifically. But you are the expert on your own life circumstances. It would be presumptuous of me to think that I know exactly what it's like to be in your shoes at work, at home, or in other circumstances in which you find yourself. So, when we work together, we bring our respective areas of expertise to the table, we put our heads together, and we figure out ways to make progress in addressing the problems that you would like to address in psychotherapy." As will be discussed further in Chapter 4 of this volume on session structure, part of the collaborative process is obtaining feedback from clients to ensure that they are "on board" with the direction in which the session is going. If a client expresses hesitation or ambivalence, such a response is taken seriously, and the cognitive behavioral therapist does not proceed further until the client's concerns have been resolved, and the client is either more in agreement with the intervention, or another intervention is decided upon.

In addition to its collaborative nature, CBT is also transparent. Transparency in CBT means that the client is "kept in the loop," such that he or she is educated about CBT principles and the rationale underlying recommendations made by the therapist. Cognitive behavioral therapists live by the somewhat humorous adage that we want to "put ourselves out of business," such that we want our clients to become their own cognitive behavioral therapists. Thus, cognitive behavioral therapists provide their clients with explanations about theory, expected mechanisms of change (i.e., the way in which we expect our interventions to work), and, when relevant, results from empirical research, so that they can begin to put their own words onto the principles that they are learning.

CBT is Conducted from a Stance of Collaborative Empiricism

We just finished a section emphasizing the collaborative nature of CBT. Here, we add the focus on empiricism. *Empiricism* means that we base the conclusions that we draw on facts, observations, or data, rather than on conjecture, hearsay, or speculation. *Collaborative empiricism* refers to a stance in which the therapist and client, together and as equal members of the team, examine all of the facts, data, evidence, observations, and so on that contribute to a situation in the client's life being as it is, and then draw the most logical, balanced, and helpful conclusion on the basis of those facts, data, evidence, and observations. Analogies that are frequently used by expert cognitive behavioral therapists are that the therapist and client are serving as co-detectives on a case, evaluating the evidence before making an accusation about a crime, or as co-scientists, analyzing the data before drawing a conclusion and disseminating results from the experiment.

Another way to understand collaborative empiricism is from a "just the facts ma'am" perspective. Cognitive behavioral therapists encourage their clients to put the greatest weight on factual information in making sense of upsetting situations. Too often, when we are faced with upsetting situations, we make many assumptions about what is happening or reasons underlying what is happening, and we base our decisions about how to address the situation on these assumptions, which may or may not be true. CBT helps people to recognize when assumptions are being made and to slow down and verify them before acting on them. At the same time, cognitive behavioral therapists do not want their clients to discount their emotional responses; in fact, in *dialectical behavior therapy* (DBT), one seminal treatment approach within the family of cognitive behavioral therapies, clients are encouraged to pay close attention to their emotional responses, because negative emotions provide important information that something is not right or needs to be adjusted (Linehan, 1993, 2015). In other words, emotional responses are a signal that something in our lives needs to be addressed, and we gather factual evidence to understand what is happening and what needs to be done. This overlap between the factual mind and the reasonable mind is called the *wise mind* by therapists who practice DBT.

CBT is Strategic

A few years back, I wrote a book on strategic decision making in CBT (Wenzel, 2013). I define a *strategy* as a thoughtful intervention that is delivered in psychotherapy that has its basis in theory, empirical research, and clinical experience. In my book, I outlined four principles of CBT strategy: (a) that it follows directly from the case formulation; (b) that it is implemented in collaboration with the client; (c) that it is delivered in a way that is meant to move treatment forward; and (d) that it is seen through in its entirety, rather than abandoned partway through on the basis of assumptions that the therapist may be making. Points (a) and (b) have been described in previous sections. However, allow me to expand upon the latter two points.

Some scholars who reviewed my 2013 book did not "get" what I meant by point (c)—that the intervention the therapist selects must move treatment forward. Isn't that the point of any intervention in treatment? Why wouldn't a therapist do something that would move treatment forward? Obviously, this point requires some explanation. This point, as well as many additional ones that I will describe in this book, arises from my experience as a supervisor of therapists in programs designed to achieve competency in CBT. To facilitate the supervisory experience, I regularly listen to CBT sessions and rate them according to the Cognitive Therapy Rating Scale (CTRS; Young & Beck, 1980). At this point in my career, I have had the privilege of working with several hundred supervisees who aimed to acquire competency in CBT, which means that I have reviewed around 2,000 recordings of CBT sessions. Thus, I have gathered a great deal of "data" on the efficient and effective delivery of CBT.

There were times when I reviewed these recordings of CBT sessions that it seemed as if the therapist selected an intervention strategy "out of thin air." It did not seem to follow from the formulation, nor did it seem relevant to the material that was being discussed in session. When I would gently question therapists in this position about the rationale for the strategy that was chosen, in most cases, they would respond sheepishly that they did not know why they chose the intervention. In some cases, they wondered whether they thought that they should be doing something, simply because they were attempting to "do" CBT; in other cases, they assumed that their client would *not* respond to a particular CBT strategy and were proceeding forward in a vague, general manner, trying not to do anything for which the client might not be ready. These sessions were almost invariably rated lower on the CTRS than sessions in which I heard a coherent strategy that advanced the client's treatment goals. This principle of strategy, then, encourages therapists to be thoughtful about and have a clear rationale for the interventions that they deliver—so that the intervention advances treatment. When I supervise therapists who hope to achieve competency in CBT, the most frequent question I ask is, "What strategy were you delivering in this session?" If they have difficulty succinctly articulating the strategy, then in many cases the intervention that they have delivered is not cogent enough to move treatment forward in that session.

I can imagine that the novice cognitive behavioral therapist might be having quite a reaction to these two paragraphs, entertaining thoughts, such as "I'll never get this" or "This is not what I expected." If these are your reactions (or if you are having a similarly aversive reaction), please take heart. CBT trainers want you to be successful. CBT trainers feel passionately about the approach being disseminated. The last thing we want is for CBT to be inaccessible to therapists or to clients. I liken the acquisition of skill in CBT much as I do to learning how to drive a car. When we are in our teenage years, and our parents are driving with us, we are encouraged to focus solely on the "nuts and bolts" of driving—paying attention to the road and to the core aspects of driving without engaging in superfluous activities, such as talking to others or listening to the radio. Over time, however, the "nuts and bolts" of driving become automatic, freeing up our cognitive resources to devote to other things. Such is the same with CBT. Once the basic "flow" of the session has been practiced, it will become second nature to the therapist-in-training, freeing up cognitive resources to think conceptually and strategically, such that the intervention chosen will, indeed, be associated with a distinct expected mechanism of change. In fact, ways to implement strategic CBT will be discussed in all of the subsequent chapters, so after reading this book in its entirety, I expect the reader to emerge with a sense of confidence about implementing interventions that will, indeed, move treatment forward.

The final piece of CBT strategy—the fact that it is seen through in its entirety without being abandoned—also deserves some comment. Again, on the basis of my experience supervising therapists who hope to become certified cognitive behavioral therapists, I have seen on many occasions that therapists can get "cold feet" when they are trying to deliver a strategic intervention. In other words, they start to wonder if the client is having a negative reaction to the intervention, or the client goes in a different direction (as clients often do), and they conclude that the intervention is no longer appropriate and instead decide to follow the client's lead. Let me state at the outset that I am *not* suggesting that a cognitive behavioral therapist should ignore a client's lead; indeed, following the client's lead is an important part of a client-centered approach, which I believe unequivocally that CBT is, and is a point on which I elaborate further in Chapter 3 of this volume. Rather, before veering off in a direction other than the one in which you and the client agreed, collaboratively, to pursue, I suggest that you pause, and then continue thoughtful collaboration, saying something such as "We'd been talking about [insert topic], but I notice that [insert topic] is coming up here. What do you think is best—should we table what we are discussing about [insert topic] and shift our attention to [insert topic]?"

The results of asking such a question are usually striking. In the vast majority of the cases, clients will express gratitude for "keeping them on track," saying something such as "This is exactly what I need—someone to step in when I start to veer off in a different direction. That's part of my problem and why I'm looking for help." What I take such a comment to mean is that, if I had not thoughtfully posed the question of the direction to take when the client began to veer in a direction that was different than the one that formed the basis for the strategic intervention, then I would have assumed that I should abandon the intervention, thereby reinforcing what very well might be a quintessential example of the client's unhelpful way of addressing his or her life problems. We cannot evaluate whether a therapeutic intervention is successful unless we implement it fully and evaluate the degree to which it is effective. If we implement it "half way," or abandon it part-way through, then we set up a "self-fulfilling prophesy" for it to be unsuccessful, and our actions will have inadvertently contributed to the lack of efficacy associated with the intervention.

Thus, strategic cognitive behavioral therapists see their interventions through in their entirety. If the client veers off in a different direction, they ask the client directly whether he or she thinks that the new direction is more appropriate to take. If the client maintains that the new direction takes precedence, from a collaborative stance (see previous CBT tenet), they follow where the client is going, though they make a note of the intervention that they were delivering, so that they can revisit it in the future. This latter point is important (i.e., revisiting the intervention in the future), so that it does not model a haphazard approach to life's problems. However, if the client agrees that the new direction is a tangent that is less important than the topic at hand, then the therapist has modeled a new way of maintaining focus and organization in addressing the client's life problem.

Work Done Between Sessions is Just as Important as Work Done In Session

If we do not want our clients to be in therapy indefinitely, then it is important that they develop the ability to generalize the learning that they achieved in session to their lives outside of sessions. The most direct way to achieve this aim is for clients to do some systematic work between sessions. Historically, this between-session work has been called *homework*, although many CBT experts are moving away from this term and are instead using language such as *action plan* or *practice*. Research shows that there is a tight association between the degree to which therapists emphasize homework in session, as well as the degree to which clients embrace homework, and, ultimately, outcome in CBT (Kazantzis, Whittington, & Dattilio, 2010). Much more discussion about (and tips for maximizing!) between-session work will be described in Chapter 4 of this volume.

Summary

CBT is a psychotherapeutic approach that is meant to help clients achieve substantial (and positive) changes in their ability to regulate emotion, solve problems, and live a quality life. When they deliver CBT, cognitive behavioral therapists are mindful of these six tenets and use them to guide the decisions that they make during the session. Some therapists-in-training find that these tenets are very sensible and that they are generally already living their lives according to them. In these cases, they generally experience a smooth transition to delivering CBT with their clients. Other therapists-in-training find these tenets to be a bit foreign and different than their view of what psychotherapy should be. If you are in this latter group, it is okay. In fact, by working through this CBT for Beginners program, you will be accomplishing a very important goal of CBT—that of *psychological flexibility*. Psychological flexibility is defined as "the ability to contact the present moment more fully as a conscious human being, and to change or persist in behavior when doing so serves valued ends" (Hayes, Luoma, Bond, Masudam, & Lillis, 2006; p. 7). In other words, by giving CBT a "fair shot," working through this workbook, and gaining practice in the delivery of CBT to clients, you will be exemplifying an open stance to learning something new that is a bit inconsistent with your preferences and proclivities. Regardless of whether you choose to continue practicing CBT when you are done with the program, you will have bettered yourself as a clinician by truly immersing yourself into an approach to theory and practice that has significantly influenced the field and by developing a tolerance for trying something that is out of your comfort zone.

Common Misconceptions About CBT

Although I regularly encounter many therapists who are eager to learn and acquire skill in CBT, I encounter a fair number of therapists who have reservations. Oftentimes, these reservations have their basis in stereotypes that have emerged about this approach, and they are surprised when I give them a different perspective. In this section, I outline some of the most common misconceptions that I have encountered, and I supply alternative perspectives that have their basis in my clinical and scholarly experience.

CBT is Superficial and is not "Deep" Enough for Complex Clinical Presentations

As you will see as you work through this book, CBT provides a framework for therapists to deliver many skills and tools to clients, which are expected to lessen their emotional distress and improve their ability to engage in proper self-care, solve problems, and follow through with action plans. Most clients believe that the acquisition of these skills is invaluable and remark that they wished they would have been taught these skills by their parents or teachers when they were children.

However, some people believe that this is where CBT's usefulness ends, such that CBT is a sound approach for clients who need concrete tools, but for those who have "deeper" issues or complex clinical presentations, it falls short. In reality, CBT, indeed, goes far, far beyond the simple delivery and acquisition of skills and tools. As mentioned previously in the discussion of case formulation, the underlying theory provides a rich framework for understanding the development, maintenance, and exacerbation of clients' clinical presentations. As you will see when you read Chapter 2 of this volume, this theory allows for an understanding not only of the typical thoughts, emotions, and behavioral responses that clients exhibit when they are faced with a situational stressor in their lives, but it also provides a framework for understanding beliefs and habitual behavioral patterns that underlie these situational responses. Many cognitive behavioral therapists believe that clients realize the greatest amount of change when these underlying beliefs and habitual behavioral patterns serve as the ultimate target of treatment (Wenzel, 2012). Such underlying beliefs and behavioral patterns are, indeed, quite "deep," having been molded over time by previous experiences and that often feel as though they are the very core of the individual. You will not learn a great deal about belief modification in this book. Nevertheless, as you acquire skill in the "basics," there is a wealth of resources available for you to gain competence in the delivery of belief modification techniques.

In addition, cognitive behaviorally-based treatment packages have been developed *specifically* to address complex and chronic clinical presentations, many of which are assumed by people unfamiliar with CBT to be a better match for insight-oriented psychotherapies. For example, *schema therapy* is a treatment approach developed by Jeffrey Young, who had trained and collaborated with Aaron T. Beck (Young, Klosko, & Weishaar, 2003). In his clinical experience, clients with personality disorders, chronic depression, and/or a history of trauma are often characterized by distinct cognitive orientations called *schemas* (e.g., mistrust, abandonment) that create enough rigidity that it is difficult for them to form a strong therapeutic relationship or otherwise embrace what "traditional" CBT had to offer. Using traditional CBT as a foundation, Dr. Young integrated approaches and techniques from other types of psychotherapies, such as *Gestalt therapy* and *object-relations therapy*, to activate and reshape these schemas. Research shows that it is highly efficacious in treating clients with personality disorders, including borderline personality disorder (Masley, Gillanders, Simpson, & Taylor, 2012). Although a full description of schema therapy is beyond the scope of this book, it is introduced here as one example of a cognitive behavioral approach that is "deep" and is efficacious and appropriate for complex clinical presentations.

There is a Checklist of Things I "Must" Do if I am to be Doing CBT the "Right" Way

Many of my supervisees worry about whether they are doing CBT the "right" way, and conversely, they wonder if they forgot to implement an aspect of session structure or a cognitive behavioral intervention, that they have then implemented CBT the "wrong" way. In reality, there is very little that "must" be done in any one session for it to be a CBT session. Instead, CBT structure and cognitive and behavioral strategic intervention serve as guidelines or heuristics to make sessions (and the overall course of treatment) run more or less effectively. In my experience, there are really only a few core features of CBT that are present in almost all courses of therapy with clients:

1. The therapist attempts to understand the client's clinical presentation in light of cognitive behavioral theory (i.e., develops some sort of a case formulation).
2. The therapist and client work together to decide how best to use the time in session, as well as the goals to focus on across the courses of treatment (i.e., the active, organized, and systematic approach to addressing the client's life problems).
3. The therapist and client work together to decide how best to translate the work done in session to the client's life (i.e., between-session work).

In other words, therapists deliver in their intervention in a thoughtful and systematic manner—one of the principles of strategy that I introduced in the previous section. Even so, I can think of select instances in which a therapist was, indeed, "doing" CBT even if one of these three features was not in place, such that even when one or more of these features was not in place, CBT was not necessarily being done the "wrong" way.

For example, even the most seasoned cognitive behavioral therapists will have instances in which a client is in crisis, or a client expresses a need to unload, and the "agenda" of therapy is put on hold. In other words, the active, organized, and systematic approach to addressing the client's life problems does not always occur in every single CBT session. I vividly remember a time when I found myself in this position, when a client with whom I was delivering CBT for panic disorder with agoraphobia presented for session in tears, indicating that a close friend had committed suicide the previous day and left him a "good-bye" voice mail. We, of course, put our CBT work on hold, and at the client's request, he spent the session remembering fondly shared experiences with this friend. We resumed our CBT work in the following session, though for a number of subsequent sessions I took care to check in on how he was feeling about the loss of his friend. At the close of treatment, the client and I both viewed the session discussing his friend's suicide as an especially powerful shared experience, and he provided feedback to me that the processing of his grief was one of the most important therapeutic gains that he made during the course of treatment, even beyond the tangible gains he made in reducing the symptoms of anxiety and avoidance for which he sought treatment.

Moreover, there will undoubtedly be instances in which clients explicitly indicate that they are uninterested in between-session work (I certainly have had a few across the course of my career!). In all of these instances, CBT can still be "done" and done well, even if it is not done according to the format described in textbooks. The key, as you will see throughout this workbook, is to ask clients to think critically about the learning that they are acquiring and the way in which they will generalize this learning to their lives, even if it is not through "formal" homework exercises.

In addition, many therapists-in-training equate certain specific tools or strategies to "doing CBT." This most commonly occurs with the strategy, cognitive restructuring, and a tool called the *thought record*, which can be used to facilitate cognitive restructuring. As will be described in much more detail in Chapter 5 of this volume, *cognitive restructuring* is a strategy in which the therapist works with the client to identify, evaluate, and if necessary, modify unhelpful thinking. An example is when a client concludes that a person does not like her, because the person did not say hello to her when they crossed paths at the grocery store. Although there is certainly a possibility that the person with whom the client crossed paths does not like her, there are many other possible explanations, such as the possibility that the person did not recognize her, the possibility that the person's mind was preoccupied with something else, the possibility that the person was in a hurry, and so on. When people focus only on the most negative possibility (in this case, that the person with whom the client crossed paths does not like her), they usually experience unpleasant and unnecessary emotional distress, and there is an increased likelihood that they will do something self-defeating (e.g., give the cold shoulder to the person the next time their paths cross). Cognitive restructuring helps clients to soften their interpretation of perceived negative events that they experience, which should help them to make sounder decisions regarding ways to handle these events. The *thought record* is a tool in which clients record situations like this that prompt negative emotions, the way in which they were interpreting the situation, and an alternative, more balanced view of the situation.

Cognitive restructuring is, indeed, a central strategy that cognitive behavioral therapists use in treatment. However, it is by far not the *only* strategy. Many of the chapters of this book describe and will give you practice in other core strategies associated with CBT, such as behavioral activation, exposure, problem solving, communication skills training, mindfulness, and acceptance. In fact, a client could go through an entire course of CBT and participate only in behavioral interventions, rather than cognitive interventions, and his therapist would still be "doing" CBT. Moreover, if a therapist implements cognitive restructuring, it need not be executed using a *thought record*; the aims of cognitive restructuring can be achieved simply through conversation between the therapist and client, using a mobile phone application, or in other creative ways that I will describe in Chapter 5 of this volume.

A major "take-home" point with which I hope you will leave after reading this book is that CBT is extremely versatile. The delivery of CBT is driven by theory and the case formulation, not by any specific structural feature, technique, or tool. In fact, unless you are following a treatment manual for a very specific and singular clinical presentation, no two courses of CBT will look alike. You will be able to implement CBT on the basis of your client's needs and preferences, your own personal style, and the creativity and ingenuity that emerges from the synergy inherent in the collaborative therapeutic relationship that develops between the two of you.

Certain Aspects of CBT are Off-putting to or "Too Much" for Clients

Some therapists-in-training worry that the structure of CBT will be off-putting to clients. For example, as you will see in Chapter 4 of this volume on session structure, one way to encourage organization and efficiency in session is for you and the client , together, to set an agenda, or an expectation of the topics and issues that will be addressed in the session. Over my years of supervision in CBT, I have heard therapists express concern that agenda setting will stifle spontaneous discussion of issues that unexpectedly arise in the course of discussion, or that clients will view agenda setting as so rigid that it will prevent them from feeling comfortable with their therapist and developing a strong therapeutic alliance. Other therapists-in-training express concern that their clients are too fragile for the more "directive" aspects of CBT, such as a "formal" intervention strategy like cognitive restructuring of behavioral activation, or for a homework exercise between sessions.

In my experience, these concerns most often reflect assumptions inherent in the therapist him- or herself, rather than truth. Of course, we do not want to dismiss these concerns, as if realized, they have the potential to affect the therapeutic relationship and the degree to which clients embrace the interventions we offer them. But, from the perspective of collaborative empiricism, it is important to check out these concerns with the client. Much more often than not, when cognitive behavioral therapists say something, such as "I'm wondering if what I'm suggesting doesn't seem right to you, or is rubbing you the wrong way?" clients respond by saying that they actually appreciate the spirit of the intervention, and while it might be a bit uncomfortable or different than the way they are accustomed to living their lives, they value the learning experience.

Cognitive Behavioral Therapists are Uninterested in the Therapeutic Relationship

I hope that you have already seen in my writing to this point that this sentiment is, indeed, a misconception and that cognitive behavioral therapists place great importance on the therapeutic relationship. Over 40 years ago, Dr. Aaron T. Beck published his seminal book, *Cognitive Therapy of Depression* (Beck, Rush, Shaw, & Emery, 1979), and in this book, he devotes a full chapter to the importance of a strong therapeutic relationship. Nevertheless, this misconception is perpetuated. Perhaps the following anecdote will clarify why this situation has come to pass.

When I was writing this book, I delivered a three-day lecture on CBT for Anxiety-Related Disorders at the Beck Institute for Cognitive Behavior Therapy, a non-profit institution founded by Dr. Beck and his daughter, Dr. Judith S. Beck, that serves as the premier training organization in CBT. As he often does, Dr. Beck attended a portion of the workshop, so that he could meet workshop participants, answer their questions about CBT, and consult on difficult cases. One of the workshop participants asked a question about the importance of the therapeutic relationship. Dr. Beck sighed and admitted that he made a mistake in his early writings about CBT. Elaborating upon this provocative statement, Dr. Beck indicated that he had, indeed, carefully read the works of seminal mental health providers, such as Carl Rogers, about the centrality of the therapeutic relationship in psychotherapy. Moreover, he agreed wholeheartedly with these writers that a strong therapeutic relationship is essential for successful psychotherapy. However, his mistake was that when he wrote about CBT, he assumed that the reader would already have this knowledge and training, so that the reader could build from a client-centered foundation and add the specific CBT framework and strategic approach to his or her clinical work. Unfortunately, over time, the absence of extensive discussion about the therapeutic relationship in his books was interpreted as a stance that cognitive behavioral therapists believe that the therapeutic relationship of minimal importance. As you will see in Chapter 3 of this volume, the CBT literature is now addressing this misconception with several published books and innovative research designs that illustrate the important role that a strong therapeutic relationship plays in CBT.

Certain Topics are "Off-limits" in CBT

I cannot tell you the number of times I have had a supervisee say something to me, such as "I really have a strong reaction to the client. But I'm not allowed to address that, right? Because focusing on transference is off-limits in CBT, right?" My unequivocal response to this sentiment is, "Nothing further from this is the truth. In my opinion, the *best* CBT is often done in the context of something that is happening between you and the client right there in the therapy session." The ensuing discussion illustrates yet another way that the therapeutic relationship plays a central role in the course of psychotherapy.

I have many reasons for my stance on this issue. First, research shows that the strength of the therapeutic alliance accounts for 20% to 25% of the variance in outcome in psychotherapy (Martin, Garske, & Davis, 2000). Although these data are often used by cognitive behavioral therapists to support the notion that the therapeutic relationship is insufficient to fully influence outcome in psychotherapy, at the same time, these data also suggest that a strong therapeutic relationship is of crucial importance and should be cultivated. In other words, attending to what is happening in the therapeutic relationship is not the only task at hand in CBT, but it is an important one not to be dismissed.

Second, one intriguing research study (Strauss et al., 2006) discovered a "V-shape" association between tension in the therapeutic relationship and outcome in CBT. Moreover, it found that when a *rupture* (i.e., "a tension or breakdown in the collaborative relationship between patient and therapist" [p. 80]; Safran, Muran, & Eubanks-Carter, 2011; see also Safran, Crocker, McMain, & Murray, 1990) in the therapeutic relationship occurred, if it was repaired successfully, outcome was better than had a rupture not occurred at all. The eminent cognitive behavioral therapist, Cory Newman (who was also an author on this study) shed further light on these findings to suggest that too little tension in the therapeutic relationship means that therapy is too easy, and that the client will likely not achieve the maximum benefit. Too much tension, in contrast, means that the therapeutic relationship has been compromised, and that the fundamental foundation of psychotherapy is not in place for gains to be made in session (Newman, 2007).

Third, the "real-time" unfolding of an issue in the therapeutic relationship has the potential to illustrate the CBT model and its associated strategies first-hand to clients. Take, for instance, a true story that occurred in my practice many years ago. I was seeing a single, female client who was involved in a romantic relationship that most of her friends and family believed was not good for her. She and I were preparing to break for eight weeks of my maternity leave, and she indicated that she had planned to end the relationship. I saw her the week I returned from maternity leave, and during that session she indicated that she had, indeed, ended the relationship, but that she resumed it a few weeks later. My initial response was, "Oh, I'm surprised" (admittedly not my best therapeutic moment).

This client's reaction to me at the time of the subsequent session, however, was telling. During my bridge from the previous session (see Chapter 4 of this volume for more on this aspect of session structure), I asked the client what "stuck with" her from the previous session. She looked at me harshly and said, "I felt so judged by you." I immediately acknowledged her reaction, thanked her for being so forthright, and asked if we could make this the first topic of discussion (meaning that I did not abandon agenda setting; see Chapter 4). When we discussed the issue from a compassionate but factual standpoint, the client realized that I did not, inherently, say anything judgmental (though we both laughed that my "I'm surprised" reaction might not have been the savviest). Rather, she realized that she had an array of negative self-judgments about resuming the relationship, and she attributed those to my ambiguous "I'm surprised" reaction. It was only after she checked out the facts (per collaborative empiricism) and was able to draw a more accurate and balanced conclusion on the basis of her fact-checking that she was able to see that I was not at all judging her with my reaction. Moreover, in my view, it ultimately, strengthened our relationship and the cognitive behavioral work we were doing together, as we sometimes lightheartedly referenced this moment during the course of therapy as a reminder that I would not pass judgment on her, and that it is important to check out the facts before assuming that we know what others think of us.

In addition to therapists' concerns about addressing issues that arise in the therapeutic relationship (or in their reactions toward their clients), I have also heard therapists-in-training assume that issues associated with "the past" are "off-limits." It is true that CBT was developed as a "here-and-now" approach to psychotherapy, with the rationale that cognitive behavioral therapists want their clients to feel the benefit of psychotherapy as immediately as possible, and that it is often unnecessary to dig deep into the past when current life problems are what have prompted the client to pursue services. Nevertheless, this does *not* mean that the past is *not* important. As you will see in greater detail in Chapter 2 of this volume, as they develop the case formulation of their clients' clinical presentations, cognitive behavioral therapists pay close attention to past formative life experiences that shape clients' core beliefs and habitual behavioral patterns. Furthermore, when a client has experienced a past trauma, the trauma is, of course, discussed in the process of implementing exposure, a strategy described in more detail in Chapter 6 of this volume. Moreover, some clients present to therapy with the observation that past life events continue to affect them and request that they spend time discussing these past life events. Because CBT is collaborative, these clients' wishes are respected, and time is made in the course of treatment to satisfy this desire.

Perhaps the best way to respond to this concern is that cognitive behavioral therapists do not engage in endless exploration of the past simply for its own sake. When the past is addressed in treatment, it is done so with the purposes of (a) developing a sophisticated case formulation; (b) responding to their client's request or an important part of his or her clinical presentation; and (c) gaining understanding of the way in which past experiences affect the client in the present, so that an appropriate strategic intervention can be identified and implemented.

Summary

CBT's active, problem-focused, and time-sensitive nature is sometimes mistaken as not being "deep" enough for complex cases and has been criticized for lacking attention to the cultivation of a strong, nurturing therapeutic relationship. I have provided some reasons as to why I believe these beliefs are unfounded, and throughout the remainder of the book, I will continue to provide examples that speak to CBT's richness, versatility, and balance between development of the therapeutic relationship and cognitive and behavioral change. At this point in your introduction to CBT, I invite you in the box below to reflect on these misconceptions and consider the ways in which the material I have presented so far has affected your view of CBT.

BOX 2 REFLECTION ON MISCONCEPTIONS ABOUT CBT

Please consider your reactions to the five misperceptions about CBT that were just presented. Did you share in any of these beliefs? If so, how has your view of them shifted on the basis of the material presented so far? What aspects of these beliefs do you still hold? Why?

MISCONCEPTION #1: CBT is Superficial and is not "Deep" Enough for Complex Clinical Presentations.

MISCONCEPTION #2: There is a Checklist of Things I "Must" Do If I Am to be Doing CBT the "Right" Way.

MISCONCEPTION #3: Certain Aspects of CBT are Off-Putting to or "Too Much" for Clients.

MISCONCEPTION #4: Cognitive Behavioral Therapists are Uninterested in the Therapeutic Relationship.

MISCONCEPTION #5: Certain Topics are "Off-Limits" in CBT

CBT Successes

Many therapists-in-training are inspired when they hear success stories of instances in which CBT made significant positive changes in people's lives. I, myself, am passionate about CBT precisely because of the profound changes that I have witnessed in my clients and the positive feedback I have received over the years about the impact that CBT had in their lives. Allow me to share some "real life" examples that illustrate just how powerful CBT can be. Per the guidance specified by the American Psychological Association, identifying details of these success stories have been changed to protect clients' confidentiality.

Example #1: "Anna" was 26 years old when I first started seeing her for obsessive compulsive disorder (OCD). I saw her on three separate occasions, each time with her OCD manifesting in a different manner. Cognitive behavioral therapists do not view a recurrence of symptoms as a failure; instead, they view clients with vulnerabilities who return to treatment as successes, because they are in tune with the way in which their mental health problem waxes and wanes, and they take proactive steps to address an increase in symptoms during times of stress (O'Donohue & Cucciare, 2008). This way of understanding chronic mental health problems certainly applied to Anna.

Anna was highly responsive to the first course of treatment, readily completing cognitive and behavioral CBT homework and demonstrating the impressive acquisition of CBT's underlying principles. Her OCD symptoms (which can sometimes be treatment resistant) decreased to a sub-clinical level. The second two times she returned to treatment, she needed only a handful of sessions, and I was gratified to see that she almost entirely took the lead and "walked herself through" CBT principles, strategies, and tools that she had acquired, developed, and practiced in our previous work together. Before she commenced the third series of sessions with me, Anna indicated that she briefly saw another psychotherapist because her new psychiatrist required her to see a psychotherapist in his practice. She remarked that she quickly discontinued her work with the other psychotherapist because she found herself educating the psychotherapist about basic cognitive and behavioral principles, such as the importance of tolerating uncertainty and seizing opportunities for exposure. This is another testimonial of the sophisticated knowledge that clients can obtain in CBT.

About two times a year, Anna contacts me to provide updates on her family and the way in which she continues to use cognitive behavioral tools in her life, articulately reflecting on CBT's theory, principles, and application. She regularly refers potential clients to me when others disclose to her that they are struggling with anxiety or depression. In her most recent message, she indicated: "Words cannot adequately express my true appreciation for CBT and the difference it made in my life. It is such a gift."

Example #2: "Matthew" was a 44-year-old very successful systems analyst who sought treatment for depression and a general sense of being "stuck" in life. He reported tremendous work stress; in fact, he once calculated that he worked at "160%" effort with the amount that he was on call after hours. Although Matthew responded well to cognitive restructuring, behavioral activation, and problem solving interventions (all of which are described later in this volume), he struggled with the concepts of mindfulness and acceptance. He diligently completed mindfulness exercises in and outside of session, but he also remarked that he did not understand their "point." We had many thoughtful discussions in session about the fact that he was a problem-focused, outcome-oriented individual who had trouble shifting to a "process" orientation.

When Matthew ended treatment, he no longer met criteria for depression, and he reported increased satisfaction with his life outside of work (though he still reported that he "hated" his job and felt stuck in it). If the story ended here, he would be considered a treatment success, though not necessarily one that would stand out to be included in a section such as this one. What makes his story interesting is that he contacted me a few years later to obtain recommendations for mental health treatment for his daughter. At that time, he indicated that he continued to pursue mindfulness after treatment ended (in part because he was determined to "master" it). Over time, he witnessed first-hand, in an experiential manner, the wisdom that I was hoping he would achieve from our mindfulness work. He had attended several mindfulness workshops in the months after our work had ended, and he was completing certification to become an instructor of these workshops. He remained in his full-time job as a systems analyst, but he was approaching his life (including his work) in a very different manner than when he first presented for treatment. What was striking was that this profound change occurred after treatment had ended.

Example #3. "Zack" was a 21-year-old young man who lived with his parents and was on medical leave from college for severe depression. He was not working, and he reported that he spent his time sleeping during the day, playing video games from when he woke up in the mid-afternoon until the early hours of the morning, and smoking marijuana (in fact, late in the course of treatment he admitted that he had smoked marijuana before most of our sessions early in the course of treatment!). He reported persistent suicidal ideation, indicating that he had ruined his life by making bad choices and that he did not see a future for himself.

Zack was initially disengaged from treatment and indicated that he was only participating in psychotherapy because his psychiatrist refused to prescribe his medications unless he was having weekly sessions with a therapist. I taught him skills for cognitive restructuring, behavioral activation, sleep hygiene, and proper self-care, but he very rarely followed through with CBT homework between sessions. Despite this apparent lack of motivation and connection with CBT, he was thoughtful in session and readily resonated with the cognitive behavioral model (see Chapter 2 of this volume) when I provided psychoeducation about it. He seemed to enjoy speculating about the development of negative beliefs about himself and the consequences of times in which those beliefs were activated. In addition, I took care to cultivate many aspects of our therapeutic relationship, using humor and metaphors when appropriate, showing interest in activities that were important to him (such as his online video-game community), and providing a great deal of encouragement when he made even small changes in self-care. During this portion of treatment, I learned that Zack was extremely witty and perceptive (characteristics that I like to think that we shared!) and I very much began to look forward to my sessions with him.

Zack eventually got a job as a server at an upscale restaurant, which not only gave him a sense of purpose and accomplishment, but it also allowed him a more tangible opportunity to apply the principles of cognitive restructuring (even if he continued not to complete written homework) and recognize the consequences of negative beliefs about the self. The new job also allowed him the opportunity to expand his previously limited social network, and we applied cognitive and behavioral skills to cultivating these relationships.

Zack ended treatment when he decided to go back to school (and keep his job), which limited his availability. By the end of treatment, his depression had decreased from severe to mild, and he was no longer smoking marijuana on a daily basis. He came back to see me two years later when he was dealing with the breakup of a relationship (which had been his first "real" girlfriend—a prospect he indicated that he could not have imagined when he first entered treatment). He was in his last year of college and had been admitted to the prestigious honors program at his university. An avid Star Wars fan, he indicated that he had been "using my Jedi CBT skills" when he was faced with challenges and adversity. He attended three sessions to review and apply what he had learned to deal with the breakup of the relationship, and at the time of his final session, he reported only minimal depression and very occasional marijuana use.

Example #4: "Cate" was a 48-year-old family physician who had participated in psychoanalysis for many years. She described herself as having major issues with her family-of-origin, including an alcoholic father and a mother who invalidated her emotions, sending her the message that she was the "problem child" amongst the five children in the family. She described many instances of emotional abuse and neglect at the hands of her parents and bullying by her two older siblings. She indicated that she attained a great deal of insight into her "family issues" from her previous course of treatment, gaining an understanding of complex family dynamics, her role in the system, and triggers that brought her back to childhood. At the same time, she recognized that she continued to be plagued by unhelpful thinking about her family-of-origin, which she noticed exacerbated her emotional distress whenever she was approaching a trip across the country to visit them.

Cate and I completed 16 sessions of CBT across five months, focused on cognitive restructuring, core belief work, and social problem solving to address recurrent conflict that arose when she visited her family-of-origin. She was a diligent client, completing her homework between each session and successfully implementing cognitive and behavioral principles with members of her family-of-origin and her life in general. She cancelled her 17th session after a trip across the country to visit her family-of-origin, thanking me for my time and indicating that she benefitted a great deal from CBT. Although I certainly regarded her as a CBT success, I wondered if I had done something that she found off-putting or if I had gotten something wrong in our previous session, given the relatively abrupt way in which she ended her work with me.

Cate contacted me two years later to work on another issue. When she presented for that session, we discussed the ending of her previous course of therapy. She gave me the feedback that she in no way found anything that I did off-putting or off-base; instead, she described our work as "transformative" and indicated that she was so overcome by the effect that our CBT work had on her life that she needed some time away to process it. She indicated that she had visited members of her family-of-origin four times in the intervening two years and that her attitude toward them and interactions with them had completely changed for the better, in a way that she did not think was possible in light of the long history of transgressions by members of her family-of-origin. Interestingly, she remarked that she would have expected that the transformation to have come about through her psychoanalytic work, rather than her cognitive behavioral work, and she lamented the fact that she invested so much time in the former approach to treatment when she achieved such great change in five months' time. Cate indicated that she returned to therapy with me to address a very "private" and "embarrassing" issue—prescription drug abuse—and that she trusted me and the CBT approach wholeheartedly, on the basis of our previous work and therapeutic relationship, to address this problem.

Example #5: "Claire" was a 32-year-old reading specialist who participated in workshops I designed to apply cognitive behavioral principles and strategies to high-performing teachers who were being trained to serve as "teacher-leaders" who served as mentors to first-year and at-risk teachers. She had gone through four workshops in which she learned about stress management and cognitive restructuring. At the time of the fifth workshop, she approached me (after never having spoken to her directly before this time) and stated, "I just want you to know that what I'm learning about CBT saved my life." She went on to explain that over the holiday break, she suddenly lost her father to a fatal car accident. She had been raised by her father since she was two-years old and viewed him as her best friend, closest confidant, and as someone she could not live without. However, she was able to use what she had learned about CBT during her time away from school to self-soothe, engage in healthy self-care, and reach a state of acceptance. She indicated that she would not have been able to do this without the help of CBT.

These are just a few examples of the serendipitous ways in which CBT impacts the lives of people who participate in and embrace it. I receive at least a few updates a week from current and past clients who describe what I call "CBT successes," including flights that they had previously been too fearful to take, successful job interviews, and adjustments to college life. When I receive these updates, I sit back, smile, and think: "This is why I do what I do."

Of course, in the spirit of presenting information as factually and with as much balance as possible, I should also be forthright that, on occasion, I receive the feedback from a client that CBT does not feel like a good match. Some clients indicate that they really are looking for "someone to talk to" and nothing more. Others remark that they are overwhelmed by the work that seems to be involved in CBT. A client I have been seeing during the final two months of the writing of this book has indicated to me that she relies on her therapist to tell her what to do and give advice, which is much more directive than the more Socratic, collaborative manner in which I practice (although she remained in CBT with the insight that perhaps this is an issue on which she can work with CBT).

This feedback is of utmost importance to acknowledge, and if the client remains in your practice, to use in the spirit of modifying your approach. By doing so, you are modeling the importance of client feedback in CBT and true therapist-client collaboration. Even when I have received feedback such as that described above, the vast majority of my clients stay in my practice. I focus first and foremost on cultivating the therapeutic relationship (see Chapter 3 of this volume), allow the client to set the agenda for the session, and take care not to supply an overabundance of psychoeducation or ideas for exercises to pursue between sessions. In many cases, something uncanny happens. Within a few sessions of this more open-ended approach, these same clients who had reservations about CBT often say something to me, such as "Gee, I've noticed that I just think so negatively about things lately, I would love to do something about that" or "Boy, I think I really need some tools for keeping myself together when I get overwhelmed, because I just lost it, and it didn't go over well." When I hear these remarks, I gently ask permission if I, now, can share with them a bit about what CBT has to offer. I also give them assurance that we will work together, as a team, to package it in a way that is manageable for them and consistent with their values and preferences.

The "bottom line" is that if you choose to practice CBT, I expect that you will receive a great deal of positive feedback from clients that would be gratifying for any clinician. However, it is okay to receive negative feedback as well—your client has every right to determine the type of treatment that he or she views as the best match. In these instances, know that if you respond in an open and genuine manner, there is no reason why these clients cannot be retained in treatment. Moreover, on the basis of my own clinical experience, it is entirely possible that many of these clients will request interventions consistent with CBT after they have had the opportunity to form a therapeutic relationship and feel comfortable in the space of psychotherapy.

How to Use the Remainder of this Book

The next six chapters correspond to different aspects of the delivery of CBT. In the next chapter (Chapter 2) you will learn about cognitive behavioral theory in the spirit of understanding how to develop case formulations of your clients' clinical presentations and corresponding treatment plans. You will think about the cognitive behavioral model in relation to your own life and subjective experiences, and you will identify one problem area to which you might apply the CBT strategies that you will learn throughout the book. In Chapter 3 of this volume, you will read about the central importance of the therapeutic relationship, reflect on supportive and nurturing relationships in your own life, and consider specific ways that you can translate these concepts into your work with your clients. Chapter 4 of this volume describes various approaches to session structure that you can use with your clients (and apply to your own life).

Chapters 5 through 7 of this volume describe standard CBT strategic interventions that cognitive behavioral therapists commonly use with their clients: (a) cognitive restructuring; (b) behavioral interventions, including behavioral activation, problem solving, and exposure; and (c) mindfulness and acceptance. I will ask you to practice some of the exercises that often accompany these interventions and get a sense of what it is like to practice them between readings. I always say that I will not ask my clients to practice anything that I have not tried myself. The practices in these chapters will allow you to achieve this aim, which has the potential to increase credibility in your clients' eyes and provide you with unique insight that you can share as you implement strategic interventions with your clients. Finally, Chapter 8 of this volume focuses on relapse prevention, or ways to help yourself and your clients consolidate the gains from your CBT work, commit to continued practice even when treatment (or this book) has ended, and identify signs indicating that more help or a refresher is needed. It will allow you to reflect on ways you achieved personal growth through the insights and exercises in this book, ways you have grown as a clinician, and ways to take your CBT practice to the next level.

So far, I have been highlighting the application of CBT principles, strategy, and techniques to yourself for experiential practice. I view this personal application as invaluable in truly understanding what these principles, strategies, and techniques are all about. However, I realize that the clients with whom you work may be (and are even likely to be) in a very different place in life than you are. Thus, I also include discussion of application to individual cases in these chapters. Throughout the book, we will follow two cases to illustrate the application of these principles, strategies, and techniques. One case is a relatively "straightforward" case, or a client who is motivated for treatment, is receptive to CBT, and completes practice between sessions; the other case is a relatively "difficult" case, or a client who is ambivalent about treatment, is skeptical about CBT, and who sometimes completes practice between sessions. I present therapist-client dialogue to show you how to introduce the principles, strategies, and techniques with clients, and, at times, I provide space for you to consider the next steps you might take with these clients. In addition, I describe tips for maximizing the effectiveness of the interventions that are presented.

Each of these chapters includes space for you to consolidate what you have learned and experienced. Often, I invite you to reflect on your learning and outline the specific ways in which your learning will influence your clinical practice, as well as your life, more generally.

As we close out this chapter, I invite you to participate in one final reflection focused on the way in which your view of CBT shifted just after the simply act of reading this chapter. Is CBT what you had expected? Did you experience any surprises? What are you looking forward to most in this experiential learning program? Are there any aspects of CBT about which you are apprehensive, and if so, why?

BOX 3 POST-CHAPTER 1-REFLECTION ON CBT

Is CBT what you had expected?

Did you experience any surprises?

What are you looking forward to most in this experiential learning program?

Are there any aspects of CBT about which you are apprehensive, and if so, why?

CHAPTER 2 CASE FORMULATION AND TREATMENT PLANNING

Case Formulation and Treatment Planning

CHAPTER 2

When you are going on a journey, you might find that it is helpful to have a sense of where you are starting from, where you are going, how you will get there, and the kinds of things you will do or see along the way. Psychotherapy is no different. As mentioned in the previous chapter, the *case formulation* is the application of psychological theory to understand your client's clinical presentation. The case formulation allows you to understand the key psychological factors that contribute to and maintain the problems that your client would like to address in treatment (Persons, 2008; Persons & Hong, 2016). It certainly provides an understanding of where you are starting from in your journey with your client, but it also gives a preview of what you might see along the way in your journey. In addition, it raises possibilities of what might be different for the client when treatment has ended.

Cognitive behavioral therapists use the case formulation to inform specific goals for treatment, or the precise destination(s) that the client is hoping to reach on his or her journey. These specific goals are compiled into a *treatment plan* that summarizes the client's main problem areas and specific manifestations of each problem area, ways to measure progress in these problem areas, and the corresponding cognitive behavioral intervention strategy that will bring the client to his or her desired destination (Dobson & Dobson, 2009; Wenzel, 2013). In other words, the treatment plan makes the final destination "crystal clear" to the therapist and client, and it answers the question: "How will we get there?"

In this chapter, you will learn about cognitive behavioral theory and observe first-hand how to apply it to understand your own experiences. In addition, you will reflect honestly on the degree to which any of these factors need adjustment to optimize your own functioning or life satisfaction, and you will commit to a plan to address it. By doing this, you will gain practice in developing a concrete treatment plan. I ask you to reflect on the way in which these exercises have relevance to your work with clients. I then follow with examples of case formulation and treatment planning and ask you to consider the way in which you would proceed with these cases. I end with a discussion of tips for maximizing the effectiveness of case formulation and treatment planning as you continue to optimize your delivery of CBT to your clients.

Cognitive Behavioral Theory

The understanding of cognitive behavioral theory is at the crux of the delivery of CBT. Not only does theory guide us in understanding our clients' clinical presentations, but it also points us toward (potentially) fruitful interventions and allows us to develop hypotheses about the way in which our interventions work. Thus, by having a sound knowledge of cognitive behavioral theory, you will be able to select interventions that have the potential to be the best match for your clients, and you will be able to explain to your clients exactly why you expect this to be so.

However, there are many facets at work in cognitive behavioral theory—in fact, there really is no one unified cognitive behavioral theory that can explain the cognitive behavioral treatment of the vast array of clinical presentations that you will see in your practice. In this section, I outline two layers of cognitive behavioral theory that I use to develop case formulations in my own practice.

Basic Theory

Figure 2.1 depicts the basic cognitive theory that captures people's psychological experiences associated with specific life situations. According to this theory, the way in which we think about a situation (i.e., the way we interpret what is happening, or the way we make meaning of it) plays a large role in our subsequent emotional, physiological, and behavioral reactions. Take, for example, your thinking associated with acquiring the skill necessary to deliver CBT to your clients. If you are thinking: "Great! This training program will really help me deliver quality therapy to my clients," it is likely that you will be a bit excited (emotion), that you might even experience a physiological reaction associated with excitement (e.g., alertness), and that you will commit to reading this book and completing the exercises (behavior). However, if you are thinking: "Ugh! This will be a lot of work, and I have no time," it is likely that you might feel a bit down, anxious, or frustrated (emotion), that you might feel tired or sluggish (physiology), and that you procrastinate reading the book and completing the exercises (behavior). Thus, cognitive behavioral therapists believe that it is not so much a life situation that simply makes us feel and behave in a certain way, but that it is the meaning that we attach to these situations that plays a large role in explaining our responses.

Notice that I said it is the meaning that we attach to these situations that *plays a large role in explaining our responses*. I did *not* say that the meaning that we attach to these situations *causes our responses*. I am careful with this terminology for two reasons. One reason is that researchers who study basic emotional processes have demonstrated that there is an intricate interdependence between cognitive and emotional systems, and that in many instances, emotions influence cognitive processes (Lench, Darbor, & Berg, 2013; Lench & Levine, 2005; Schwarz & Clore, 1983; Storberk, & Clore, 2007). A good example of this is the client with an anxiety disorder who experiences increased anxiety and physiological reactivity, such as increased heart rate and rate of breathing, out of nowhere. This sometimes happens with anxious clients simply because they are prone to these emotional and physiological experiences, probably due to a combination of biological vulnerability and conditioned responding. However, many anxious clients do not attribute these emotional and physiological reactions to random elevations; they then conclude that something is terribly wrong and that they are in danger. In this example, the emotional and physiological responses, then, preceded the thinking, or the meaning that was attributed to the situation. For this reason, I have included bidirectional arrows in Figure 2.1 to depict that changes in one of these constructs often has effects on the others.

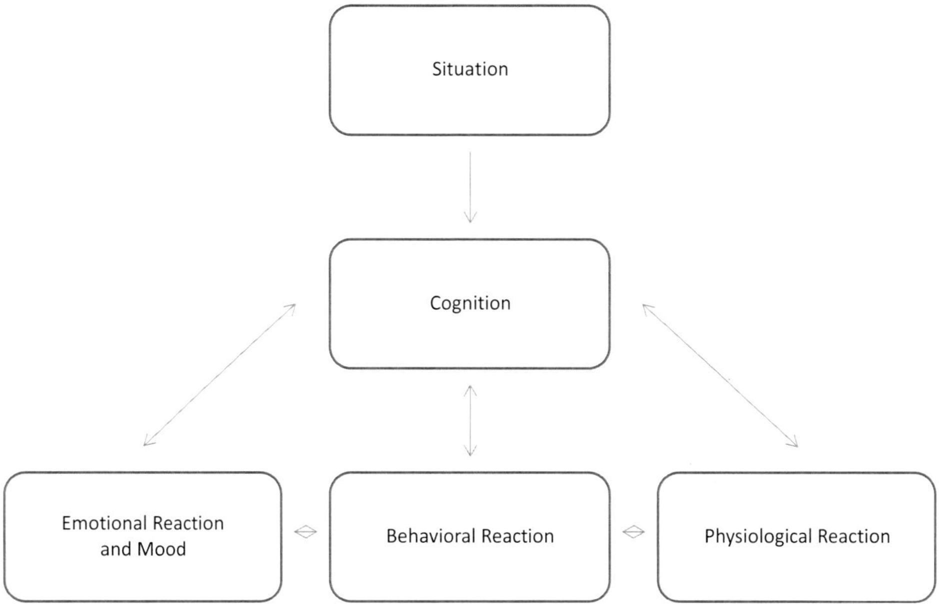

Figure 2.1 Basic Theory

Reproduced with permission from Greenberg, McWilliams, & Wenzel (2014, p. 132).

The second reason that I am careful not to attribute causal language to the role that thinking plays in emotional responding is from research on the change processes associated with CBT. If unhelpful thinking is viewed as the central piece of a client's clinical presentation, then it would be logical that the acquired ability to modify unhelpful thinking—a central activity in CBT (see Chapter 5 of this volume on cognitive restructuring)—would be associated with successful outcome in CBT. These is certainly some research that supports this premise; for example, one study found that a systematic decrease in scores on a standard depression inventory was associated with the systematic increase in the application of a tool associated with the modification of unhelpful thinking (Braun, Strunk, Sasso, & Cooper, 2015). Research by Stefan Hofmann suggests that change in cognition mediates the outcome in the cognitive behavioral treatment of anxiety disorders, meaning that, statistically, change in cognition was the pathway by which successful outcome was achieved (Hofmann, 2004; Hofmann et al., 2007). However, many other studies have reported a lack of compelling evidence for the statistical medication between changes in unhelpful cognitive and outcome in CBT (Burns & Spangler, 2001; DeRubeis et al., 1990; Stice, Rohde, Seeley, & Gau, 2010). This means that the modification of other problematic psychological processes (e.g., behavioral inactivity, lack of acceptance, to name a couple of candidates) might be just as central, or at times even more central, to explaining a client's mental health problems and explaining why CBT is successful. At present, the basic cognitive model that highlights thinking, or cognition, is still very relevant in the literature, in clinical practice, and in supervision, but I expect this model to evolve as new research that has implications for theory is published.

Take a moment in the box below to reflect on the way the basic theory plays out in your own life. Consider a situation that was upsetting to you, and identify the cognitive, emotional, and physiological components that were evoked.

BOX 1 APPLICATION OF THE BASIC THEORY TO YOURSELF

Think about an upsetting event that you experienced recently, and identify its components according to the basic theory.

SITUATION:

THOUGHT (OR INTERPRETATION OR MEANING):

EMOTIONAL RESPONSE:

PHYSIOLOGICAL RESPONSE:

BEHAVIORAL RESPONSE:

What do you notice about the ways in which these components come together?

Did your thinking lead to emotional, physiological, and behavioral responses, or was it the other way around?

If one of the psychological components—the thinking piece, the emotional piece, the physiological piece, or the behavioral piece—were to change, how would that change the way in which you experienced the situation?

Expanded Theory

The basic theory is a terrific model for making sense of our reactions to specific life situations, such as stressors, challenges, disappointments, and surprises. However, there are underlying cognitive and behavioral patterns that provide further context to the reactions we have in these situations. This is the "deep" part of CBT that I mentioned in the previous chapter.

Figure 2.2 presents the expanded theory and its associated components. According to this model, most of us are characterized by helpful and unhelpful underlying beliefs. Examples of helpful beliefs include: "I'm a good person," "I'm competent at what I do," "Other people are generally kind-hearted," and "The world offers many opportunities." In times of relative calm, these helpful beliefs predominate. So, when helpful beliefs are active, we interpret challenges and disappointments in a relatively benign way, experience appropriate but manageable emotional responses, and make adaptive choices to address the issue. However, in times of stress, when our psychological, physical, and/or financial resources are down, unhelpful beliefs become activated. Examples of unhelpful beliefs are: "I'm a horrible person," "I'm incompetent at what I do," "Other people are out for themselves and will take advantage of you," and "The world

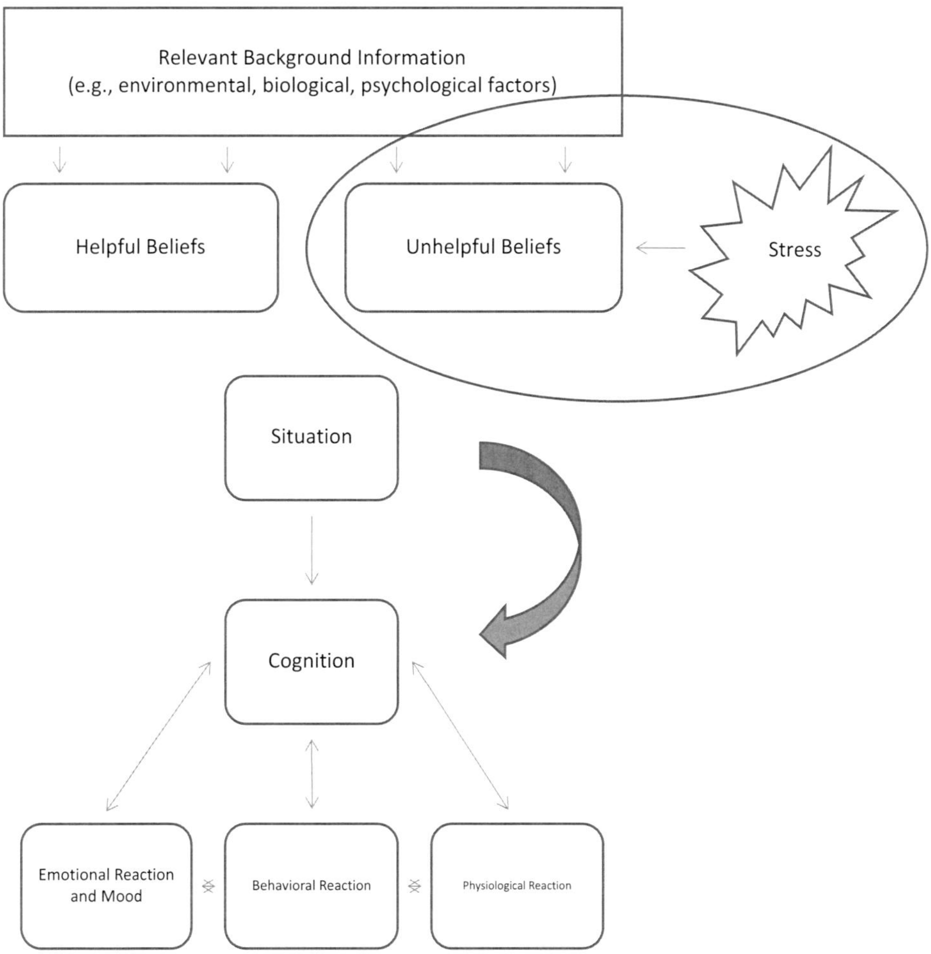

Figure 2.2 Expanded Theory

Reproduced with permission from Greenberg, McWilliams, & Wenzel (2014, p. 135).

is dangerous." Not surprisingly, when unhelpful beliefs are active, we interpret challenges and disappointments in quite a negative way, experience intense and sometimes unmanageable emotional responses, and make poor choices to address the issue.

I have circled the constructs of unhelpful beliefs and stress because it is these two constructs that often explain the thinking experienced in particular situations (represented by the large arrow that points from the circle to the cognition construct). Consider, for example, a person who is learning CBT and whose active unhelpful underlying belief is: "I'm a failure." When faced with the practice of a particular CBT strategy, say for a course, he might have the thought: "I'm going to get negative feedback from my supervisor." Now consider a person who is learning CBT and whose active unhelpful underlying belief falls in a very different realm, such as:"I'm unlikeable." When faced with the practice of a particular CBT strategy for the same course, she might have the thought: "The instructor is going to be disappointed with me." Both thoughts are negative, having to do, in a general sense, with a poor performance. But notice that the person with the "I'm a failure" belief focuses his thought on negative feedback, whereas the person with the "I'm unlikable" belief focuses on the instructor's interpersonal-affective reaction. The subjective nature or "feel" of thoughts that emerge in particular situations often relates directly back to the type of underlying belief that is active.

In response to upsetting underlying beliefs, people often develop *compensatory strategies* to protect themselves from (or compensate for) the discomfort associated with acknowledging them. Let's continue our example of the person who is trying to learn CBT but whose "I'm a failure" belief has been activated. One way this person can cope with this belief is to "overdo" his learning by reading additional books on CBT, watching video demonstrations, and role-playing with his classmates—in other words, by doing everything in his power to acquire the skill and not fail. However, I can also imagine that the belief is upsetting enough that this person might do the opposite, such that he procrastinates and puts minimal effort into the practice and exercises. Here, this person creates a self-fulfilling prophecy, kind of like an "I told you so" about the veracity of the unhelpful belief. A third, even more damaging compensatory strategy would be to avoid the activation of the belief altogether. This would be the case if the person discontinued with his graduate studies, or if he would have never attempted graduate studies in the first place so as not to face the possibility of failing.

So far, we have highlighted some beliefs about the self that we frequently see in clients, such as "I'm a failure" and "I'm unlikeable." In my clinical experience, I would estimate that beliefs about the self are the most common that you will identify during the course of treatment. However, it is important to recognize that many clients hold equally powerful beliefs in other domains, which can logically explain some of the symptoms with which they present and emotional distress that they describe. For example, some people have had upsetting past life experiences with other people, such as a parent who repeatedly put them down or a peer who bullied them. Examples of beliefs that can be formed from these kinds of experiences are "Others can't be trusted" or "Others will hurt you." They might compensate for those beliefs by demonstrating mistrust and guardedness toward others, only allowing a "select few" into their inner circle. Other people have unhelpful beliefs about the way in which the world works, such as "The world is dangerous" or "We're all on our own in this world." A person with the first belief might live life very conservatively, expecting an unmanageable disaster or catastrophe around every corner. A person with the second belief might live life in a selfish manner, looking out for his or her own interests at the expense of the interests of others. Finally, people can have unhelpful beliefs about the future, such as "Things won't work out in the end," and compensate for those beliefs by not taking on challenges or quitting when times get tough.

How does a person's cognitive behavioral profile develop in the first place? As seen from Figure 2.2, many factors contribute to it. For example, most people recall key environmental factors that sent definitive messages about themselves, others, the world, and the future, and that ultimately shaped beliefs that they hold about them. For example, a person who did well in school and received feedback from teachers that he could go on to do anything he wants might develop a belief, such as "I'm competent." However, say this same individual also had an older brother who was arrogant and successful and who repeatedly put him down. This individual, then, might also have internalized messages consistent with the belief "I'm incompetent." This example illustrates how a negative, unhelpful belief can develop seemingly in the face of a history of success experiences. To illustrate the development of another domain of core beliefs, a person who was popular in school and had many friends might develop a belief, such as "I'm likeable." In contrast, a person who recalls being excluded from the group and shunned might develop a negative belief such as "I'm undesirable." These key environmental factors can be single events; such as a trauma; they can be repeated events over time, such as bullying, or they can be a general state of affairs, such as living in poverty.

Although these environmental factors and events are perhaps those that are most commonly identified as key factors that shape the developing of underlying beliefs and behavioral patterns, they are not the only ones that are important. *Biological factors* can also influence a person's cognitive behavioral profile. For example, there is some sort of genetic component to mental health disorders (the precise percentage of variance that can be accounted for by genetics varies as a function of the particular type of mental health disorder under consideration). Take Anna, for example, my former client who I described as a CBT success in Chapter 1 of this volume. Her father had committed suicide, which is almost certainly indicative of having some sort of mental health disorder, and her mother was in treatment for an anxiety disorder. Anna probably inherited a strong tendency toward anxiety and emotion dysregulation more generally, which could contribute to beliefs about being vulnerable and helpless, and compensatory strategies to avoid experiencing intensive and uncomfortable emotional distress (e.g., reassurance seeking). Thus, mental health professionals almost always gather information about a family history of mental health problems in order to construct hypotheses about the contribution of genetics to their clients' clinical presentations.

However, biology does not stop at genetics. People who struggle with medical illnesses, deformities, and other conditions can develop profound views of themselves, others, the world, and the future, as well as distinct strategies to compensate for these beliefs. Take one of my former clients, Finn, as an example. Although Finn struggled with chronic mental health problems throughout his life (at one point even being diagnosed with a psychotic disorder), he was resilient individual who, at 52 years old, pursued outdoor passions, such asrock climbing and snowboarding. He went into a profound depression after being in a car accident that left him unable to fully regain the use of his legs. As a result, positive beliefs about his physical strength, his ability to fully embrace extreme sports, and, more generally, his prospects for happiness were shattered after the accident, leaving him with beliefs, such as "The future is hopeless" and "I'm nothing now." This is a good example of a case in which the client's underlying beliefs shifted dramatically on the basis of an event that occurred mid-life.

A third domain of biological factors that should not be ignored are hormonal factors. Women's hormones, in particular, are an oft-neglected domain of factors that can explain emotional distress (Sichel & Driscoll, 1999). For example, many women who seek treatment from me express a suspicion that their depression, anxiety, and anger follow a repeated pattern with their menstrual cycle. Such an observation can lead women to engage in specific coping strategies at specific times of the month. Other women experience significant and dramatic changes in hormone levels during pregnancy and menopause. These hormonal shifts can cause a great deal of stress, which increases the likelihood that unhelpful underlying beliefs are activated. In addition, they can serve as life events, themselves, that feed into negative beliefs, such as "I'm out of control."

Finally, there are many possible *psychological factors* that have the potential to shape a person's cognitive behavioral profile. Table 2.1 lists examples of some psychological factors that have been demonstrated in the empirical literature, or observed in clinical practice to be associated with the expression of mental health disorders. Let's take the example of self-efficacy, the first psychological factor that is listed in both columns, psychological strengths and psychological vulnerabilities. *Self-efficacy* is defined as a person's belief that he or she can deal successfully with life situations and make positive changes in his or her life, such as completing a task or reaching a goal. As might be expected, people high in self-efficacy might carry underlying beliefs, such as "I'm competent" or "I'm successful." In contrast, people low in self-efficacy might carry underlying beliefs, such as "I'm incompetent" or "I'm a failure." Many of the other psychological factors included in this table, such as thoughtfulness (strength) vs. impulsivity (vulnerability), compassion (strength) vs. judgementalness (vulnerability), and good problem solving ability (strength) vs. poor problem solving ability (vulnerability) affect the kinds of life experiences people have in relationships, in the job, or in school that contribute to and reinforce various helpful and unhelpful beliefs.

Thus, the expanded cognitive behavioral theory provides a rich context of environmental, biological, and psychological factors that help to explain a person's clinical presentation, as well as the structure of his or her underlying beliefs and compensatory strategies to cope with beliefs

Table 2.1 Psychological Strengths and Vulnerabilities

PSYCHOLOGICAL STRENGTHS	*PSYCHOLOGICAL VULNERABILITIES*
• High self-efficacy	• Low self-efficacy
• Persistence	• Tendency to "give up"
• Thoughtfulness	• Impulsivity
• Compassion (toward the self and others)	• Judgmentalness
• Good problem solving ability	• Poor problem solving ability
• Good work ethic	• Poor work ethic
• Flexibility	• Perfectionism
• Proactivity	• Procrastination
• Creativity	• Rigidity
• Optimism	• Pessimism
• Confidence	• Lack of confidence
• Ability to let go	• Rumination
• Assertiveness	• Passivity
• Good behavioral habits (e.g., sleep, diet, exercise, no more than moderate alcohol use)	• Poor behavioral habits (e.g., sleep, diet, exercise, excessive alcohol use)

that are painful and distressing. This model is certainly not the only way to understand clients' clinical presentations. For example, cognitive behavioral therapists who work primarily from a behavioral orientation to treat their clients' depression pay close attention to the "vicious cycle" between depressive symptoms and inactivity, attributing depression to a lack of response-contingent positive reinforcement from one's environment (see Chapter 6 of this volume; Ferster, 1973; Lewinsohn, 1974). Cognitive behavioral therapists who practice from this framework, then, devote their resources to determining the function that the depression-reinforcing behaviors serve in the face of various environmental contingencies. Nevertheless, the basic and expanded models presented here are almost always taught in foundational courses on CBT and provide a foundation for practice for most cognitive behavioral therapists even if they adhere more closely to a more specific theoretical model associated with a particular type of cognitive behavioral intervention or specific clinical presentation.

Case Formulation: From Theory to Clinical Application

Recall the definition of *case formulation* presented in Chapter 1—the application of cognitive behavioral theory to explain a "real-life" client's "real-life" clinical presentation. When I lecture, I like to say that case formulation "brings the theory to life" in the individual. The case formulation forms the "heart" of CBT for any one client. It captures the most important cognitive, behavioral, and other psychological factors that account for the greatest percentage of variance in explaining the client's clinical presentation. It provides a logical framework to explain why clients have arrived at where they are when they present for treatment, the types of experiences and interactions that maintain their problems, and the types of experiences and interactions that make their mental health problems relatively better and relatively worse. It also summarizes a person's history of key environmental factors that might have contributed to his or her underlying beliefs and associated compensatory strategies, as well as biological and psychological strengths and vulnerabilities that shaped the person's cognitive behavioral profile.

Worksheet 2.1 is an example of a summary sheet that can be used to record key information that contributes to the case formulation. You will see that it contains both positive, or strength-based information that can signal resilience, as well as negative traits and experiences that can signal vulnerability. You will be able to keep this copy blank, photocopy it as needed, and use it with your clients.

Worksheet 2.1

Case Formulation Worksheet

RELEVANT BACKGROUND INFORMATION
Positive environmental experiences:
Negative environmental experiences:
Relevant biological vulnerabilities:
Psychological strengths:
Psychological vulnerabilities:
UNDERLYING BELIEFS
Helpful beliefs:
Unhelpful beliefs:
Life stress:
Buffers against life stress:
SITUATIONAL EXAMPLE
Upsetting situation:
Thought (or interpretation or meaning):
Emotional reaction (please rate intensity on a scale of 0 = no noticeable emotional reaction; 10 = most intense emotional reaction that one can imagine):
Physiological reaction:
Behavioral reaction:

I believe that it is essential for me to go beyond the simple description of the constructs that make up the cognitive behavioral model and the associated case formulation, as case formulation is one of the most daunting tasks even for the seasoned clinician. I appreciate that, at this point in the book, the way in which the case formulation is used might be a bit unclear. Here, then, I would like you to take a moment to participate in an experiential exercise. In Box 1, earlier in the chapter, I asked you to consider the way in which the basic model could explain a situation in which you noticed a distinct emotional reaction. Now I would like you to extend your critical evaluation of the cognitive behavioral model and to complete a full case formulation (captured in Worksheet 2.2) for your own life.

Worksheet 2.2

Case Formulation Worksheet: Application to Yourself

RELEVANT BACKGROUND INFORMATION
Positive environmental experiences:
Negative environmental experiences:
Relevant biological vulnerabilities:
Psychological strengths:
Psychological vulnerabilities:
UNDERLYING BELIEFS
Helpful beliefs:
Unhelpful beliefs:
Life stress:
Buffers against life stress:
SITUATIONAL EXAMPLE
Upsetting situation:
Thought (or interpretation or meaning):
Emotional reaction (please rate intensity on a scale of 0 = no noticeable emotional reaction; 10 = most intense emotional reaction that one can imagine):
Physiological reaction:
Behavioral reaction:

I realize that this exercise has the potential to create some discomfort. Although the case formulation worksheet calls upon you to identify positive environmental experiences, psychological strengths, and helpful underlying beliefs, there is equal opportunity to identify aversive environment experiences, psychological vulnerabilities, and unhelpful beliefs that are difficult to acknowledge. On the one hand, I sincerely hope that you take this opportunity and develop a case formulation based on your own life, so that you can acquire an appreciation for the nuances of the cognitive behavioral model and understand what the application of the model feels like, from the client's perspective. If you think it would be helpful, you can elicit the support and input from a trusted individual, such as a family member who might have insight into some of the concepts described in this book so far, or a mentor. On the other hand, in the spirit of true collaboration (which, as you know, is a fundamental tenet of CBT), if the case formulation of your own life is not something you feel ready to do, then I respect that. As an alternative, please consider developing a case formulation in Worksheet 2.2 for someone you know well in your life.

Now that you have completed the case formulation exercise in one form or another, I would like you to reflect on your experience. What did you learn? Were you surprised by anything? What did you see as missing from the case formulation worksheet? As I have stated previously, as you practice CBT, you will develop your own style, and you very well might find that additional constructs are essential in truly developing a comprehensive case formulation of your client's clinical presentation. Perhaps most importantly, what value do you see in applying this framework to your clinical work with your clients?

BOX 2 REFLECTION ON CASE FORMULATION

Were you surprised by anything about the case formulation exercise?

What constructs do you believe are missing from the case formulation worksheet? If you identified anything as missing, how would you work them in?

What value do you see in applying this framework with your clients?

Once you develop your case formulation, you will use it to guide treatment planning, as described in the next section. It will highlight the most (potentially) useful targets to address in treatment. Your goal is to enhance the helpful beliefs and psychological strengths, as well as to utilize the buffers against stress, while developing strategies to manage and/or minimize unhelpful beliefs, psychological vulnerabilities, and sources of stress.

Most new cognitive behavioral therapists find the notion of the case formulation to be intimidating. In fact, it is true that the ability to craft a sophisticated case formulation is considered a relatively advanced CBT skill. Why, then, highlight this topic in the second chapter of the book? For the very reason highlighted in Chapter 1—that case formulation is the "heart" of CBT. Without the case formulation, the likelihood increases that treatment will proceed in a haphazard manner, rather than a thoughtful and strategic manner.

This being said, it is perfectly understandable if you feel a bit apprehensive about your ability to develop case formulations. With time, you will feel more comfortable in doing so. You will have an opportunity later in the chapter to develop a case formulation with a relatively straightforward hypothetical case. In addition, it is important to understand that even the most seasoned cognitive behavioral therapists develop and refine their case formulations over time, as they have more and more interactions with their clients, and observe the way in which their clients respond to particular situations and stressors. Thus, the case formulation is a "living" model that is continually being modified. When a cognitive behavioral therapist first meets a client, many of the constructs identified for the case formation (e.g., the beliefs, strengths, and vulnerabilities) are posed as hypotheses to be verified over time. Thus, the initial case formulation need not be perfect; instead, it is viewed as a flexible working model to guide treatment.

A question that my supervisees often ask me is whether they should develop their case formulation with their client, or whether this is something that they do on their own. My response to this question is the ever-elusive "both." Cognitive behavioral therapists continually think conceptually using cognitive behavioral theory, and much of this thinking is internal. However, remember that CBT is a fundamentally collaborative and transparent approach to treatment. In fact, the renowned cognitive behavioral therapists, Willem Kuyken, Christine Padesky, and Robert Dudley (2009) developed a case formulation approach called *collaborative case conceptualization*, which focused on the collaborative development of the case formulation across several levels of inference (e.g., what is happening with the client right now; what factors contributed to the development of the client's mental health problems).

I believe that my supervisees' question stems from wondering whether they should take a worksheet, such as that depicted in Worksheet 2.1, sit down with the client, and complete it systematically. I tend to advise against such an activity, at least early in the course of treatment. Instead, what I do is that I have a visual depiction of the cognitive behavioral model on a white board in my office. When I am getting to know clients, I listen for descriptions of what could potentially be key unhelpful and helpful beliefs, key psychological vulnerabilities and strengths, and so on. Upon identification of one of these constructs, I ask my client's permission to say a little bit more about the cognitive behavioral model that underlies treatment. As I am providing a (very basic) education about the model, I take what they told me in conversation, insert it into the model, speculate about the way in which it affects the expression of the mental health problems that bring them into treatment, and ask for feedback regarding the degree to which what

I am saying fits with their experience. Most clients are surprised (and heartened) to realize that their subjective experiences can be explained by a coherent theory that provides a pathway for intervention. I let them know that we will continue to "keep an eye" on the way in which these constructs impact their daily lives and figure out ways to work with them. When clients give me the feedback that my speculations do not resonate with them, I ask them if, in a general sense, the cognitive behavioral model makes sense to them (almost everyone says that it does), and I give my word that we will continue to be on the lookout for ways in which the model manifests in their lives. In this way, I am practicing in the spirit of Kuyken et al.'s (2006) collaborative case conceptualization approach.

Treatment Planning

We have now established that the case formulation guides treatment planning. In this section, I provide some more specific guidance for treatment planning. You will find that when you ask your clients what they would like to get out of treatment, most respond with a vague response, such as "feel better" or "feel less depressed or anxious." Although such responses are laudable goals, they are general enough that it is difficult to know how to measure progress. A convention that is used by cognitive behavioral therapists is to develop *SMART goals*, with SMART being an acronym for the following:

S = Specific
M = Measurable
A = Achievable
R = Realistic
T = Time-limited

The concept of SMART goals was originally developed to advance performance of employees (Doran, 1981). However, at present, they are regularly taught to students and trainees who are studying to become mental health professionals. When I lecture about treatment planning, I always ask for a show of hands from the audience to indicate who is familiar with the SMART goals convention. In most instances, between half and three-quarters of audience members raise their hands.

Let's take each of these interrelated characteristics in turn. For a goal to be "specific," it must be operationally defined. An *operational definition* contains the precise components of a general concept, such as "feeling better." When a client expresses a general goal like this, it is helpful to follow up with questions, such as: "What would it look like to be feeling better? What would you notice that would be different? What might others notice that would be different?" In many instances, clients continue to identify components that are a bit subjective and abstract. For example, if a client's initial goal is to "feel less depressed," when asked what that might look like (i.e., when asked to be more specific), the client might say something, such as "I'd have better self-esteem" or "I would feel more motivated." Although these responses are a bit more specific than feeling "less depressed," it is still difficult to know exactly what is meant by them. Thus, not only do we want our goals to be more specific, but we would also like them to be measurable. The most straightforward ways for goals to be "measurable" is for them to be defined in behavioral, observable terms. Continuing with our example, the cognitive behavioral therapist might follow up and ask: "What would you be doing differently if your self-esteem were to improve, or you were to have more motivation?" The client might then respond with behaviors, such as "working out more" or "applying for jobs." Combining the concepts of being specific and measurable, the cognitive behavioral therapist might probe even further, asking the client how many times per week he might aim to work out, or the number of jobs to which she might apply.

I pause for a moment to provide two caveats regarding the specificity and measurability of goals. First, although I am a staunch advocate for defining goals in quantitative terms to measure progress (e.g., "work out three times a week"), at the same time, I am an equally staunch an advocate for wording goals, so that they afford some flexibility and do not set up clients for failure or disappointment. For example, even the best of us do not always follow the rule to work out three times a week; after all, we are traveling some weeks, there are holidays other weeks, we are struggling with illness other weeks, and so on. Thus, I recommend that you build flexibility, creativity, back-up plans, and self-compassion into treatment goals. For example, rather than writing a specific and measurable goal, such as "work out three times a week," a more reasonable goal might be "work out approximately three times a week, finding alternative ways to be active if circumstances prevent me from sticking with my plan." One activity in treatment that would follow from this goal would be to specify exactly what types of "alternative ways to be active" would work for the client.

A second caveat is that no matter how probing we as cognitive behavioral therapists might be, clients are adamant that there are some goals that are inherently internal, especially those that involve a reduction in the frequency of self-defeating cognitions (e.g., "reduce frequency of self-defeating thoughts"). Early in my career, I would try my darndest to translate these internal, cognitively-oriented goals to goals that were behavioral and measurable (e.g., "But what would it look like to an outside observer if you reduced the frequency of self-deprecating thoughts? Let me ask it in a different way, what would you be doing differently if you had fewer self-deprecating thoughts?"). Sometimes this line of questioning would become exhausting, as no matter how hard I tried to identify behaviors that would correspond to the cognitive goals, I was running in circles with my clients and increasing the risk that I was "beating a dead horse." This state of affairs forced me to rethink goal setting in light of the therapy that I was providing—and that is cognitive behavioral therapy, with equal emphases on the "cognitive" and the "behavioral." As a result of this reflection, I am now more relaxed about setting cognitively-oriented treatment goals with my clients, and when they are identified during treatment planning, I simply ask my clients to operationalize the frequency and impact of these thoughts that they are aiming to achieve (e.g., "reduce the frequency of self-deprecating thoughts to only a few times a week and actively applying cognitive behavioral strategies to deal with them when they arise").

The other three characteristics of SMART goals is that they are "achievable," "realistic," and "time-limited." One reason why these characteristics of treatment goals are recommended is so that the client can notice meaningful changes in his or her life in a reasonable period of time, which would be expected to correspond to a reduction in the mental health problems that brought him or her to treatment in the first place. Having time-limited goals also decreases the likelihood that clients will fall into a pattern of procrastination (Dobson & Dobson, 2009). Although, as I mentioned in Chapter 1 of this volume, some people participate in courses of

CBT that would be considered "long-term" (i.e., a year or more), it is more typical that clients participate for a shorter amount of time, such as a few to several months. Consider a client who is applying to college but specifies "graduate from law school" as a goal for treatment. That goal would likely not be achievable or realistic during the period of time in which he is participating in CBT. More reasonable goals would be to "establish the following study habits that will allow me to be successful as an undergraduate and that will set me up for graduate study: "X, Y, Z" or "gain a sound understanding of the criteria that law schools require applicants to meet."

Worksheet 2.3 displays a typical treatment plan worksheet that cognitive behavioral therapists can complete with their clients to guide treatment. It consists of four columns: (a) problem area, (b) manifestations of the problem area, (c) measurement of progress, and (d) CBT strategy. Say, for example, that a client identifies "depression" as a problem area. In the spirit of being specific, we would ask her to list a few manifestations of depression. In the second column, then, she might write manifestations, such as "waking several times throughout the night," "lack of engagement in enjoyable activities," and "pessimistic thinking." To measure progress in a way that is achievable, realistic, and time-limited, she might aim to "sleep at least 7 hours a night, waking infrequently and falling back asleep within 15 minutes," "resume a schedule of running approximately three times a week, seeing a friend for lunch or coffee at least once a week, and reading for pleasure before bed most nights," and "demonstrate the ability to reshape or distance oneself from pessimistic thinking, as evidenced by the ability to continue engaging in goal-directed activity without 'shutting down' because of pessimistic thinking." In the final column, the cognitive behavioral therapist might suggest strategies such as "sleep hygiene," "behavioral activation," "cognitive restructuring," and "cognitive defusion."

Worksheet 2.3

Treatment Planning Worksheet

PROBLEM AREA	MANIFESTATIONS OF PROBLEM AREA	MEASUREMENT OF PROGRESS	CBT STRATEGY
1.	1. 2. 3. 4.	1. 2. 3. 4.	
2.	1. 2. 3. 4.	1. 2. 3. 4.	
3.	1. 2. 3. 4.	1. 2. 3. 4.	

Although many clients link their treatment goals with their symptoms, such as depression, anxiety, or anger, cognitive behavioral therapists also work with their clients to supplement the treatment plan with goals that are consistent with unhelpful beliefs, psychological vulnerabilities, and stressors that are identified in the case formulation. For example, another problem area that could be identified by a client is the significant life stress that she is experiencing. Specific manifestations of that stress might be "tension with supervisor at work," "not meeting deadlines at work," "difficulty paying bills," and "son getting in trouble at school." Measurable markers of progress that are achievable, realistic, and time-limited might be "increase frequency of collegial and collaborative communication with supervisor," "meet all deadlines at work, or proactively renegotiate deadlines before the timed has passed," "make all minimum monthly payments on time," and "develop plan with son's teacher to address his behavior." Corresponding cognitive behavioral strategies could be "problem solving," "communication skills training," and "cognitive restructuring" (the latter of which would be used to address negative thinking that would interfere with problem solving and the delivery of effective communication).

Case Examples

Throughout this book, we follow the application of cognitive and behavioral strategies with two cases—a case that most clinicians would regard as relatively "straightforward," and a case that most clinicians would regard as relatively "difficult." I chose this approach because, too often, I receive feedback from supervisees that the cases highlighted in CBT textbooks seem very straightforward, and that, in their experience, sessions with their clients rarely proceed the way they expect on the basis of the material presented in the text. Thus, with the "straightforward" case, I will illustrate the way in which we would expect the application of these techniques to work "in theory," and with the "difficult" case, I will illustrate the "real life" obstacles that clinicians often encounter when they are applying the techniques in practice. Also, before proceeding, I provide the disclaimer that although these cases are, indeed, based on actual clients who I have encountered in my practice, all identifying information has been changed.

"Straightforward" Case

The "straightforward" case that we will follow in this book is "Ashley," a 32-year-old Caucasian stay-at-home mother of three children. She specifically sought out CBT after several previous experiences with therapy—not all of which she regarded as negative experiences, but those that she regarded as relatively ineffective because she continued to struggle with clinically significant manifestations of anxiety, despite having been in treatment. When I completed a diagnostic interview with Ashley, she met criteria for generalized anxiety disorder (GAD). The following dialogue illustrates the way in which I asked questions during our first meeting that facilitated the development of the case formulation.

Dr. Amy: I'm going to ask some questions now that will help us to understand how you got to where you are today and what has been keeping you in this state of high anxiety. Is that okay?

Ashley: Yes, definitely.

Dr. Amy: Tell me a bit about your household while you were growing up. For example, did it feel like a safe environment, where you were free to express yourself, or at times did you find yourself walking on eggshells?

Ashley: No eggshells, my parents were really supportive. And I was close to my brother and sister. I still am, actually.

Dr. Amy: [making a reflection] Ah, so you had close, supportive relationships with your parents, as well as with your siblings.

Ashley: Yeah. If anything, maybe too close.

Dr. Amy: [sensing there might be something to this comment, which could contribute to the case formulation] Oh? What do you mean by that?

Ashley: Well, my mother worried all the time. She was kind of a homebody, because she was so scared of everything—scared to drive at night, scared of crowds at local events like fireworks. That sort of thing.

Dr. Amy: [using my clinical knowledge of other clients who have remarked on anxious parents] Would you say she was overprotective?

Ashley: Overprotective, yes, definitely overprotective. Although it didn't matter much with me, because I'm a homebody, too. I take after my mother. But I think it affected my siblings more, especially my brother. She wouldn't let him do a lot of the things that other boys his age were doing, like playing football, driving with his friends without an adult, things like that. It drove him crazy.

Dr. Amy: In what ways do you believe the home environment you describe played a role in your own anxiety?

Ashley: [pausing for a moment] That's a good question. I never thought of it before. [pausing again] I think I learned that you should always be cautious, that it is better to play it safe than to be sorry.

Dr. Amy: [making a reflection] Okay, so you received the messages that it is good to be cautious, better being safe than sorry. How did that type of mindset play out in your life?

Ashley: [rolling eyes] Lots of different ways. I was so studious in college that I hardly had any fun or did anything social. I would spend days upon days, hours upon hours, studying for each test, because I was so concerned that the professor would ask a question that I was unprepared to answer.

Dr. Amy: I see. And the consequences of that were that you studied a great deal, perhaps even overstudied at the expense of having more of a balance between school and friends?

Ashley: [nodding her head, become tearful]

Dr. Amy: [speaking gently] Am I sensing correctly that you wish you had approached school a bit differently?

Ashley: [averting eye contact, tears filling her eyes] Yes. All of my memories are of studying. I only keep in touch with a couple of girls from my dorm, and even then, it's just on social media. I really didn't get to know them in the way most college students get to know each other.

Dr. Amy: And what are the ways in which that cautious mindset impacts your life now?

Ashley: [pausing] I always make the safe choices. I majored in math and a 3.9 GPA but didn't do anything with it, because I was scared to take on the debt of medical or graduate school. So now I'm not working. And, and [pausing] even my marriage is a safe choice. My sister fixed us up. I just went with it, so that I didn't have to go out there and date.

Dr. Amy: How satisfied are you in your marriage, Ashley?

Ashley: [averting eye contact again, wringing her hands, and shaking her head] I'm not. Not at all. He works such long hours that he's never around. And when he *is* around, all he seems to do is criticize me.

Worksheet 2.4

Case Formulation Worksheet: Application to Ashley

RELEVANT BACKGROUND INFORMATION
Positive environmental experiences:
Negative environmental experiences:
Relevant biological vulnerabilities:
Psychological strengths:
Psychological vulnerabilities:
UNDERLYING BELIEFS
Helpful beliefs:
Unhelpful beliefs:
Life stress:
Buffers against life stress:
SITUATIONAL EXAMPLE
Upsetting situation:
Thought (or interpretation or meaning):
Emotional reaction (please rate intensity on a scale of 0 = no noticeable emotional reaction; 10 = most intense emotional reaction that one can imagine):
Physiological reaction:
Behavioral reaction:

Take a moment now to digest this dialogue and apply what you have learned about Ashley in the case formulation form in Worksheet 2.4. You will not be able to fill in all of the boxes, and some of what you fill in might be an educated guess (i.e., a hypothesis to be tested), rather than a true fact. In the following box, reflect upon the way in which the case formulation worksheet allowed you to organize the information you learned about Ashley, as well as the types of questions you would ask Ashley if you were the therapist in this session and was continuing the dialogue.

BOX 3 CASE FORMULATION: APPLICATION TO ASHLEY

Take a moment to reflect on the way in which the case formulation worksheet helped you to organize the information in this dialogue. What was helpful?

What did you find challenging?

If you were in the position in which you were continuing the dialogue with Ashley to gather additional information for the case formulation, what kinds of questions would you ask? How do you think the information you gather from these additional questions will enhance the case formation and your treatment plan?

1.

2.

3.

There is no exactly "right" or "wrong" way to develop a case formulation or "right" or "wrong" information to include in a case formulation. Nevertheless, in Worksheet 2.5, I provide an example of some of the information that either stood out to me, or that I inferred from this initial conversation between the two of us. Here, I explain my reasoning for the inclusion of these insights, so that beginning therapists can have a view into the mind of an experienced clinician.

Worksheet 2.5

Case Formulation Worksheet: Dr. Amy's Application to Ashley

RELEVANT BACKGROUND INFORMATION
Positive environmental experiences: *Close-knit, supporting, intact family-of-origin*
Negative environmental experiences: *Mother modeled excessive caution and overprotectiveness.*
Relevant biological vulnerabilities: *(Hypothesis) Anxiety disorder in mother*
Psychological strengths: *Good work ethic, diligence, conscientiousness*
Psychological vulnerabilities: *(Hypothesis) perfectionism, rigidity*
UNDERLYING BELIEFS
Helpful beliefs: *?*
Unhelpful beliefs: *(Hypothesis) The world is dangerous; I am vulnerable* *(To examine further): You should always be cautious; better to be safe than sorry*

Life stress: *Marital dissatisfaction* *(Hypothesis) Staying at home with three young children*
Buffers against life stress: *Close-knit family of origin*
SITUATIONAL EXAMPLE
Upsetting situation: *(From past) Upcoming test in college*
Thought (or interpretation or meaning): *The professor will ask a question I'm unprepared to answer*
Emotional reaction (please rate intensity on a scale of 0 = no noticeable emotional reaction; 10 = most intense emotional reaction that one can imagine): *Fear (no rating specified)*
Physiological reaction: *None specified*
Behavioral reaction: *Overstudying*

I regarded Ashley's family-of-origin as a positive environmental experience for many reasons, as they were intact (i.e., there was no divorce, separation, or estrangement of which we know at this point), and she experienced them as close-knit and supportive. At the same time, Ashley clearly indicated that her mother was overprotective and excessively cautious in the way in which she lived her life. When Ashley described her mother as someone who "worried all the time" and who was "scared of everything," I developed the hypothesis that her mother has an anxiety disorder that, therefore, could serve as a biological vulnerability. Ashley's reference to overstudying is a potential indicator for both psychological strengths and vulnerabilities. On the one hand, her self-description suggested that she has a good work ethic, is diligent, and is conscientious. At the same time, my clinical experience with clients who describe such a history is that they also struggle with perfectionism and rigidity. However, because I did not hear Ashley make direct reference to examples of these characteristics, I regarded them as hypotheses to be tested as I get to know her better during the course of treatment.

During our conversation, Ashley mainly focused on the negative aspects of her past and current life experiences. Focusing first on negative beliefs, upon questioning, she clearly indicated that she developed the beliefs that "you should always be cautious" and that it is "better to be safe than sorry." I listed these beliefs as unhelpful, but I denoted them with "to examine further," because I suspected that they hold Ashley back in life, rather than truly protect her, but I could not know for sure on the basis of this brief conversation. I also listed "The world is dangerous" and "I am vulnerable" as unhelpful beliefs on the basis of two factors: (a) the implications of what she had directly expressed to me, and (b) my clinical experience with clients with GAD. As a CBT beginner, you might not have this clinical experience, so it is fine for you to make guesses and regard them as hypotheses to be tested in the future. Conversely, Ashley did not directly express any helpful, or positive beliefs. I suspected that she certainly possesses some helpful beliefs, in light of the facts that she comes from a loving family and was successful in college. However, I did not have enough information to even form a hypothesis, so I included a question mark in that field (which is entirely appropriate to do if it seems that it would be premature even to make a hypothesis). I saw two current life stressors that had the potential to activate unhelpful beliefs: (a) the marital dissatisfaction that Ashley clearly mentioned in the conversation, and (b) a hypothesis, based on my clinical experience, that it is stressful for a mother to stay at home with three young children when her husband works long hours. At the same time, Ashley indicated that she continued to be close with her family-of-origin, so this closeness likely serves as a buffer against life stress and as context for the activation of helpful beliefs.

In this conversation, Ashley was mainly describing general characteristics of her family-of-origin and her current life, although she was more specific when she relayed information about her college years. I was able to translate that to a situational example in which unhelpful cognitive and behavioral patterns were elucidated. Specifically, Ashley described what would happen when she was anticipating a test in college (situation). Her thought was that the professor would ask a question she was unprepared to answer. She described herself as being "scared to death" of this scenario, so I listed fear as the emotion (though I did not obtain a rating of the intensity of the fear that she experienced, nor of her physiological reactions, because she was describing a situation that occurred many years ago). However, Ashley clearly indicated a distinct behavioral response—that of overstudying.

If you indicated other constructs of beliefs on your case formulation of Ashley's clinical presentation, it is okay. You might very well have observed something that I did not observe, or hypothesized something on the basis of your understanding of the research literature or from your clinical or life experience that I did not hypothesize. As stated previously, the beauty of case formulations is one of that they evolve over time as you get to know your client, as your hypotheses are confirmed or disconfirmed, and as new information is gathered. In fact, the development of the case formulation is one of the most enriching exercises that are done in group supervision, because the research knowledge and clinical and life experiences of many clinicians can be pooled to develop a rich understanding of a client's clinical presentation.

Before moving onto the more difficult case, I can imagine some beginning cognitive behavioral therapists wondering what makes this case relatively "straightforward." Here are some reasons why, at least at the outset, when I first met her, I regarded as having a relatively straightforward clinical presentation:

1. Though she exhibited some symptoms of depression, Ashley carried one and only one diagnosis—GAD—and she did not exhibit features of other disorders that, historically, have been considered difficult to treat in psychotherapy (e.g., antisocial or borderline personality disorder, psychosis).
2. Ashley did well in college, suggesting that she has more than enough intellectual capacity to appreciate even the most sophisticated aspects of CBT. This was evidenced in a tiny way when I asked her if she believed that her home environment played a role in her anxiety, and she gave a thoughtful response that directly illuminated some beliefs that she holds about being cautious and better safe than sorry.
3. Although the fact that Ashley overstudied is regarded in the case formulation as a problematic behavior, it also suggests that she is conscientious and willing to do homework which, as you will see in Chapter 4 of this volume, bodes well for success in CBT.
4. Ashley answered the questions in an open, straightforward, and non-defensive manner, which made it straightforward for me, as her therapist, to get to know her and formulate a rudimentary case formulation rather quickly.

"Difficult" Case

The "difficult" case that we will follow in this book is "Marilyn" a 54-year-old single woman of mixed race (Filipino father, Caucasian mother), who had participated in several courses of therapy for chronic depression. Two previous mental health providers had also diagnosed her with borderline personality disorder, a diagnosis with which she disagreed. Marilyn worked at a botanical garden and lived alone in a small house, admitting that she hated her job and that she was very lonely when she came home from work each evening. She often "threw back a few cocktails" to curtail the loneliness and sense that life was passing her by. She described her upbringing as one in which "children were meant to be seen rather than heard" and perceived her parents as highly critical of her, and as favoring her older brother because he was male. The following dialogue illustrates the way in which I asked questions during our first meeting that facilitated the development of the case formulation.

Marilyn: Therapy has never been helpful. Nothing has ever worked. All my therapists tell me that I am doing something *wrong* and that I need to change. But how can I change if I don't even know what is *right*?

Dr. Amy: [demonstrating empathy] It sounds like therapy has been frustrating for you in the past.

Marilyn: Yes, yes it has. I've spent so much money, and for what? Life has passed me by. I'm never going to find a husband. I'm too old to have kids now. I just don't get the things that other people get in life.

Dr. Amy: [speaking gently] It sounds like things are really hard for you right now, Marilyn. [Marilyn nods her head.] [deciding to move toward a specific manifestation of her distress that I might be able to conceptualize as a situational example for the case formulation] Can you give me a specific example of something that you're finding hard in your life right now, at this very time?

Marilyn: [having difficulty giving me a specific example, and growing agitated] It's just everything—work! Dating! My mom! Life!

Dr. Amy: [providing some hope for our work together] It sounds like there are many areas of your life that are upsetting. That's okay; that's what I'm here for. Together, we can sort them out and develop specific goals for ways in which you'd like these areas of your life to be different.

Marilyn: [responding with an unexpected amount of anger and hostility] What makes you think that it will be so easy for you to do that? What makes you think you can provide any help to me at all?

Dr. Amy: [using a soft, even, non-defensive tone of voice] I don't at all know that it will be easy, Marilyn. But I do know that you reached out to me to give CBT a try. That suggests to me that you want to give therapy another shot. Perhaps see if this experience will be different than the others?

Marilyn: [sinking back into her chair, looking forlorn] Yeah, I guess so. You're right. I just really don't have a lot of hope that anything *can* change.

Throughout the session, I attempted to assess Marilyn's thoughts, emotional reactions, and coping strategies associated with current life difficulties, as well as underlying beliefs associated with painful childhood experiences and former romantic relationships that she described. In most instances, Marilyn responded in a similar manner as that depicted in the dialogue, with a sense of hopelessness, disdain for previous courses of therapy, and mild hostility toward me. As a result, I adjusted the speed of my information gathering, focusing primarily on cultivating the therapeutic relationship, which will be discussed in greater length in the subsequent chapter. Nevertheless, I developed a preliminary case formulation, captured in Worksheet 2.6, albeit with many areas for which I had very little data and that I knew I would observe as my work with Marilyn progressed (given the somewhat unorthodox way that our first session went, I will not ask you to make your own attempt at developing a case formulation!).

Worksheet 2.6

Case Formulation Worksheet: Dr. Amy's Application to Marilyn

RELEVANT BACKGROUND INFORMATION
Positive environmental experiences: *None reported*
Negative environmental experiences: *Perceived parents as critical; perceived parents as favoring of her older brother because he was male*
Relevant biological vulnerabilities: *Family history of mental health problems not taken*
Psychological strengths: *(Hypothesis) Persistence*
Psychological vulnerabilities: *Pessimism, judgementalness; (hypothesis) rigidity, excessive alcohol use*
UNDERLYING BELIEFS
Helpful beliefs: *?*
Unhelpful beliefs: *The future is hopeless; Life has passed me by; I don't get the things that other people get in life* *(To examine further): negative beliefs about the self*

Life stress: *Stressful work environment* *Social isolation*
Buffers against life stress: *?*
SITUATIONAL EXAMPLE
Upsetting situation: *Reflection on previous courses of therapy*
Thought (or interpretation or meaning): *Therapy hasn't been helpful*
Emotional reaction (please rate intensity on a scale of 0 = no noticeable emotional reaction; 10 = most intense emotional reaction that one can imagine): *Frustration (observed)*
Physiological reaction: *None specified*
Behavioral reaction: *Hostility toward new therapist*

Marilyn did not report any positive environmental experiences during our session, so I indicated as such on the case conceptualization form. With regard to negative environmental experiences, I indicated that Marilyn perceived her parents as being critical, and favoring her older brother because he was male. Notice that I used the word "perceive." Because Marilyn demonstrated a tendency to have strong reactions to whatever she was talking about (e.g., previous courses of therapy, her life in general), I did not want to take at face value that her parents, indeed, exhibited these behaviors until I had more specific examples from Marilyn to support these points. Nevertheless, Marilyn's perception of her parents' behavior is important to note, as these perceptions could very well have shaped the way in which she viewed herself and others, even if they were not necessarily accurate. I did not have the opportunity to take a family history of mental health problems, so I indicated as such on the case formulation form. Regarding psychological strengths, I hypothesized that Marilyn is characterized by persistence, as evidenced by the fact that she has attempted many courses of therapy and is now seeking CBT even though she has not found therapy to be helpful in the past. Regarding psychological vulnerabilities, I listed pessimism and judgmentalness, because I observed them clearly throughout the session. I hypothesized that she was also characterized by rigidity on the basis of my experience with clients with chronic depression and borderline personality features. I also regarded excessive alcohol use as a poor behavioral habit, noting the importance of conducting further assessment to determine exactly how frequently and how much she was drinking at night.

Because of the way in which Marilyn responded to me in our initial session, I did not have much information to speculate about underlying beliefs. In addition, because she did not describe anything positive in her life during the session, I was unable to even form a hypothesis about positive underlying beliefs. She did, however, make many statements that reflected a sense of hopelessness and pessimism. Thus, I included a general belief reflecting hopelessness (i.e., "The future is hopeless"), as well as two more specific beliefs using the words that she supplied (i.e., "Life has passed me by," "I don't get the things that other people get in life"). This hopelessness was manifested in the situational example, in which she regarded therapy as unhelpful when she reflected on her previous therapy experiences, resulting in what I observed as frustration and somewhat hostile behavior toward me. Although she did not overtly express any negative beliefs about the self, I indicated on the case formulation form that this should be an area to examine further, on the basis of my experience with clients who have struggled with chronic depression and social isolation. Regarding life stress that can activate or buffer against these beliefs, Marilyn mentioned that she hated her job, so I listed "stressful work environment." Because she referenced "loneliness" on many occasions, I also listed social isolation as an additional life stressor.

Despite the fact that I did not ask you to develop a case formulation of Marilyn's clinical presentation, I ask you here to reflect on my work with Marilyn thus far, as well as the type of information that you would like to get from her, if you were continuing to work with her.

BOX 4 CASE FORMULATION: REFLECTION ON MARILYN

Take a moment to reflect on my preliminary case formulation of Marilyn's clinical presentation. With which aspects do you agree and disagree?

What did you find challenging in my dialogue with Marilyn?

If you were in the position in which you were continuing the dialogue with Marilyn to gather additional information for the case formulation, what kinds of questions would you ask? How do you think the information you gather from these additional questions will enhance the case formation and your treatment plan?

1.

2.

3.

What makes Marilyn's case relatively difficult? Below I list factors that contributed to my view of her case in this manner.

1) Marilyn reported chronic depression that had not responded to several courses of treatment. This history raises the possibility that Marilyn would likely not respond completely to CBT in a small number of sessions.
2) Marilyn exhibited signs of borderline personality disorder, which is characterized by intense negative affect and unstable patterns in relationships, including the therapeutic relationship, and she indicated that two previous therapists had diagnosed her with the condition. Borderline personality disorder has, historically, been regarded as a mental health disorder that is difficult to treat (National Collaborating Centre for Mental Health, 2009), although, fortunately, cognitive behavioral therapists have made great gains in developing unique treatment approaches for these clients (Linehan, 1993).
3) Marilyn did not answer questions in a straightforward manner. Instead, she spoke in "all-or-nothing" generalities and had difficulty providing specific examples when prompted. As you will see in Chapter 5 of this volume on cognitive restructuring, many cognitive behavioral interventions are most effective when clients can identify specific examples from their lives, in which their symptoms have caused life interference and can work with their therapists to devise specific ways to intervene.
4) Marilyn demonstrated a negative attitude toward treatment. Research shows that clients who approach treatment with negative attitudes or low expectations usually have poorer outcomes than clients with more positive attitudes or higher expectations (Devilly & Borkovec, 2000; Joyce & Piper, 1998; Safren, Heimberg, & Juster, 1997; Sotsky et al., 1991; Wenzel, Jeglic, Levy-Mack, Beck, & Brown, 2008; see Shapiro & Shapiro, 1997, for a review). It could be, for example, that clients with a negative attitude create a self-fulfilling prophesy for themselves, such that they do not fully participate in or embrace the therapeutic interventions that are delivered to them, so these interventions do not achieve their full potential, resulting in poorer outcome. Behavioral manifestations of such negative attitudes toward treatment include homework noncompliance and a high rate of missed sessions.
5) Marilyn demonstrated mild hostility toward me, which had the potential to make it particularly difficult for me to develop a strong therapeutic relationship with her (see more about the therapeutic relationship in Chapter 3).

Tips for Maximizing Effectiveness

Many mental health professionals, when they are first getting to know a client and gathering information about them, ask relatively straightforward questions about the family background (e.g., marital status of parents, number of siblings) and current life situation (e.g., the type of job they have, people in their social support network). Although this information is important to know, cognitive behavioral therapists go beyond this factual information and ask questions about messages clients have taken from their previous and current life circumstances, and strategies they developed to learn to cope with life circumstances that are difficult. Such questions are asked strategically in order to develop the case formulation. Table 2.2 lists some of the kinds of strategic questions that cognitive behavioral therapists can ask during a first appointment with a client. The main point is that gathering details about your client's life facilitates the case

Table 2.2 Questions to Facilitate the Case Formulation

- "Tell me about an experience from your past that really shaped the person who you are today."
- "Tell me about an experience from your past that can shed light on the issues that bring you here to see me today."
- [when the client is discussing a troubling past experience] "What message did that experience give you about yourself? Others? The way the world works? Do you still carry that message with you today?"
- [when the client is discussing a troubling past experience] "How did you cope with that? What coping strategies did you develop from that? How do you use those coping strategies now?"
- "What did you learn about marriage and parenting from observing your parents?"
- "What did you learn about friendships from your peer relationships while growing up?"
- "What did you learn about accomplishment or achievement from your academic experiences? From your work experiences?"
- "What is your greatest strength? Describe the circumstances in which you developed that strength."
- "Tell me about a transformative experience in your life. What did you learn from it? What have you taken with you from it?"

formulation *especially* when you ask about beliefs and habitual coping, or compensatory strategies that may have formed from those details.

When I ask these questions of my clients, we usually stumble upon a fairly significant underlying belief, even in the first session. When I hear the client express such a belief, I ask the client's permission to educate him or her about the cognitive behavioral model. As stated previously, in my office on a white board, I have a model that looks something like Figure 2.2. I encourage beginning cognitive behavioral therapists to do the same. Thus, when I take the opportunity to educate clients about the cognitive behavioral model, I point to the constructs on my white board, using the examples that they, themselves, supplied in response to my questions. I indicate to my clients that it is typical to work with the situational manifestations of problematic cognition and behavior so that they can begin to get relief from their emotional distress, respond to stressors more adaptively, and solve problems relatively immediately. However, I tell them that we will be on alert for manifestations of helpful and unhelpful beliefs, and compensatory strategies that often provide thematic context for situational thoughts and behaviors, and that it is my expectation that the most lasting change in CBT occurs when we are able to shift beliefs that are unhelpful to beliefs that are more balanced and adaptive.

There will undoubtedly be times in which you have an initial session with a client who is ambivalent about treatment, who has a negative attitude about treatment (as did Marilyn), or who simply does not want to be in treatment. In these instances, if clients are not responding to your strategic questions to facilitate the case formulation, do not be concerned that you are doing something wrong. Focus on cultivating the therapeutic relationship (which is the focus of Chapter 3 of this volume). Demonstrate genuine interest in the client's life and experiences. It is difficult to deliver effective CBT without a sound therapeutic relationship. Many times, clients just need to develop a level of comfort and trust with the therapist before they are ready to truly engage in the process. Other clients have a history of maltreatment or betrayal by others and likely carry powerful beliefs, such as "People who I get close to just leave me" or "People I let in will use the information they learn against me." They need to accumulate evidence that you, as the therapist, will be different.

Application to a Client

Although you likely perceive your case formulation skills to be rudimentary, I would like you to take a moment to apply the concepts learned this chapter to one of your clients. As I have emphasized throughout the chapter, the case formulation need not be "perfect" or exact; rather, the purpose of the exercise is to gain some practice from yet another perspective, after you have applied it to yourself and to the relatively straightforward case described in this chapter. Thus, to complete this exercise, choose a client on your caseload and apply the cognitive behavioral model to understanding his or her clinical presentation, using the case formulation sheet in Worksheet 2.7 as a template to record your observations. You can choose to complete the exercise for a client whom you have been seeing for some time, for whom you have already gathered much of the relevant information, or for a client whom you have just met recently, which would allow you to practice applying the framework as you are beginning to understand his or her presenting issues and developing a treatment plan. In Box 5 below, reflect on the exercise.

Worksheet 2.7

Case Formulation Worksheet: Application to A Client

RELEVANT BACKGROUND INFORMATION
Positive environmental experiences:
Negative environmental experiences:
Relevant biological vulnerabilities:
Psychological strengths:
Psychological vulnerabilities:
UNDERLYING BELIEFS
Helpful beliefs:
Unhelpful beliefs:
Life stress:
Buffers against life stress:
SITUATIONAL EXAMPLE
Upsetting situation:
Thought (or interpretation or meaning):
Emotional reaction (please rate intensity on a scale of 0 = no noticeable emotional reaction; 10 = most intense emotional reaction that one can imagine):
Physiological reaction:
Behavioral reaction:

BOX 5 REFLECTION ON CASE FORMULATION OF YOUR CLIENT

What do you conclude about your client from this exercise?

Was case formulation easier or more difficult to implement than you had expected? Why?

What types of questions do you need to ask your clients to hone your case formulation skills?

How will completing this exercise influence your therapeutic work with your client?

CHAPTER 3 THERAPEUTIC RELATIONSHIP

Therapeutic Relationship

CHAPTER 3

Think of your most nurturing and supportive relationships. What about them allowed you to feel comfortable being yourself, explore your environment, feel cared for, and accomplish things in life? To what degree do you attribute your success in life to the support you experienced from these relationships? A major goal of this chapter is to help you to put words onto the central qualities of these important relationships, so that you have a heuristic to guide you in your cognitive behavioral work with clients. Below, I invite you to reflect on these important relationships and the specific aspects of these relationships that you found so appealing and helpful.

BOX 1 **INITIAL REFLECTION ON IMPORTANT SUPPORTIVE RELATIONSHIPS**

Please think about one or more important supportive relationship in your life—past or present. Write down the name(s) of that person. In a few sentences, write down what it is about the relationship(s) that have been so appealing and helpful.

These relationships likely overlap with, but are not identical to, the therapeutic relationship in psychotherapy. In point of fact, the therapeutic relationship is one of the most unique relationships that exists between two people. The *therapeutic relationship* is just as it sounds—the relationship between you, the therapist, and your client. It consists of three main components. Within the CBT literature, the component that has, by far, received the greatest amount of attention is the *therapeutic alliance*, itself composed of three pieces: (a) the *bonds* between the therapist and client; (b) the *goals* for the course of therapy; and (c) the *tasks* of therapy, or what the therapist and client do together in order to achieve the goals (Bordin, 1979). Research on the therapeutic alliance in CBT suggests that it steadily increases throughout the course of treatment and that it predicts successful outcome (see Martin, Garske, & Davis, 2000). Although many clinicians hold the belief that a sound therapeutic alliance must be in place first, before embarking on the work associated with CBT, in actuality, research shows that early gains achieved by the work done in CBT, in turn, enhances the therapeutic alliance (DeRubeis, Brotman, & Gibbons, 2005; DeRubeis & Feeley, 1990; Webb et al., 2011). In other words, as clients begin to see changes in their lives and attribute those changes to the work they have done in CBT, they report a stronger sense of alliance with their therapist. These results have clinical significance for the practicing cognitive behavioral therapists for two reasons: (a) they demonstrate that cognitive behavioral therapists need not withhold powerful CBT interventions at the beginning of treatment before the therapeutic alliance has been developed; and (b) they show that taking time to link early gains made in treatment to the goals, tasks, and bonds in therapy can go a long way in promoting good outcome.

The other two components of the therapeutic relationship receive much less attention in the CBT literature, but are nevertheless important (Durvasula, 2015). *Transference* occurs when the client has a distinct reaction to you, which is often reminiscent of something that happened in an important relationship in his or her past. Practitioners of some schools of psychotherapy, such as psychodynamic psychotherapy, believe that good outcome in treatment is most likely to occur when transference is identified and successfully addressed during the course of psychotherapy. Although the identification and resolution of transference is not a central task in CBT, the transference reaction can, without a doubt, serve as a vehicle for in-session CBT work to be done to resolve the issue, allowing the client an opportunity to observe the first-hand application of CBT skills in resolving relationship tension and achieve important learning that can be applied to close relationships in the client's life outside of session. In addition, *interpersonal sharing* occurs when the client and therapist, alike, share their genuine feelings and thoughts about their relationship and the work that they are doing together. It is my belief that it is this sort of intangible connection that brings any type of psychotherapy to a higher level and sets up the therapist and client for a successful therapeutic experience (and an experience that can make a difference in both their lives).

Over the years, CBT has been criticized for minimizing the importance of and attention to the therapeutic relationship. Critics view it as mechanistic and impersonal, almost as if the therapist is following a recipe. In some instances, I understand where this criticism comes from. Many supervisees tell me that, when they are first learning CBT, they believe that they believe they must keep a "checklist" in mind (and sometimes, they write out a checklist on a piece of paper that they consult!), listing the components of session structure (see Chapter 4 of this volume) and some of the steps of the most standard CBT strategies. It is understandable that they do this; after all, they are caring, conscientious individuals who want to deliver CBT with the utmost integrity to their clients. However, the downside of doing this is that checklists have the potential to stifle spontaneity, and heartfelt interaction.

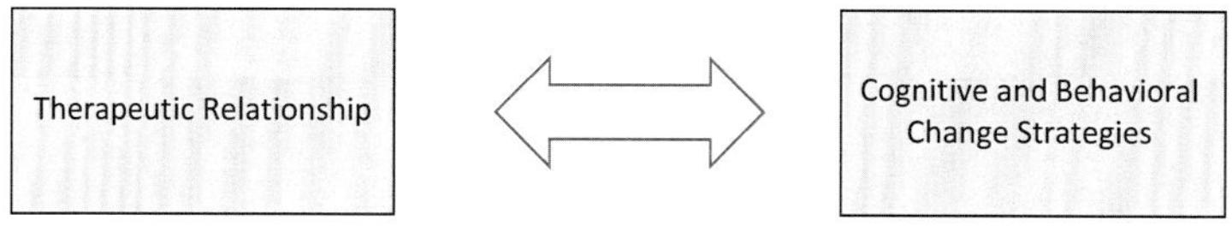

Figure 3.1 Balance Between the Therapeutic Relationship and Cognitive Behavioral Change Strategies

I hereby give permission to the therapists-in-training who are reading this book to focus first on forming a genuine connection with clients before implementing CBT structure and strategy. Remember what I said in Chapter 1 of this volume—that there is very little you can do in session that is *not* in the spirit of CBT when you approach the session in a thoughtful manner guided (at least loosely) by cognitive behavioral theory. The therapeutic relationship is the foundation from which more specific cognitive behavioral interventions stem. Figure 3.1 is an example of the way in which I conceptualize the balance, or overlap, between the therapeutic relationship and cognitive behavioral change.

As they acquire skill in CBT, therapists-in-training learn that they can *simultaneously* achieve these goals. Consider the difference between the following dialogues, in which the therapist is implementing the standard CBT intervention of reviewing homework.

DIALOGUE #1

Therapist: Is it okay if we review your homework?
Rachel: Sure, it's right here.
Therapist: [reading what the client has written on a *thought record*, which will be discussed in greater length in Chapter 5 of this volume] You've done a thorough job, Rachel. Well done. What did you get out of completing this homework?
Rachel: Well, I learned that the way I think really affects my mood at any given moment.
Therapist: Yes, I agree with you. I was hoping that you would see that from this exercise. Is it okay if we talk more about ways to work with these thoughts once you identify them?
Rachel: Definitely, yes.

DIALOGUE #2

Therapist: I've been thinking a lot since we last met about the things in your life that are upsetting you, Rachel. Just curious—did you write about any of them on your *thought record*?
Rachel: Sure, it's right here.
Therapist: [reading what the client has written on a *thought record*, which will be discussed at greater length in Chapter 5 of this volume] You've done a thorough job, Rachel. Well done. [pausing] Oh, I see here that you had an upsetting experience at the party on Saturday night. I know how worried you were about that event.
Rachel: It was really hard. I saw so many people on "that" side of the family. They are all so judgmental!
Therapist: I see that from what you've written here. I'm sorry that the family gathering ended up being so difficult for you. Would you like to talk about that some more?
Rachel: Oh yes, definitely.

Therapist: I also see here that you wrote about the job interview. I've been pulling for you, Rachel. Can we talk more about that as well? I'm really interested to hear how that went.

Rachel: [face brightening] Okay! I think it went really well.

Therapist: [responding in a genuine, heartfelt manner] Oh, that's so good to hear. When we talk about it, let's focus on how our work together prepared you for it and what you can learn for similar experiences in the future. Sound good?

Rachel: Okay!

Therapist: And just to round out our game plan for today, I have some other ideas of where we can take the work you've done here—figuring out how to reshape the thoughts, so that they are working for you, rather than working against you. We can apply what I have to the family gathering situation, the interview, and any other situations that you see fit. Is that okay?

Rachel: [responding enthusiastically] Yes, perfect!

Take a moment to reflect on the differences that you see in these two dialogues.

There is nothing inherently unappealing about Dialogue #1. The cognitive behavioral therapist is quite dutiful in acknowledging the homework that the client completed, praising her for her work, asking her to reflect on what she learned from it (which, as you will see in the next chapter, consolidates learning), and asking permission to make working on thoughts a topic to focus on in session. There is nothing to suggest that the client is responding negatively to the therapist. In fact, the therapist could be speaking in a very warm, inviting, non-judgmental manner—all qualities that enhance the therapeutic relationship.

However, I believe that Dialogue #2 brings something "extra" to the therapeutic relationship that is developing between the therapist and client. The therapist opens with a statement indicating that she has been thinking about the client and all that is on her plate, which demonstrates genuine concern for the client's well-being. Then the therapist communicated curiosity as to whether the client was able to use these life situations in completing her homework. The therapist expressed empathy when the client mentioned that a family gathering was difficult for her, and she also expressed interest in how a job interview went. Many clients give the feedback that these personal touches—overt expressions of empathy and interest by the therapist—are noticed and truly appreciated.

There are many aspects of CBT that inherently add to the therapeutic relationship. As mentioned in Chapter 1 of this volume, *collaboration* is a key tenet of CBT, such that the therapist and client work together as equal members of a team to address the client's life problems that have brought him or her to treatment. Thus, the therapist is neither directive in an authoritative manner, nor is the therapist so passive that he or she contributes little insight, structure, or reaction to what the client is saying. Collaboration communicates respect for the client's autonomy, opinions, and intimate knowledge of his of her life situation. A second aspect of CBT that enhances the therapeutic relationship is the solicitation of *feedback*. If clients are to be truly treated as equal members of a team, then it is important to touch base with them periodically to ensure that they believe the therapeutic interventions being delivered have promise and are a good match for their needs. In addition, it is important to check in to assess whether they are having a negative reaction to anything that the therapist has said or done, so that the potential transgression can be addressed from a cognitive behavioral framework. The solicitation of feedback communicates that the therapist is truly interested in using the client's preferences to shape the course of treatment. A third aspect of CBT that facilitates the therapeutic relationship is *guided discovery*, a process in which the therapists asks guided questions that allow the client to grapple with his or her own issues and take ownership over his or her own conclusions, rather than being told by the therapist what to do or how to think. Therapists who practice guided discovery provide clients with tangible assistance with their life problems, while, at the same time, allowing for client autonomy and individualized pacing.

That being said, these aspects of CBT are essential but not sufficient in truly cultivating a strong therapeutic relationship. Consider the blog post by the renowned psychodynamic therapist, Jonathan Shelder (2015). In comparing CBT with psychodynamic psychotherapy, the latter of which, has traditionally been viewed as an approach in which the therapeutic relationship is central in creating change, he highlighted an article about CBT which indicated that in order to build a strong therapeutic alliance, cognitive behavioral therapists work collaboratively with clients, ask for feedback and demonstrate warmth and interest in case, in their clients. Shelder wrote in response:

> I expect that much from my hair stylist or real estate broker. From a psychotherapist, I expect something more. The CBT thought leader seemed to have no concept that the therapy relationship is a window into the patient's inner world, or a relationship laboratory and sanctuary where lifelong patterns can be recognized and understood, and new ones created.

Dr. Shedler might be judging CBT a bit harshly in this piece—I certainly do not know of the CBT "thought leader" to which he is referring, and I cannot evaluate whether he is accurately evaluating the original piece describing CBT and the therapeutic relationship that he read. However, Dr. Shedler (perhaps a bit provocatively) brings out the important point that there is something intimate about the therapeutic relationship that goes beyond collaboration and feedback. I believe that this (perhaps intangible) intimacy is important for therapists to acknowledge, respect, embrace, and even savor. It is this point on which I would like to take a moment to elaborate.

The therapist has the privilege of witnessing and even experiencing the client's vulnerability. The client invites the therapist into his or her interpersonal world, so that the therapist can develop an intricate understanding of how the client approaches relationships. Together, they create a possibility for the client to have a learning experience that will provide a template for the development and maintenance of close relationships in the future. In many instances, clients disclose painful or embarrassing information about themselves, their family members, or their life experiences that they have never disclosed to another person. Such disclosure creates a bond between the client and therapist that could be unlike any other bond that the client has in his or her life. I encourage therapists I supervise to honor and respect this unique opportunity and be mindful of the initial level of trust that the client demonstrated by choosing the therapist to be a partner in the therapeutic process.

Because of the importance of the therapeutic relationship, it is crucial that beginning therapists be oriented to principles of the therapeutic relationship that are essential features of all types of psychotherapy. Many of these principles are those that characterize an array of supportive relationships, not only the relationship between the therapist and client. However, when they are harnessed in a manner that creates a safe environment to discuss and address sensitive, and even painful issues, and that fosters the opportunity for learning a new way of being with a trusted individual, the therapeutic relationship can serve as an important mechanism of change in its own right.

Although many of the features described in this paragraph might seem self-evident, it is essential that therapists stay mindful of them in session and consciously respond in a manner that reflects these principles. First, a therapist communicates to the client that he or she has heard what the client has said and grasps the internal reality of the client. This understanding can be communicated through reflection, paraphrasing, summarizing, and expressions of empathic understanding. Many clients who present for therapy believe that their concerns are overlooked, or dismissed, or ignored by others in their lives, so leaving a session with the sense that they have been heard and understood can be a powerful experience for them. Second, the therapist approaches the client with a positive, inviting disposition that communicates that the therapist is sincerely interested in the client's well-being. This disposition is communicated to the client when the therapist is mindful of the principles of genuineness, warmth, concern, and unconditional positive regard. Fortunately, these features are often ones that we, as caring clinicians, do naturally, but at the same time, it is important to be mindful of making overt demonstrations of them. Third, to fully engage clients in the therapeutic process, the therapist asks open-ended questions that invite clients to elaborate on their experiences and share openly. Open-ended questions create space for clients to reflect on their experiences and consider new ideas or new perspectives on their life problems. Finally, the therapist demonstrates a sense of confidence in the therapeutic abilities and in the methods that he or she is using, which instills a sense of hope in clients that their lives can be different. A strong therapeutic relationship characterized by these features communicates the following messages:

- "I care."
- "I'm interested in what happens to you."
- "I'm invested in what happens to you."
- "I want life to be different for you, just as much as you do."
- "I'm in this with you."
- "I can help you."
- "I want to help you."
- "I will help you find a way out, even when it is hard for you to find a way on your own."
- "You get credit for your own victories, but I will savor them right along with you."

Throughout the course of treatment, be on the alert for indications of the way in which the client views the therapeutic relationship. When clients view the therapeutic relationship in a positive manner, such as when they reflect fondly on the support they received from the therapist about a particular issue with which they were struggling, the goals of therapy can be enhanced. For example, at the time of the writing of this book, I was working with a client who struggled with significant public speaking anxiety. I strongly encouraged him to attend meetings sponsored by Toastmasters, a group with chapters worldwide that allows people the opportunity to hone their public speaking skills. The rationale underlying this intervention was to seize opportunities for exposure, or the systematic contact with a feared situation (see Chapter 6 of this volume), as well as refinement in his public speaking skills. He had avoided a couple of Toastmaster's meetings but eventually attended one, and to his surprise, he won a small award for the "Best Table Topic," a short speech in which he introduced himself. He sent me a message entitled "This one's for you!," attached a picture of the award, and wrote: "Thank you for your support. I couldn't have done it without you!" Through this message, it was clear that we were "in it together" and that he viewed this as a victory for both of us. Not only did such an expression of delight provide an indication of the success that we were having together in our therapeutic work, it also provided a great deal of gratification for me, personally, reminding me of the reason why I went into this profession, and reinforcing the fact that the work I am doing is meaningful.

However, there will be some instances in which the client provides feedback suggesting that something is "off" in the therapeutic relationship, and the openness and respect with which you respond to it can go a long way in "turning things around," ultimately enhancing outcome. You will see the way in which this unfolds as you follow the "difficult" client throughout the rest of this volume. I realize that it feels daunting, as a caring mental health professional, to receive negative feedback from clients. However, as I mentioned in Chapter 1 of this volume, at least one study has demonstrated that outcome in CBT is *enhanced* when a rupture in the therapeutic relationship is repaired successfully. Thus, viewing a problem in the therapeutic relationship as an opportunity for important interpersonal learning and for a good outcome, would go a long way in helping you to maintain a balanced view of what is happening between you and the client, and to plan in a strategic, non-judgmental way to ultimately enhance the therapeutic relationship.

The Therapeutic Relationship: Reflection and Experiential Exercise

As you can see, a strong therapeutic relationship is essential for success in psychotherapy. In this section, you will have the opportunity to reflect on your learning and on ways to apply this to your own relationships, both in and out of session.

BOX 2 **REFLECTION ON LEARNING**

Please use this space to reflect on the central features of a strong therapeutic relationship in order to consolidate your learning on this topic.

Name the three features of a strong therapeutic relationship described in the previous section that you view as most important in psychotherapy. Why are these features particularly important to you?

(continued)

(continued)

1.

2.

3.

What do you see as an important feature of a strong therapeutic relationship that was *not* introduced in the previous section. Why is this feature particularly important to you?

What themes did you notice in your responses? Were there certain aspects of the therapeutic relationship that seemed more important to you than others? In what ways did you see these aspects as serving as a catalyst for change throughout the course of psychotherapy?

Intellectual exercises such as reading about important features of the therapeutic relationship and consolidating learning by providing reflections on the therapeutic relationship are one important cornerstone of learning. However, as I have mentioned previously, therapists-in-training often lament the lack of experiential learning opportunities that allow them to experience and practice, first hand, the therapeutic skills, tools, and strategies that are described in psychotherapy textbooks. You did this in Chapter 2 of this volume by developing a CBT case formulation as applied to yourself (or to a close other). Here, I would like you to have the experience of practicing these fundamentals of a strong therapeutic relationship, rather than simply reading about them. Use the following steps as a guideline:

1. Recall the three most important features of the therapeutic relationship that you developed in Box 2 above. Describe, specifically, three behaviors that fit with your style and that you believe would exemplify each of these features. Table 3.1 provides space for you to list these behaviors.
2. Choose a client with whom you are working on a regular basis with whom you can implement the behaviors identified in Step #1.

3. Across the course of three sessions, implement the behaviors systematically. That is, in one session, implement the behaviors associated with one of the key features of the therapeutic relationship that you identified, and observe the effects. In a second session, implement the behaviors associated with the second of the key features of the therapeutic relationship that you identified, and observe the effects. And, in a third session, implement the behaviors associated with the third of the key features of the therapeutic relationship that you identified, and observe the effects. Although you might find it a bit artificial to separate the implementation of the three sets of behavior, it is important to do so in this experiential exercise so that you can isolate the effects of each one of the three key components of the therapeutic relationship that you identified as being most important.
4. Record your observations in the second part of Table 3.1.
5. In Box 4 below, please supply your reflections to specify the specific ways in which the results of your reading, previous reflection, and practice will influence the manner in which you approach the therapeutic relationship with your client.

Table 3.1 Therapeutic Relationship Practice

IMPORTANT THERAPEUTIC RELATIONSHIP FEATURE	*SPECIFIC BEHAVIORS AND OBSERVATIONS*
Week #1:	Specific behavior #1:
	Specific behavior #2:
	Specific behavior #3:
	OBSERVATIONS
Week #2:	Specific behavior #1:
	Specific behavior #2:
	Specific behavior #3:
	OBSERVATIONS
Week #3:	Specific behavior #1:
	Specific behavior #2:
	Specific behavior #3:
	OBSERVATIONS

Congratulations—you have just conducted an important exercise as a practitioner-scientist! You systematically implemented a change in your clinical practice that has its basis in theory and/or research, and you systematically observed its effects on your client, on you, and on the therapeutic relationship. On the basis of these observations, you can now adjust your behavior to continue to enhance the therapeutic relationship with not only the client with whom you implemented the exercise, but all of your clients.

BOX 3 **REFLECTION ON YOUR EXPERIENTIAL EXERCISE**

What do you conclude from your experiential exercise?

What, specifically, will you do differently in the future to cultivate (and if necessary, repair) the therapeutic relationship in the future?

How has your view about the therapeutic relationship changed after participating in this experiential exercise?

Case Examples

In the following sections, consider the way in which the two in-depth cases in the volume so far respond to my efforts to cultivate the therapeutic relationship. You will have an opportunity to reflect on the way in which you would further cultivate the relationship in each of these instances.

Straightforward Case

Recall that Ashley left her initial session struggling with clinically significant symptoms of anxiety, but optimistic that she could achieve significant change in CBT. After her first session, she made an appointment for the next week. The following conversation occurred at the beginning of the session, when I conducted a brief mood check and a bridge from the previous session (i.e., components of session structure; see Chapter 4 of this volume) before deciding on a specific focus for the session.

Dr. Amy: Ashley, hello, welcome back! It's so good to see you again.

Ashley: [looking relieved] It's really good to be back.

Dr. Amy: I've really been looking forward to continuing our work together, so we can get a jump start on addressing the anxiety that you described last week.

Ashley: Oh, me too.

Dr. Amy: Before we get started, I'd like to get an anxiety rating from you, so that we can begin to track our progress across the course of our work together. Is that okay with you?

Ashley: Sure! You know me, I love math. I was a math major.

Dr. Amy: [chuckling] Yes, you were, so I think you might like this. Each week, I'll ask you to rate your average level of anxiety on a 0-10 scale, with 0 being the absence of anxiety, and 10 being the most that you can imagine experiencing. Periodically, we'll review your ratings to determine whether what we are doing in treatment is corresponding to a reduction in anxiety. What do you think of that?

Ashley: I think that's really good, actually. I'm not sure that I have ever given these kinds of ratings before.

Dr. Amy: Terrific, let's gather the ratings, and we'll be sure to track our progress. What rating would you assign for the time between our appointment last week and today?

Ashley: Mmmmm, I guess I would say 8? Pretty bad.

Dr. Amy: [projecting a concerned look] Oh, I'm sorry to hear that, Ashley. But one silver lining of all of this is that I believe I have some helpful strategies to offer you in managing anxiety.

Ashley: I'm really looking forward to talking more about that. Because I've been having a hard time lately.

Dr. Amy: Of course, Ashley, we'll talk much more about that today. [pausing] Before we start today, can you share some reflections about your visit last week?

Ashley: It was so helpful to lay everything out. I really think CBT is the right type of therapy for me.

Dr. Amy: I'm so thrilled to hear that, Ashley. I agree that the issues you'd like to address are a terrific match for CBT. I believe that I will have a great deal to offer you.

Ashley: I'm ready to get started.

Dr. Amy: Although you sound quite positive about CBT, I'm wondering if there were any aspects of CBT, or what we had discussed last week, that you have reservations about?

Ashley: No, not at all.

Dr. Amy: [demonstrating an openness to hearing negative feedback] I'm glad to hear that, Ashley. However, as we progress with our CBT work, you might find that you have some questions of clarification, or that you develop some reservations. If that occurs, would you be comfortable bringing those to my attention?

Ashley: Oh yes. I definitely will.

Dr. Amy: [keeping the mood relatively light and providing a big smile] Great, well then I think you and I will make a good team.

Ashley: So do I.

Dr. Amy: [linking back to the comment she made earlier regarding talking more about Ashley's high level of anxiety in order to set a session agenda] Ashley, during the mood check you mentioned that your anxiety is high right now, at the level of an 8, and I indicated that I would share more with you about what CBT has to offer to help you. What else were you hoping to discuss here today?

Ashley: [demonstrating a visible shift toward sad affect in her facial expression] I'd like to talk more about what's happening with my husband, if it's okay. Our couple's therapy really doesn't seem to be helping at all.

Dr. Amy: [demonstrating empathy in her facial expression] You got it, we can certainly spend some time talking about what is happening with your husband, and determining whether there is anything we can be doing in here to help that situation.

Ashley: [looking relieved] That would be really helpful. Thanks.

Dr. Amy: What should we focus on first—developing a plan to address your anxiety, or your marriage?

Ashley: Um, let's focus on the anxiety first, since that is what brought me here. But, you'll start to see that the anxiety and my problems with my husband go hand-in-hand.

Dr. Amy: Understood, Ashley. Let's be on the lookout for those points of overlap, as I suspect that it will be at those points that our work will be particularly helpful to you.

Ashley continued to present as a relatively "straightforward" client in this dialogue for several reasons. First, she spontaneously expressed many optimistic sentiments about her therapeutic work thus far and CBT's promise (e.g., "It's really good to be back," "I really think CBT is the right type of therapy for me," "I'm ready to get started."). Second, consistent with what was observed in the dialogue in Chapter 2, Ashley readily responded to my interventions. For example, when I asked her to supply an anxiety rating during the brief mood check, she expressed a positive predisposition toward doing so, and she easily chose a rating. In addition, she readily provided a reflection on the previous visit (thus forming a bridge from the previous session) and contributed to a session agenda (see Chapter 4 of this volume for more about session structure).

It is natural to assume that the therapeutic relationship is wholly intact with clients such as Ashley (and, indeed, there is no evidence to suspect that it is not). However, it is nevertheless important to be just as cognizant of ways to build, maintain, and enhance the therapeutic relationship with clients such as Ashley as it is with difficult clients, as doing so has the potential to improve outcome that much more. In the box that follows, consider the way in which you would use your knowledge of the features of the therapeutic relationship to continue to attend to your relationship with Ashley.

BOX 4 CONTINUED ATTENTION TO THE THERAPEUTIC RELATIONSHIP: APPLICATION TO ASHLEY

If you were in the position in which you were continuing the dialogue with Ashley to build the therapeutic relationship, name three things you would do or say, the rationale for doing or saying them, and the way in which you would expect them to affect outcome.

1.

2.

3.

Notice the questions in Box 4 that prompted you to indicate the rationale for saying or doing what you choose to say or do, and to describe the way in which you would expect them to affect outcome. These questions are prompting you to think strategically. Although there will certainly be many instances in therapy in which you react from your "heart" or your "gut," it is equally as important that many of your reactions have a strategic basis for their implementation, in order for you and your client to move relatively efficiently toward your treatment goals and intervene in a way that maximizes the likelihood of positive outcome in light of the client's case formulation. There is nothing about a strategic intervention that precludes it from being genuine and heartfelt. CBT is delivered optimally when the therapeutic relationship is nurtured and when, simultaneously, important new learning occurs that advances the client toward his or her treatment goals, and that broadly reinforces CBT's theoretical principles.

Difficult Case

Marilyn had left her initial session somewhat dejected, as she had focused a large extent of her energy on expressing how unhelpful she thought previous courses of therapy had been. At the end of that session, she was unsure if she should schedule another appointment. I asked her permission to conduct an "experiment," such that she would agree to come in for four additional sessions, keep an open mind, and engage fully with the cognitive behavioral tools that I had to offer her. At the end of the fourth session, we would evaluate the degree to which CBT held promise for her and was different from her other courses of therapy. This technique is reminiscent of the *behavioral experiment* (described more in Chapter 5 of this volume), which allows for clients to gather "real-time" evidence in their lives to support or refute a conclusion that they have drawn about their life circumstances.

My focus with Marilyn was primarily on developing the therapeutic relationship, which I anticipated would allow me to demonstrate some basic CBT tools, and which would, in turn, instill hope that things could be different for her. The following excerpt occurred when she returned for the second session.

Marilyn: This week was a little better. I had a lot of ice skating on my schedule, which always helps.

Dr. Amy: [demonstrating genuine interest, as I very much admire people who pursue unique hobbies and interests] Ice skating? I didn't realize that you skate.

Marilyn: Yeah, I've been doing it since I was a child. I'm active in the local skating club.

Dr. Amy: [continuing to demonstrate genuine interest] I'd really be interested in hearing more about that.

Marilyn: I'm a figure skater. I don't really compete now that I'm older, but I teach figure skating. I'm still in the performances, because I'm either leading the little kids, or I'm playing a role that most people can't play, because it's too technical.

Dr. Amy: That's fascinating, Marilyn. I don't hear very often that people are so immersed into figure skating.

Marilyn: [perking up] But it's not all figure skating. I coach some people in speed skating, too.

Dr. Amy: You do? How interesting!

Marilyn: [resorting back to her depressive tendencies] Well, I guess it passes the time. I don't have a lot else to do outside of work.

Dr. Amy: Honestly, Marilyn, I'm really glad that you shared this bit of information with me. I truly admire people who engage in athletic pursuits, particularly those that are a little different than the ones we typically hear about. And I don't have an athletic bone in my body. So I live vicariously through others who can achieve what I cannot.

Marilyn: [smiles a little bit, as if she is starting to feel a connection]

After this interaction, I had the sense that that session was off to a good start, as we found a topic with which we could genuinely connect (i.e., Marilyn's ice skating), and I genuinely found that I had admiration for her with her athletic ability. This brief conversation helped me to feel closer to Marilyn, and perhaps even have more empathy toward her than in the previous session, and I was eager to share some of what I thought I could offer her with CBT and how I thought I could be of help to her. The following dialogue captures this direction and illustrates additional issues that arose in the therapeutic relationship.

Marilyn: I guess skating is a pretty big part of my life.

Dr. Amy: [asking permission to share some knowledge about CBT] Can I share with you what strikes me about your love of skating and how it might be helpful in CBT?

Marilyn: [looking surprised] Sure, okay.

Dr. Amy: There are two main foci in CBT—the "C" part, which stands for cognitive, or the thinking part. I can tell you more about that in a minute. But there is also the "B" part, or the behavioral part. When clients struggle with depression, as you have shared with me, one typical goal of the behavioral aspect of CBT is positive engagement in one's environment. In other words, we believe that an antidote to depression is actively pursuing and engaging in activities that are expected to bring you joy, pleasure, and meaning in your life. One thing we can do together is to look more closely at the degree to which you're getting this benefit from skating. If we see there is anything that we can adjust to increase the benefits further, and we can see what we learn from this to infuse it in other areas of your life. What do you think of that?

Marilyn: [looking skeptical] I guess so, but I've been skating my whole life, and I'm still miserable.

Dr. Amy: [going out of my way to provide validation] Understood, Marilyn. I certainly wouldn't want to suggest that your experience has been otherwise.

Marilyn: You know what, this is really starting to be no different than my work with other therapists!

Dr. Amy: [demonstrating genuine interest and non-defensiveness] How so, Marilyn? I'd truly be interested in hearing your thoughts about this, as my aim is to work together with you to shape this experience into one that is different than your previous experiences.

Marilyn: You all just think that you have all the answers! Just skate more, Marilyn, then you'll feel better. Just do this, or do that! It's not that *easy*!

Dr. Amy: You're right; it's not easy at all, and I truly apologize if I gave you the impression that I thought it was. [asking permission] Would you like to hear what was running through my mind as I was reflecting on the way in which your skating could really be an asset in CBT, along with the reasoning behind my thinking?

Marilyn: [looking skeptical] Well, okay.

Dr. Amy: It's important to me, both personally and professionally, to make sure there's a scientific rationale that supports the suggestion I make. Your skating fits in so nicely with a core strategy we use in CBT for depression, called behavioral activation. The idea is that doing things that make you feel good, such as those that give you a sense of pleasure, or those that give you a sense of accomplishment, should provide positive reinforcement for your efforts, which should lessen your depression. I do hear you, however, that it might not seem like you've gotten that kind of benefit from skating so far. Would it be okay with you if we take a closer look to see if there is a way that we can make this theory work *for* you, before deciding it doesn't apply?

Marilyn: I guess. I mean, I'm not optimistic. Nothing has worked so far.

Dr. Amy: [speaking warmly] I understand, Marilyn. You've had a number of courses of psychotherapy that have not yielded the results for which you were hoping, and you want this to be different. Believe me, so do I. What I'd like us to do is to see, together, if we should rule out what we know has worked for many other people before moving onto Plan B. Does that make sense?

Marilyn: I guess so. I just don't want to spend a lot of time and money, only for us to decide that this isn't working.

Dr. Amy: Fair enough, Marilyn. I give you my word that we will be evaluating consistently as we go along the degree to which our theory and interventions are relevant to your specific situation. And I also give you my word that we can shift gears and put together an alternative plan if it seems as if what we're doing is not a good match.

Marilyn: [again, looking hesitant] Okay, I guess we can proceed with your plan.

Marilyn continued to present as a relatively "difficult" client in this dialogue for several reasons. On the one hand, she responded to my warmth and genuine interest in her unique interest in ice skating. On the other hand, she expressed a great deal of skepticism, wondering how her skating could achieve the aims of behavioral activation (see Chapter 6 of this volume), and observing that her experience felt no different than her experience with other therapists. In response to these concerns, I was cognizant to (a) maintain an open, inviting stance to communicate that her feedback and observations were welcomed and would be respected in our therapeutic work, rather than dismissed; (b) validate her concerns; (c) ask permission in a non-defensive way if I could provide the rationale behind my suggestion, so that I could educate her about the CBT model and process, and determine whether my suggestions might resonate with her a bit more within that context; and (d) subsequently provide that rationale. Marilyn agreed to continue with the line of intervention that I was proposing, although her tone of voice and facial expression suggested that she was reluctant about doing so. Thus, I took care to note this reluctance, so that I could verify it in the future if she expressed or demonstrated similar indicators. My train of thought throughout my work with Marilyn to this point was that I did not want to abandon the CBT approach because of what I was interpreting as resistance, but at the same time, I aimed to (a) devote even more time and attention than with the typical client to cultivate the therapeutic relationship, and (b) take care not to invalidate or dismiss her concerns about whether the principles or strategies of CBT applied to her.

Clearly, Marilyn's commitment to treatment was tenuous, and although there were moments of connection between the two of us, she also continued to demonstrate skepticism and guardedness toward me. In these types of cases, it is wise to keep cultivation of the therapeutic relationship as the paramount goal and not to push an "agenda" of CBT too strongly. In Box 5 that follows, consider the way in which you would use your knowledge of the features of the therapeutic relationship to continue to attend to your relationship with Marilyn.

BOX 5 **CONTINUED ATTENTION TO THE THERAPEUTIC RELATIONSHIP: APPLICATION TO MARILYN**

If you were in the position in which you were continuing the dialogue with Marilyn to build the therapeutic relationship, name three things you would do or say, the rationale for doing or saying them, and the way in which you would expect them to affect outcome.

1.

2.

3.

Tips for Maximizing Effectiveness

In the other chapters in this volume, I provide specific tips for maximizing the effectiveness of the strategy or skill under consideration in that chapter. I am more hesitant to do so in this chapter on the therapeutic relationship because every therapist is unique, which means that every therapist will have his or her own style that is brought to the therapeutic relationship. For example, what are the most salient personality traits that people notice in you? Are you a gregarious, extroverted person, or are you a more subdued, introverted person? Although these personality styles can be construed as "polar opposites," both can be significant assets in developing and maintaining a strong therapeutic relationship. The key with translating your personality strengths to the therapeutic relationship is to do so in a genuine, thoughtful manner.

So, although I cannot advise you, specifically, on ways to maximize your therapeutic relationships on the basis of your own style, I can share some of my own experiences, ways in which I thoughtful apply my own salient personality traits as I develop relationships with my clients, and obstacles that I have encountered in my own therapeutic relationships. Personally, I am an extroverted, high-energy person who attends to small details, tells stories and recounts metaphors, and uses humor to illustrate important points to my clients in session. When my client tells me a small detail about his or her life, I make an extra effort to remember that and inquire about it in subsequent sessions. For example, if a client likes a particular sports team, I pay attention to whether that team won a game between sessions and comment on it the next time I see that client. If a client likes a particular musical act, I note when that act is coming to town and ask that client if he or she is going to go to the show. At times, my clients and I share common interests, and I will readily ask my clients a question, or make an observation about that interest (e.g., I have had many discussions about fantasy football over the years about various players and their performance). I take care not to make this discussion too lengthy, or focus too much on myself; indeed, these are often brief conversations that I have when I am walking with clients from my waiting room to our seats in my office. My rule-of-thumb is that if we are still "chatting" informally a few minutes after we have settled into our seats, ready to begin the session, I make an expressive statement that is supportive or encouraging (e.g., "Oh Rachel, I'm so glad you had the opportunity to enjoy that concert."), and I transition, using my words and tone of voice, into our therapeutic work (e.g., "Well, that was certainly one positive event that happened between sessions. Let's check-in on your mood and see what else would be useful for us to focus on today."). The feedback that I've gotten from clients is that they appreciate and are surprised by my memory of details from their lives, that they appreciate my interest in their lives, and that they view me as human when I share a bit of detail of my own life.

That being said, as with any style, it is important to be alert for drawbacks or indications that one's style might be a sufficiently poor match for the client's style that it would impede the development of the therapeutic relationship. When I am first educating clients about CBT, I know that I can come across quite enthusiastically, so I say something about this in an above-board manner, such as"You'll probably hear in my voice that I am quite passionate about CBT. The reason for this is that I have observed the difference it has made in the lives of so many people with whom I have worked." However, I also am aware that I can be construed as coming across quite strongly. In fact, when I was participating in my clinical training in graduate school, I received written feedback that I have a "high stimulus value" and that I would be wise to be cognizant of the fact that it could be overwhelming for clients. That piece of feedback remains "front and center" in my mind to this day, and if I notice subtle, nonverbal indications that my client is becoming overwhelmed by my emotion, or by the information that I am presenting, I slow down, lower the volume of my voice, and obtain feedback from the client. When my client is discussing a painful life experience and expressing a great deal of affect, I specifically tone down and create space for the client to fully experience affect, and work through what is happening. In the box below, consider your own three most salient personality traits that you would "bring to the table" in the therapeutic relationship, along with strengths associated with these traits that would likely enhance the therapeutic relationship, and any potential drawbacks that could interfere with the therapeutic relationship.

BOX 6 YOUR PERSONAL STYLE AND THE THERAPEUTIC RELATIONSHIP

What are three salient traits that people notice about your personality? How could each trait enhance the therapeutic relationship? How might each trait interfere with the therapeutic relationship?

TRAIT #1:

TRAIT #2:

TRAIT #3:

In addition to being aware of the strengths and drawbacks of your personality style, it is also important to be clear, in your own mind, regarding your comfort level with self-disclosure. There is no right or wrong answer to this issue; every therapist is different. Moreover, you will likely adjust the type of information that you disclose as a function of the type of client you are seeing. For example, when I am seeing clients who are describing issues that have arisen with their children, I am more likely to disclose that I have a daughter, and perhaps even that I have dealt with a similar issue, than I would with clients who do not have children. Many of my clients know "fun facts" about me, such as my favorite sports team and my favorite area restaurants.

At times, clients will ask questions that tap into information that is private. I recall one instance in which a client with an extensive history of trauma, who had recently gone through an upsetting experience that reactivated her posttraumatic stress symptoms, angrily asked me, "Can you even understand what I have gone through? Have you ever experienced anything even remotely as bad as I have experienced?" Even if you feel comfortable disclosing such personal information, it runs the risk of shifting the focus of treatment from the client onto you if you have had a similar experience, and it runs the risk of distancing the client from you if you have not had the experience. My response was something like, "I'm human, Rachel, just like you. And unfortunately, tragedy and disappointments are part of the human experience, mine included, just like joys and triumphs. I will certainly draw on my own experience to develop an understanding of what you are going through, and at the same time, I will rely on what you tell me to have an even greater appreciation." In the box below, reflect on your own views about self-disclosure and how you can imagine handling instances in which clients ask you for information that you view as private, or that you are uncomfortable sharing.

BOX 7 YOUR VIEWS ON SELF-DISCLOSURE

Consider your own views on self-disclosure. What personal details, if any, are you willing to share with most clients? How do you think sharing these details will develop or enhance the therapeutic relationship?

What personal details are you not willing to share with most clients? Why not?

Suppose a client asks for personal detail that you are uncomfortable sharing. How might you handle that?

CHAPTER 4 SESSION STRUCTURE

Session Structure

CHAPTER 4

Think about the most effective ways to go about solving a problem or completing a task. Do you dive in haphazardly, following urges and meandering in whatever direction captures your attention? Or do you think first about some sort of a game plan for doing so, so that you do not overlook important details and make systematic progress in accomplishing what you hope to accomplish?

Although most people would likely agree that a planned, systematic approach is preferable, in reality, most of us are swayed, at times, by emotions, urges, disorganization, and procrastination when we are trying to get things done. It is human nature! In many instances, these obstacles are particularly evident in the context of psychotherapy, when clients are facing complex life problems. Oftentimes, none of these problems have a clear or comfortable solution, and many of these problems are disconcerting and even painful to face. Moreover, some clients who present for mental health treatment report especially great struggles with problem solving inefficiency, disorganization, and emotional overwhelm, so they would benefit greatly from a systematic approach to thinking about, organizing, and addressing their life problems.

Cognitive behavioral therapists believe that interventions to structure the therapy session provides an important opportunity for clients to learn these skills. These structural components bring a focus to the session, creating a thread that weaves sessions together and that points clients in the direction of their treatment goals. They also allow for clients to move from mere discussion of their life problems to progress toward solving them, learning ways to cope with them, and preventing similar problems from happening in the future.

In this chapter, I describe the components of CBT session structure. As I discuss session structure components, I present the two cases that we have been following to this point in the volume, illustrating their straightforward and less-than-straightforward application. I also weave in tips for maximizing effectiveness and common obstacles that therapists encounter when implementing them. In addition, on some occasions, I invite you to reflect on the ways in which these aspects of session structure have contributed to effective problem solving in your own life; on other occasions, I encourage you to consider the ways in which you can apply your learning about session structure components with your clients. In the section on homework, I suggest an experiential exercise, so that you truly develop a sense of what it is like for clients to complete homework between sessions. Moreover, I encourage you to practice applying the components of CBT session structure in an experimental manner with your clients, similar to what you did in Chapter 3 of this volume with components of the therapeutic relationship.

CBT Session Structure Components

In this section, I describe the main components of CBT session structure. These components include:

- A brief mood check
- A bridge from the previous session
- The setting of a session agenda that includes homework review
- Discussion of agenda items
- Development of new homework
- A final summary and feedback

Before considering each one in turn, I encourage you to recognize that CBT session structure can and should be flexible, and that you are still "doing" CBT even if you do not implement one or more of these components for whatever reason. You need not implement them in a rigid manner, such as in a particular order, or in a way that stifles spontaneous and genuine conversation between you and your client. Rather, these components are meant to be guides that help you to facilitate the overall mission and principles of CBT in your session.

In addition, during your first sessions with your clients, I encourage you to *socialize* your clients into these CBT session structure components. By socializing, I mean that you explicitly educate your client about the session structure components and their rationale, model them, and ask for feedback from your client about them. Socialization of clients into session structure components (as well as other aspects of CBT) helps the client to develop accurate expectations for the way in which therapy will proceed. If you conduct a few sessions without much structure as you gather information and formulate a treatment plan, clients might begin to develop the idea that CBT is loose and unstructured, and that the primary purpose is for them to ventilate about their problems. If this is the case, they might be surprised when you shift toward implementing session structure. However, when clients are educated about what CBT entails and all that it has to offer, and when session structure is modeled from the very first session, in my experience, most clients will express that many of its features sound attractive, and that they are optimistic that it will lead to improvement.

Of course, you will experience occasions in which a client indicates that he or she does not resonate with one or more aspects of CBT session structure. In the spirit of collaboration, you will almost always respect the client's wishes and discontinue implementing that aspect (or those aspects) of CBT session structure. You are still "doing" CBT. In fact, some of the best CBT is done when the cognitive behavioral therapist responds openly and creatively to client feedback. I would caution, however, against abandoning one or more aspects of CBT session structure because it makes you feel uncomfortable, or because you wonder if it will be aversive to client (but have no concrete evidence to support that notion). In the former instance, try experimenting with CBT session structure, much as you did with aspects of the therapeutic relationship in Chapter 3 of this volume. Observe the degree to which you become more comfortable with it, as well as the degree to which it becomes more second nature, with repeated practice over time. In the latter instance, communicate your hypothesis to your client (e.g., "I'm wondering if it seems odd to you to get a mood check at the beginning of the session? Can I get some feedback?") and adjust the session structure component on the basis of client feedback, rather than an assumption that you are making. Later in this chapter, I give you an opportunity for this very type of experimentation and observation.

These subsections are organized a bit differently than the way in which I set up the previous two chapters. Rather than waiting until later in the chapter to illustrate the application to our relatively straightforward and our relatively difficult case and describing tips for maximizing effectiveness, I weave reference to these cases and tips throughout to directly illustrate ways to implement session structure components when they are being discussed.

Brief Mood Check

The brief mood check, typically conducted at or near the beginning of a session, is a quick tool to collect quantitative information about symptoms that are the focus of treatment. The idea is that clients supply these ratings at the time of each session, and over time, they and their therapists can track the degree to which clients' mood is changing throughout the course of treatment, as well as the degree to which CBT is resulting in positive changes in their lives. Notice that I am using the words "quantitative" and "ratings." In the spirit of conducting themselves as practitioner-scientists, cognitive behavioral therapists collect "data" that are as objective as possible in order to make informed determinations about their clients' mood and associated symptomatology. If a therapist simply asks a client "How are you feeling?" or "What is your mood like today?", it will be difficult to determine using qualitative responses to these questions whether symptoms have changed appreciably from session-to-session.

Data for the brief mood check can be gathered in different ways. Many expert cognitive behavioral therapists recommend that clients complete one or more standardized self-report inventory prior to each session. Examples of self-report inventories that can be used for this purpose include the *Beck Depression Inventory-II* (BDI-II; Beck, Steer, & Brown, 1996) or the *Patient Health Questionnaire-9* (PHQ-9; Kroenke, Spitzer, & Williams, 2001). The advantage of using self-report inventories such as these is that they have well-established psychometric properties (e.g., reliability, validity) and norms that allow test givers to compare their clients' scores with various groups of people, which allows clinician to be able to conclude whether their clients' symptoms are falling in the normative range on a particular construct, or whether their symptoms are elevated to a mild, moderate, or severe degree. Although some inventories, such as the Beck Scales (of which the BDI-II is the most well-known inventory), are proprietary and must be purchased in order for them to be administered to clients, others such as the PHQ Screeners (of which the PHQ-9 is the most well-known inventory; http://www.phqscreeners.com/), are freely available.

You need not be limited to self-report inventories when collecting data during the brief mood check. For example, you can develop your own Likert-type scale, defining each end of the scale for a particular construct (e.g., depression or anxiety on a 0–10 scale, with 0 being the absence of the symptom under consideration, and 10 being the highest level of severity that the client can imagine). Other constructs lend themselves well to a frequency rating, such as the frequency of panic attacks or anger outbursts. Still other constructs lend themselves to a simple count, such as the number of drinks taken in the time since the previous session, the average number of hours slept, or the number of binges and purges.

Thus, there are many ways to approach the brief mood check, all of which have merit. In my practice, I typically gather ratings of depression and anxiety, as they are the two most common emotional experiences reported by clients whom I see professionally. In addition, when I explain the rationale for the brief mood check and obtain ratings from clients on the depression and anxiety scales, I ask them if they believe that there are other constructs that we should be tracking across sessions. In addition to the examples I have supplied, other common constructs that I track include marital dissatisfaction, irritability, and severity of hopelessness or suicidal ideation. Whatever you and your client decide to track, I encourage you to write down the scale you are using and make sure that you are using the same scale across sessions to facilitate straightforward comparison. This suggestion stems from my experience in reviewing audio recordings of therapists who are training to become cognitive behavioral therapists, as I have heard instances in which one week they define a scale in one way (e.g., 0 = absence of depression; 10 = the highest level one can imagine experiencing), and the next week they define a scale in a different way (e.g., 0 = low mood; 10 = the best mood one can imaging experiencing). Not only does the changing nature of the scale become confusing to clients, but it also precludes comparison of progress across sessions, because different ratings mean different things.

A straightforward demonstration of the brief mood check was presented in the previous chapter on the therapeutic relationship, when I demonstrated the way in which I approached the beginning of Ashley's second session, described in Chapter 3 of this volume. Most clients readily respond when they are asked to provide a small number of ratings to track progress. In fact, some clients, after they have participated in at least a handful of sessions, remark, "I knew you were going to ask me about my mood, so I was thinking about it on the way over here." Comments such as these are important pieces of feedback, as they demonstrate that you have adequately socialized clients into this aspect of CBT session structure, and they also suggest that you have consistently modeled and implemented this aspect of CBT session structure.

Undoubtedly, however, you will encounter clients who exhibit or communicate a negative reaction to the brief mood check. Some clients remark that they do not know what numbers to choose and have the sense that they are "pulling numbers out of the air." In these cases, it can be helpful to spend extra time defining key anchors in whatever scale you are using. Other clients indicate that the scale is overwhelming to them; in these cases, it is okay to simplify the scale (e.g., using a scale that runs from 0–3 instead of 0–10). Still other clients will have a negative reaction that can be explained by their pathology and the unhelpful way in which they react to many situations. This was the case with Marilyn, who, as you have seen to this point in the book, was highly skeptical of CBT and of me as her new therapist. The following dialogue occurred when I began to socialize Marilyn into participating in the brief mood check.

Dr. Amy: Marilyn, one of the things I'd like to do at the beginning of each session is to get a couple of mood ratings from you, so that we can track the degree to which CBT is making an impact on your life. [asking permission] Can I share more with you about what those mood ratings look like?

Marilyn: [looking skeptical] Mood ratings, I don't know. [shaking her head] It all sounds so impersonal to me.

Dr. Amy: [trying another angle] Oh, I would hate for you to have the sense that anything about this process is impersonal. Can I share more with you about the reasoning behind it and the way in which I make these mood ratings *especially* personal to each one of my clients?

Marilyn: [giving permission but still looking hesitant] I guess.

Dr. Amy: The reason why I gather these ratings is because I want to be very respectful of the time and effort that you put into therapy. If the mood ratings change in the direction that we hope, then we know that we're on the right track. But it's important for us to know if they *aren't* changing, so that we can make adjustments. And also, together, we can decide what aspects of your emotional experiences are the most relevant to track, so that the ratings truly are customized for your situation.

Marilyn: You really have an answer for everything, don't you?

Dr. Amy: [reacting non-defensively and smiling] I doubt I have the answers for *everything*, Marilyn, but I do have a lot about CBT that I can share with you. And I like there to be a good reason behind all of the things that I am suggesting.

Marilyn: [looking exasperated] Fine, okay. What rating do you want me to give?

Dr. Amy: [responding collaboratively] I can certainly make some suggestions on the basis of my work with other clients. But I'm curious as to the symptoms, emotional experiences, or life circumstances that are most upsetting to *you*, as those have the potential to be the most relevant experiences to keep our eye on.

Marilyn: [sinking back into her chair] Oh, I don't know. I don't care. Ask me whatever you want to ask me.

Dr. Amy: [checking out the assumption that Marilyn finds mood ratings to be aversive] Marilyn, I'm getting the sense that the mood ratings that I am suggesting don't feel right to you? Is that the case?

Marilyn: [looking exasperated] I don't know! I just don't know how you can expect me to put a number on how I am feeling.

Dr. Amy: [making a reflection] Fair enough, Marilyn. The mood ratings I'm describing seem a bit odd to you. [forging collaboration] Would you be willing to give them a try? Or do you think we should skip them altogether? You're in the driver's seat, so I will respect your preferences.

Marilyn: [sighing] No, it's okay. I'll give them a try. I came to you because I really want to try CBT. And this is part of it.

Dr. Amy: [acknowledging Marilyn's concession, but communicating respect that supplying mood ratings might not be consistent with her style] I appreciate your willingness to try it out, Marilyn. How's this for a plan—maybe we can just get one or two ratings that are the absolute most relevant to your circumstances, and we can see how it goes over the next couple of sessions. If it still feels aversive for you to supply the ratings, or if, more generally, it seems that they aren't really giving us the information we were hoping to get, then we can revisit this issue?

Marilyn: Okay, I'd appreciate that.

All things being equal, I am a staunch advocate for obtaining quantitative mood ratings. As therapy progresses, clients are often interested in assessing progress, and the mood ratings lend themselves well to visual depictions (i.e., graphs) of the ways in which symptoms are changing. When clients see, graphically, the way in which the symptoms or problems that they are targeting in treatment are changing, they often become empowered, and it reinvigorates their commitment to and motivation for treatment. However, if clients express a displeasure at supplying mood ratings, and they continue to reject them after you provide a compelling rationale, ask if they will be willing to supply them for a few weeks and then evaluate their usefulness, then cognitive behavioral therapists heed their wishes.

What do you see as the value of the brief mood check? Have there been things in your own life that you have tracked in a quantitative manner to assess progress periodically? In the following exercise, please write about these experiences. Then, indicate the ways in which you plan to implement the brief mood check with your clients.

BOX 1 **REFLECTIONS ON THE BRIEF MOOD CHECK**

Think about something in your life that you have tracked quantitatively (e.g., grades, weight). What was it like to track it? What benefits did you see in doing so?

What do you see as advantages of doing a brief mood check with your clients? What, if any, disadvantages do you see?

How, exactly, will you implement the brief mood check with your clients?

Bridge from Previous Session

The bridge from the previous session is an opportunity for the therapist and client to become reoriented to the work they have done in the previous appointment. Not only does this allow the therapist and client to weave a thread that runs across sessions, thereby increasing the coherency of the course of treatment, it also models persistence and follow through. Moreover, the bridge also provides the opportunity for the therapist to check in with the client regarding any negative reactions to the previous session.

It is tempting to ask a simple question, such as"Did you find the previous session helpful?", during the bridge from the previous session. My clinical experience suggests that most clients will provide a simple (and perhaps even enthusiastic) "yes" to this question. Although it is gratifying for any therapist to know that his or her client found the previous session helpful, such a question-answer sequence does not provide specific information (such as exactly *what* was helpful about the previous session, which could be replicated in the current or future sessions). Moreover, it does not provide an opportunity for the *consolidation of learning*, or for the client to put in his or her own words what has been learned, which allows clients to translate cognitive behavioral principles and strategies to their lives when they are not in session. Instead, I recommend that therapists ask one or two open-ended questions about their experience with the previous session that allows their clients to reflect on cognitive behavioral principles. Table 4.1 lists examples of these types of questions.

The idea is that the question or questions you ask in the bridge from the previous session will allow clients to dig deep and develop insight into the way in which cognitive behavioral principles manifest in their daily lives, and the way in which the interventions delivered in session can translate to their lives. Invariably, you will have clients who indicate that they do not remember what was discussed in the previous session. Although such a scenario can, of course, be discouraging for therapists, it also provides an opportunity for the therapeutic relationship to be enhanced, to model the systematic and organized approach to solving life's problems, and to identify any obstacles that might be interfering with the full embracement of treatment, so that those obstacles can be solved.

The first time a client says to me that he or she cannot remember the previous session, I respond in a mildly humorous way (consistent with my personal style; see Chapter 3 of this volume), such as with an emphatic "Oh man!" or "It happens," followed up by a "Well, let's put our heads together and see if we can remember together." I take care not to say something, such as"Oh, it's okay," as I want to be sure that I do not communicate a message that therapy will be effective even if clients do not remember what is discussed from session to session. Thus, I aim to achieve a balance between making a non-shaming, empathetic statement and communicating that, ultimately, it will be important for them to remember what happened in the previous session, so that CBT makes a difference in their lives. I usually ask for permission to go back to my notes and read to them what I wrote down about the previous session (which also facilitates the aim of transparency in CBT), and they are almost always grateful that I have done so.

Table 4.1 Questions to Facilitate the Bridge from the Previous Session

- What did you take away from the previous session?
- What did you learn from the previous session that ended up making a difference in your life?
- What stuck with you from the previous session?
- In what way did the principles discussed in our previous session show up in your life between our sessions?
- Can you share some reflections on our previous session?
- Was there anything about the previous session that bothered you?
- Did I say or do anything in the previous session that rubbed you the wrong way?

Another issue arises when clients *repeatedly* indicate that they do not remember the previous session. When this occurs, it raises the possibility that (a) clients are not benefitting as much as they could from treatment, (b) there is something about their clinical presentations or stressors in their lives that are preventing them from fully accessing or embracing treatment, or (c) the targets that have been addressed in treatment so far are not the optimal match for what the client needs at that time. These are also possibilities to be discussed openly and collaboratively with the client. Thus, when a client indicates several times that he or she does not remember the previous session, I ask for permission to talk about this further, so that we can ensure that he or she is truly benefitting from CBT. In fact, whenever an issue arises during the bridge from the previous session that deserves further consideration, it is best to add it to the agenda (see the next section), rather than launching into spontaneous discussion. This will ensure that you do not get swept away into devoting most of the session time to the issue before carefully considering the best use of time to address all of the issues that you and the client were hoping to address.

A note is in order about the last two rows of Table 4.1. Earlier in this section, I suggested that you ask open-ended questions to facilitate the consolidation of learning. When the consolidation of learning is the goal of questioning during the bridge from the previous session, it is, indeed, best to ask open-ended questions, so that clients can put their own words onto the constructs and strategies that have been taught. However, a second purpose of the bridge from the previous session is to determine whether the client has any negative feelings or reactions that carried over from the previous session, which has the potential to affect the therapeutic relationship. Usually, close-ended questions are sufficient to assess any potential negative reactions, such as the two that are included in Table 4.1. If you detect hostility, withdrawal, or general discomfort in your client, and you suspect that it has to do with something that happened in the previous session, you might make an observation, such as "I'm noticing that you have something on your mind. How are you feeling about our previous session?" Although most clients will indicate that there was nothing that bothered them about the previous session, if they respond affirmatively, then it is important to indicate that you would like to discuss it further and demonstrate an open, inviting, and non-judgmental stance.

Let's see how the bridge from the previous session would work with our relatively straightforward and relatively difficult cases. The bridge from the previous session was modeled with Ashley in the previous chapter, when I asked her to reflect on her visit the previous week. She responded eagerly that she found it helpful to lay out her problems in the way that we did, and that she thought CBT was the "right" therapy for her. For many clients, this type of response is sufficient and the bridge from the previous session does not require any additional attention. In fact, I would estimate that the typical bridge from the previous session involves one or two questions from the therapist and one or two thoughtful responses from the client, all of which takes place in the span of just a couple of minutes.

There certainly are other clients for whom the bridge from the previous session does not run as smoothly. Marilyn would be an example of one of those clients. In the previous dialogue, she expressed skepticism about and reluctance to supply ratings for the brief mood check. In the following dialogue, she also expresses dissatisfaction about the previous session.

Dr. Amy: I'm curious Marilyn. Now that you've had some time to think about it, what was your impression of the previous session?

Marilyn: [looking guarded] I don't know.

Dr. Amy: [providing empathy] I realize that this is still early in the therapeutic process. It is only our third session. Nevertheless, I find that it's helpful to remind ourselves of our previous work, so that we can build momentum, and so that there are themes that run across our sessions.

Marilyn: [looking skeptical] What did we even *do* in the previous session? I mean, really? I'm paying you all this money for you to tell me that you like that I ice-skate?

Dr. Amy: [linking overtly to the therapeutic relationship] Actually, Marilyn, I found that part of our session to be very important. We know that the relationship between a therapist and a client is a meaningful one, and one that makes a difference in the outcome of therapy. [demonstrating genuineness] To me, learning that information about you brought out a lot of positive regard toward you, and I was very optimistic that this is something important in your life that we can build upon to help you overcome your depression.

Marilyn: Okay, if you say so.

Dr. Amy: [recognizing and "filing away" that we likely were not seeing "eye-to-eye" on the degree to which our discussion of her ice skating contributed to the development of the therapeutic relationship, but also not wanting to get side-tracked before setting an agenda] I also recall that we talked about the way in which your ice skating actually builds upon an important principle of CBT. Do you remember that?

Marilyn: [looking dejected] No, not really.

Dr. Amy: Would it be okay if we continue our discussion of what CBT has to offer you and how it can build upon the things that you are already doing in your life? And parlay that into a specific game plan for our work together?

Marilyn: Yes, I think that would be a good idea, because I still don't really know what I am doing here.

Marilyn indicated that she did not remember the previous session on a couple of occasions, both when I asked her about her general impression of the previous session, as well as when I asked her, more specifically, if she remembered the CBT principles discussed in the previous session that pertained to her ice skating. I "took the bait" the first time she made a sarcastic comment (i.e., "I'm paying you all this money for you to tell me that you like that I ice-skate?") and responded with a heartfelt observation about the way in which I saw that as enhancing our therapeutic relationship, and the way in which a strong therapeutic relationship could contribute to outcome. However, she continued to express skepticism (i.e., "Okay, if you say so"). Some readers might wonder why I did not follow up on that response, given that it suggested that we continued not to be on the "same page." My rationale was that I did not want to be swept away into discussion that had the potential to last the remainder of the session without modeling an organized approach to making a thoughtful decision as to how to spend our time, which could demonstrate effective problem solving more generally. As can be seen in the dialogue, I did ask one final question pertaining to her memory of our discussion of the way in which CBT principles applied to her ice skating; this was asked to move toward a linkage to CBT's underlying theory and an opportunity to allow her to consolidate her learning from the previous session. When she did not respond to this intervention and appeared as if she was dejected, I moved toward agenda setting, which at this point in the conversation was continued discussion of the way in which CBT could be applied to her clinical presentation and the development of a treatment plan. More about Marilyn's agenda for her third session is described in the subsequent section.

What do you see as the value of the bridge from the previous session? In what types of situations in your own life has it been helpful to recall your previous work and weave a thread across multiple sittings when you are completing a task? In the following exercise, please write about these experiences. Then, indicate the ways in which you plan to implement the bridge from the previous session with your clients.

BOX 2 **REFLECTIONS ON THE BRIDGE FROM THE PREVIOUS SESSION**

Think about a time in your life when you were attempting to accomplish a task across multiple sittings. Did you take the time to reorient yourself to your previous work? If so, what benefits did you see in doing so? If you did not do so, upon reflection, in what way might have it been helpful?

What do you see as advantages of doing a bridge from the previous session with your clients? What, if any, disadvantages do you see?

How, exactly, will you implement the bridge from the previous session with your clients?

Agenda

The *agenda* is the agreed-upon pool of topics that the therapist and client hope to address in session. The purpose of agenda setting is to do what has been mentioned at many points already in this chapter—to model a systematic approach to addressing a client's life problems. Too often, clients get overwhelmed when they are faced with everything on their plates, and they either shut down, or they meander from problem to problem, thinking about their problems vaguely and not defining them specifically, or identifying a specific piece of them to address before getting distracted by a different problem. The end result is that they make little systematic progress toward seeing change in any one of their problem areas, and they begin to develop a sense of helplessness and hopelessness.

Thus, near the beginning of the session, typically (but not always) after the brief mood check and the bridge from the previous session, the therapist asks the client to collaborate in setting a session agenda. Clients are socialized to the idea that it is their job to come prepared for session with topics or issues that they would like to address. However, in the spirit of collaboration, therapists can also suggest items for the agenda that would facilitate the thread being woven across sessions. Many therapists, when they are first learning how to deliver CBT, have a distinctive negative reaction about agenda setting. Consistent with the sentiments I described in Chapter 1 of this volume, in my supervisory experience, I have fielded concerns about agenda setting being too rigid and too off-putting to clients. These skeptics wonder whether agenda setting would stifle spontaneous conversation in session, which they believe was indicative of some "deeper" or more important issue than the items that were originally identified for the agenda. In other words, they wonder whether agenda setting is experienced negatively by the client, which could impede the development of the therapeutic relationship, or if agenda setting interferes with the introduction of more important topics that would be associated with greater gains achieved in treatment.

It is my firm view that we are not doing our clients any favors if we do *not* facilitate agenda setting. As has been stated to this point in the chapter, clients who present for treatment are usually overwhelmed by many stressors, challenges, and disappointments that they are experiencing in their lives, and they do not know where to begin to address them, along with their associated emotional distress. A session in which the client meanders from topic to topic, not considering a specific way to address the topic or drawing a conclusion from discussion of the topic before they move into the next issue, often reinforces an unhelpful way of dealing with life's problems. I tell my clients that I would not be doing my job if I did not model and implement a different way of organizing, talking about, and doing something about the issues that are causing so many difficulties in their lives.

That being said, unlike what is sometimes perpetuated in stereotypes about CBT, agenda setting need not be rigid. Consider the differences between these two approaches to agenda setting, with our client, Finn, the man who experienced a major depressive episode after being hit by a car and losing the use of his legs:

SCENARIO #1

Dr. Amy: Finn, what would you like to put on our agenda for today's session?

Finn: I guess I'd like to talk about a Labor Day barbeque that I've been invited to. I'm just really nervous about it. I think they're just inviting me because they feel sorry for me. I don't really think they want me there.

Dr. Amy: Of course, let's spend more time talking about that. Is there anything else you'd like to put on the agenda for today?

Finn: Um, the lawsuit. That's really stressing me out. There have been some new developments.

Dr. Amy: Okay, the Labor Day party and the new developments in the lawsuit. Is it okay if we also discuss the homework that you completed in-between sessions?

Finn: Yeah, sure. I brought it with me.

Dr. Amy: Great, let's make sure we reserve some time to review that as well. What shall we start with?

Finn: The lawsuit. That's what's been causing the most stress in the past week.

Dr. Amy: Alrighty. Let's start there.

SCENARIO #2

Dr. Amy: What's on your game plan for today's session?

Finn: I guess I'd like to talk about a Labor Day barbeque that I've been invited to. I'm just really nervous about it. I think they're just inviting me, because they feel sorry for me. I don't really think they want me there.

Dr. Amy: Oh, I remember you mentioning this get-together in passing last week. For sure, let's talk more about that. Before we jump in, what else do you want to accomplish here today?

Finn: [groaning] Um, the lawsuit. That's really stressing me out. There have been some new developments.

Dr. Amy: Oh boy. I realize that all has been quiet on the lawsuit front for a few weeks, and you've gotten such a nice reprieve. I'm sorry to hear that that things are amping up again. Let's definitely spend some time hearing about the new developments, and seeing if we can apply what we've done so far to address them.

Finn: Yeah, that would be great. I really need some help with that.

Dr. Amy: We have the Labor Day party and the new developments in the lawsuit on our game plan. Is it okay if we also discuss the homework that you completed in-between sessions? I'm really interested to see what you came up with, importantly, whether it made a difference in your life.

Finn: [looking brighter] I think it did, actually. I was looking forward to coming in and telling you about it.

Dr. Amy: [making a genuine response] Oh good, I'm looking forward to it too. So, we have three important things to discuss, and I want to be sure that we can give adequate time to each of them. Where would you like to start?

Finn: The lawsuit. That's what's been causing the most stress in the past week.

Dr. Amy: You got it, we'll start there. And I'll tell you what—I'll make sure that I keep an eye on time, so that we can be sure to address all three of these topics since they are all important for you to talk about today?

Finn: Thank you so much. I really don't want to leave here without touching base on all of them.

On the surface, there might not seem to be a big difference between Scenarios #1 and #2. Both of them are solid examples of agenda setting, including identifying items for the agenda, ensuring that all items are identified before launching into discussion, and prioritizing which item the client prefers to address first. However, there are some subtle differences, which I believe contribute to conversational flow, and, ultimately, to the enhancement of the therapeutic relationship. For example, in Scenario #1 I use the term "agenda," whereas in Scenario #2, I use the term "game plan." Perhaps, for many clients, this difference would not even be noticed. However, consistent with my personality and the way in which I cultivate the therapeutic relationship, I veer toward using informal terms, such as"game plan," rather than more formal terms, such as "agenda." Does this mean that a formal term such as"agenda" is off limits? Absolutely not. I have used the term "agenda" many-a-time in my practice. Regardless of the terminology used, the goal is for the interaction between the client and the therapist to be as natural, comfortable, and genuine as possible.

There were other subtle differences between agenda setting in Scenarios #1 and #2. In Scenario #2, before indicating that apprehension about the Labor Day party would be an appropriate agenda items, I said, "Oh, I remember you mentioning this get-together in passing last week." This statement was expressed genuinely, as I remembered that Finn was anxious about the party, but it was also stated strategically to communicate that I had paid close attention to what he had expressed in the previous session, and that I was interested in his subjective experience. In addition to his experience in anticipating the Labor Day party, Finn also expressed stress associated with the forthcoming lawsuit (regarding the accident that rendered him unable to use his legs). Rather than simply indicating that we can add this to the agenda, as I did in Scenario #1, I stated, "Oh boy. I realize that all has been quiet on the lawsuit front for a few weeks, and you've gotten such a nice reprieve. I'm sorry to hear that that things are amping up again." These statements, again, communicated genuine concern for and interest in Finn's life circumstances, thereby enhancing the therapeutic relationship. Thus, the straightforward implementation of an aspect of CBT structure, such as agenda setting, can be an opportunity that is ripe for the development of the therapeutic relationship.

One word is in order about when the review of homework occurs in session. In these examples, I asked permission to include homework review on the agenda. In other CBT textbooks, you might very well read the recommendation that homework review occurs before the agenda is set. I appreciate how confusing that might be to a beginning cognitive behavioral therapist. This is another example of the fact that there is no one "right" or "wrong" way to "do" CBT. Every cognitive behavioral therapist has his or her own style, and the most important thing is (as you will see below) that homework is reviewed at some point in order to reinforce the notion that homework is essential for a good outcome in CBT.

This being said, allow me to elaborate upon my own personal style and reasons why I believe it is most effective to add homework review to the agenda rather than reviewing it before the agenda has been set. The most significant reason is that homework review often requires a large chunk of time. After all, it is important to spend time acknowledging the effort that clients have put into between-session work and to make sure that adequate time is devoted to allow clients to consolidate the learning that occurred from the homework. What did they learn about themselves? How would they apply their CBT tools similarly or differently in the future? Such discussion requires careful thought. If homework is only acknowledged in a cursory fashion before the agenda is set (e.g., Therapist: "Did you complete your homework we discussed last time?" Client: "Yes!" Therapist: "Good for you!"), it deprives the clients of the opportunity to put their their new learning into their own words. If you spend the time to, thoroughly, discuss with the client what was learned, what he or she will continue to apply, what he or she will do differently next time, and so on, this could take a significant amount of time. Before you know it, over half the session might be completed before the agenda is set, and only then might you learn of pressing topics that need to be addressed before the client leaves the session. In addition, depending on the particular homework exercise, the issues or circumstances that your clients write about (e.g., on a *thought record*) could serve as agenda items themselves. Finding this out as you are asking about homework review in the same conversation as agenda setting will give you all the information you need to develop a rich and compelling agenda for the session.

Agenda setting does not stop at deciding, near the beginning of the session, what you and the client hope to cover. Agenda setting is something that occurs throughout the session. What this means is that the therapist is mindful of the agenda as the session progresses. If much of the session time has passed, and only one or a small subset of the agenda items have been covered, the therapist acknowledges this (e.g., "I'm noticing that we have about ten minutes remaining, and we've mainly addressed the first issue that we were hoping to cover.") and asks the client to consider thoughtfully the way to spend the rest of the time (e.g., "How should we address the remaining two issues you were hoping to cover? Should we talk about them briefly, or should we table them for next week?"). Such questions prevent the client from getting "swept away" into discussions about one or a few items and forgetting about the other items to cover. In other words, it models the systematic approach to organizing life's problems that I am suggesting is such an important modeling experience in CBT. *Agendas can absolutely be adjusted, reformulated, and even abandoned in CBT, allowing for discussion of other topics and issues that spontaneously arise during the course of the session.* However, when this occurs, it is done so thoughtfully, collaboratively, and with a plan to address the remaining agenda items at a later time. It is not done so in a haphazard way that has the potential to replicate the unhelpful approach to solving life's problems that could very well be plaguing the client in his or her own life. Thus, if something deeper and/or important arises, then it can absolutely assume focus if the client and therapist both agree that it is best to shift the agenda.

When agenda setting is straightforward, the therapist asks a question, such as "What would you like to accomplish today?" or "What were you hoping to put on our game plan for today?" The client might come prepared with a couple of topics, and the therapist might add an additional topic to ensure that a thread is woven across sessions. In a clear-cut scenario such as this one, it is a mere couple of exchanges between the client and therapist, and the session proceeds.

However, you will undoubtedly encounter instances in which agenda setting is more challenging. At times, clients will say they have nothing for the agenda. Such a response could be indicative of a number of scenarios, such that the client is (a) not especially invested in treatment; (b) avoiding painful topics to address in treatment; or (c) reliant on the therapist to direct the course of treatment, and even solve his or her problems for him or her. All of these are therapeutic issues that deserve direct and transparent discussion. The first time a client tells me that he or she has nothing for the agenda, I demonstrate a fairly "laid-back" attitude, asking if we can put homework review on the agenda (as I do in every session if the client does not proactively suggest it as an agenda item), and making a suggestion to continue the discussion from the previous session, or to make progress toward a specific treatment goal that the client had identified. If the client repeatedly indicates that he or she has nothing for the agenda, I ask permission to put this issue, itself, on the agenda for the session. Assuming the client is agreeable (as it is important to be collaborative and not uniformly dictate items for the agenda) I re-socialize the client into his or her role for therapy (i.e., that he or she brings the specific content areas to discuss). In addition, I engage in sensitive but frank discussion to examine the hypotheses I have about factors that could be interfering with their identification of agenda items, and we begin to brainstorm obstacles to overcome those items.

In the previous chapter, I demonstrated the simultaneous development of the therapeutic relationship and the application of the beginnings of CBT session structure with Ashley, our relatively straightforward case. In point of fact, the agenda was set seamlessly during and after discussion of the brief mood check. Specifically, during the brief mood check, Ashley indicated that her anxiety was at a level of 8 out of 10, and I replied that I had some CBT strategies to share with her. After she expressed gratitude, I indicated that we could talk more about those strategies (which corresponded to an agenda item without ever saying the word "agenda"). After I did a quick bridge from the previous session, I reminded Ashley that, so far, our focus was on anxiety management strategies, and I asked her what else she was hoping to cover in the session (again, never using the word "agenda"). In response, Ashley indicated that she was having some problems with her husband that she had hoped to discuss. Once we agreed upon those two topics as the focus of the session, I asked her to prioritize the one that she hoped to address first, which is another standard component of agenda setting.

As might be expected, agenda setting was less straightforward with Marilyn. The following dialogue illustrates Marilyn's difficulties with pinpointing a specific agenda item, interspersed with statements of hopelessness. Note that this interaction follows from the bridge from the previous session, in which we had already indicated that continued discussion of what CBT has to offer would be in order. I include the final exchange of the previous dialogue and elaborate on the agenda.

Dr. Amy: Would it be okay if we continue our discussion of what CBT has to offer you and how it can build upon the things that you are already doing in your life? And parlay that into a specific game plan for our work together?

Marilyn: Yes, I think that would be a good idea, because I still don't really know what I am doing here.

Dr. Amy: Let's do that. It's truly important to me to make sure that we are on the "same page" as we proceed. In addition to discussing what CBT has to offer you, was there anything else you were hoping to cover in today's session?

Marilyn: My life is just so pathetic. That's all. Just pathetic. There's no other word for it. So there you go. Where do you start with that?

Dr. Amy: [making an attempt to narrow down the general reference to Marilyn's "pathetic" life to a topic that is more specific and tangible, which would increase the likelihood that progress could be made in a single session in addressing it] [speaking gently and empathetically] You have really communicated to me how unhappy you are over the past couple of visits, Marilyn. And as we move from assessment and treatment planning toward our therapeutic work, I very much hope that you can leave each session with something specific that can help you to chip away at that unhappiness. I wonder if there is one piece of this that we can tackle here today?

Marilyn: [speaking sarcastically] Which piece are you thinking of? The fact that I've never had a husband? Or the fact that I'll never have children? How about the fact that I'm in my 50s and in a dead-end career where I'm treated like crap?

Dr. Amy: [continuing to speak gently, evenly, and empathically] Marilyn, you mentioned that all of those areas are important for you to address in therapy at some point. I might suggest the one on which we can make the most tangible headway today. Any ideas?

Marilyn: [working collaboratively for a moment] Maybe we can talk more about my job? I really need to figure out if there is a way to find something different. But in the meantime, I also need to figure out how to have better interactions with my co-workers. I feel like I'm always the scapegoat.

Dr. Amy: [reinforcing Marilyn's movement toward specificity] I think those could be two very helpful areas of focus—problem solving with regard to finding a new job, and managing interpersonal relationships with your co-workers. Of those two, which one seems most important?

Marilyn: [falling back into her chair] I don't know! Both? None? What's the point, really? I've been in this job for almost 15 years, and I'm in my 50s now.

Dr. Amy: [making a statement of empathy, rather than pushing an agenda] You've expressed a great deal how hard this is for you, and I hear you. There might not be any easy solutions to either one of those areas. But I'm here to be by your side as we figure it out.

Marilyn: [responding to the empathic comment, making eye contact] Okay.

Dr. Amy: [using my clinical knowledge to inform my sense of a manageable task for the session] How about this for a plan, Marilyn? Why don't we finish our discussion of what CBT has to offer you? Then, we can solidify a more specific plan for the course of treatment, incorporating these issues, as well as any others that you'd like to tackle? And then, we can jump into one for which there might be something to try out in-between sessions. Perhaps some interpersonal skills for making things easier with your co-workers?

Marilyn: [looking skeptical] Okay, I guess.

Dr. Amy: [acknowledging the skepticism] If, as we're focusing on these things, you think of other issues, or it feels like we're barking up the wrong tree, will you let me know?

Marilyn: Yes, I definitely will.

Before diving into the topic that we identified during the brief mood check—what CBT has to offer Marilyn—I wanted to be sure to solidify the agenda and give Marilyn the opportunity to indicate what she had hoped to get out of the session. When Marilyn responded with despondency (and a little bit of sarcasm) about her life being "pathetic," I took care to express empathy and support, refraining from using language that would give the impression that CBT would be a "quick fix" for the extent of her life problems. However, in order to begin to build momentum and make small but tangible indicators of progress, I invited Marilyn to break down her "pathetic life" into smaller pieces, so that we could focus on one specific problem. Marilyn responded to this intervention, identifying her job as an immediate and specific problem. Even within the broad category of her job, she recognized that there were two subcomponents: (a) considering and eventually deciding upon a possible career change, and (b) developing more effective ways of interacting with her coworkers at her current job. When I asked her which one was most pressing, Marilyn responded with a bit of hostility, so I took care to make another statement of empathy and support, and I followed with a suggestion to begin to move the session forward. I recognized that we had not yet fully solidified the treatment plan, so I suggested that we discuss more about what CBT has to offer (the topic that had been identified in the bridge from the previous session), I reasoned that we could move that discussion into the finalization of the treatment plan, and then I raised the possibility of focusing on interpersonal skills with her coworkers. The rationale behind my suggestion to focus on interpersonal skills with coworkers is that it could lead to the most immediate change because the topic lent itself to the possibility that we could identify and practice one specific way of improving these relationships, which Marilyn could practice between sessions, observe an improvement in these relationships, and begin to develop a more positive expectation that her life could improve through treatment. At the end of this part of the conversation, I invited Marilyn to provide feedback if our therapeutic work was not resonating with her, once again demonstrating my openness to her input and collaboration.

What do you see as the value of working with your client in a collaborative manner to set the session agenda? In what types of situations in your own life has it been helpful to set some sort of agenda when completing a task? In the following exercise, please write about these experiences. Then, indicate the ways in which you plan to implement agenda setting with your clients.

BOX 3 REFLECTIONS ON THE AGENDA

Think about a time in your life when you had many things to accomplish in a short period of time. Did you take the time to decide how you would best use your time? If so, what benefits did you see in doing so? If you did not do so, upon reflection, in what way might it have been helpful?

What do you see as advantages of working with your clients to set an agenda? What, if any, disadvantages do you see?

How, exactly, will you implement the agenda with your clients?

Discussion of Agenda Items

The bulk of a CBT session is devoted to discussion of agenda items. As cognitive behavioral therapists discuss agenda items with their clients, they simultaneously balance the implementation of a strategy designed to help the client make headway in addressing that issue with attention to and cultivation of the therapeutic relationship. Discussion of agenda items need not proceed in a rigid, mechanistic way. Rather, conversation between the therapist and client is smooth and spontaneous, allowing for an interpersonal connection to develop. One common way in which agenda items are discussed is as follows:

- The therapist invites the client to provide more description of the first issue identified for the agenda.
- During discussion of this first issue, the therapist makes reflections to ensure that he or she understands what the client is saying and to communicate that he or she is listening.
- When appropriate, the therapist makes statements that communicate empathy and support.
- When it is clear that the client has communicated the essential information about the issue at hand and that the therapist has a solid understanding of this information, the therapist raises the possibility of a strategic intervention (e.g., cognitive restructuring, behavioral activation, problem solving, exposure) and receives feedback from the client about it.
- The therapist applies the strategic intervention to the issue at hand, allowing the client to practice the application of the strategy him- or herself.
- In many instances, the therapist and client together will identify something for the client to do or practice in-between sessions as homework (see subsequent section for more discussion of homework).
- At the end of discussion of the issue at hand, before moving onto the next agenda item, the therapist asks the client what he or she is taking away from the discussion to allow the client the opportunity to consolidate his or her learning.

Therapists need not be tied too closely to this format for discussion of agenda items. At times, agenda items are related, and they are addressed simultaneously, focused on a broader theme that encompasses all of them. In other instances, a strategy that has been implemented in the past can be applied to multiple agenda items, so the strategy is first reviewed and then applied systematically to the issues identified by the client for lengthier discussion. In still other instances, something arises in the discussion of a later agenda item that has relevance to an earlier agenda item, and the earlier agenda item is revisited. In other words, there is no set rule for the way in which agenda items are discussed. Therapists are simply mindful of the agenda that was developed to ensure that they cover everything in session that both the client and therapist think is important to cover. As they discuss agenda items, they balance attention to the therapeutic relationship and the strategic implementation of cognitive and behavioral change strategies.

When you transition from one agenda item to another, it can be helpful to wrap up discussion of the former agenda item with a periodic summary. A *periodic summary* is a summary statement that reflects the main points of the previous discussion. A periodic summary that closes discussion of an agenda item can highlight the important "nuggets" of learning that the client is taking away from the discussion or reinforcing a homework exercise or practice to do in-between sessions. It is often recommended that clients, themselves, supply the periodic summary, so that they can put their own words onto the cognitive and behavioral principles that they are learning. However, therapists can certainly provide periodic summaries as well.

It is inevitable that there will be times in which an impressive agenda is developed at the beginning of the session, but that discussion of one agenda item takes much longer than expected, and the session is about to end. This happens even to the most experienced cognitive behavioral therapists—it is nothing to chastise yourself over as you are learning to become a cognitive behavioral therapist! As stated in the previous section, it can be argued that the best agenda setting is the agenda setting that takes place across the course of the session, such that the therapist and client collaboratively adjust their expectations for what will be discussed on the basis of time and additional issues that have arisen during the course of the session. There will invariably be times in which an item identified for the agenda at the beginning of the session needs to be tabled until a later session.

In the subsequent chapters on specific intervention strategies (i.e., cognitive restructuring, behavioral interventions, mindfulness and acceptance), you will see dialogue that illustrates the way in which agenda items are discussed strategically in session. Illustrations of the discussion of agenda items, then, are reserved for these chapters. However, in the next exercise, reflect on the way in which your own sessions with clients proceed. Do you follow an agenda? How does the discussion of agenda items typically proceed? How do you handle it when new topics or issues are introduced?

BOX 4 REFLECTIONS ON DISCUSSION OF AGENDA ITEMS

How have you implemented agenda setting and subsequent discussion of agenda items in your clinical practice? How does the discussion of agenda items typically proceed?

How do you handle it when new topics or issues or introduced?

What will you work on improving or honing in the way in which you discuss agenda items with your clients?

Homework

Homework is one of the most central elements of CBT because it allows clients the ability to implement, apply, and practice the new learning and skills that have been developed in session. Research shows that there is a tight association between the degree to which clients invest in homework and the degree to which therapists emphasize homework and eventual outcome in treatment (e.g., Kazantzis, Brownfield, Mosely, Usatoff, & Flighty, 2017; Kazantzis et al., 2018; Kazantzis, Whittington, & Dattilio, 2010; Kazantzis et al., 2016). Thus, it is essential that cognitive behavioral therapists attend to homework in sessions, emphasizing its importance to clients, and creatively and collaboratively working with clients to maximize the effectiveness of homework.

Homework is considered in each session in two ways. First, the homework that had been developed in the previous session is reviewed. As mentioned in the previous section on agenda setting, my recommendation is to ask clients' permission to add homework review to the agenda to ensure that it is given adequate attention in session. In this section, I describe some ways to facilitate the effective review of homework in session. Second, at some point during the session, new homework to be completed in-between sessions is developed. Both of these aspects of homework are examined below.

Homework review. Homework review is more than the simple question and response, "Did you do your homework? You did? Great!" Of course, we like to give clients positive reinforcement for attempting and completing their homework between sessions. However, homework review deserves more attention than a simple statement of encouragement, as it provides an opportunity for clients to reflect on their learning, put their own words onto the cognitive behavioral principles that they have observed in their own lives, and commit to translating the learning and skill-building that occurred into a lifelong practice. Questions, such as "What did you learn from doing your homework?" and "In what specific ways did the homework make a difference in your life?", facilitates this consolidation of learning.

All cognitive behavioral therapists invariably encounter instances in which clients do not attempt or complete their homework. Regardless of whether clients actually do their homework, I encourage you to add homework review to the session agenda with the client's permission. There are several reasons why I make this suggestion. First, it socializes clients into the expectation that homework will be discussed in session no matter what. If the previous homework is not discussed, then it inadvertently gives clients the message that homework is not important. Thus, discussion of homework occurs is every single CBT session. This practice has the potential to shape clients' behavior in the direction of homework completion. Second, if homework is not attempted or completed, then there were obviously obstacles that were not anticipated or fully addressed in the previous session. Discussion of homework allows the client and therapist, together, to consider the obstacles that interfered with homework completion, and brainstorm ways to overcome those obstacles. Table 4.2 lists common obstacles to homework completion reported by clients. Finally, many homework exercises require sustained effort and attention across many days that take place in-between sessions. Thorough discussion of homework honors and respects the work that clients put into their homework, reinforcing the notion that they are working hard in treatment, and are doing something important that will ultimately be beneficial to them.

Table 4.2 Obstacles to Homework Completion

- Client forgot about or lost the homework exercise.
- Client did not have enough time for the homework exercise.
- Client was overwhelmed by the magnitude of the homework exercise.
- Client did not understand how to complete the homework exercise.
- Client did not truly believe that the homework would be helpful.
- Client did not have the motivation to complete the homework exercise.
- The client's homework was geared toward implementation in a particular setting or scenario, and the client did not find him- or herself in that setting or scenario.

As with any of the CBT session structure components or interventions, in many instances homework review runs relatively smoothly, but at times it can go awry. First, I demonstrate homework review with our relatively straightforward client, Ashley. Recall, in Ashley's previous session captured in an excerpt in Chapter 3 of this volume, that Ashley wanted to develop a plan to address her anxiety. After we collaboratively crafted a treatment plan, I began to teach Ashley cognitive restructuring (see Chapter 5 of this volume) to help her address unhelpful thinking that seemed to exacerbate her emotional upset. For homework, she agreed to keep a *thought record*, which (as will be described in the subsequent chapter) is a standard tool for recording instances of unhelpful thinking and its associated emotional distress. Below is an excerpt of homework review at the time of the next session.

Dr. Amy: Is it okay if we turn our attention to taking a closer look at the *thought record* that you completed for homework?

Ashley: Sure.

Dr. Amy: Terrific! I'm curious as to what you concluded from doing this homework?

Ashley: [pausing to think hard] I learned that I can have some really wacky thoughts when I am caught up in the moment and becoming really overwhelmed with things.

Dr. Amy: And what effect did you observe that wacky thinking has on your mood?

Ashley: Oh, it was very clear to me that the more wacky my thinking was, the more anxious I was feeling.

Dr. Amy: And in the times that you had the wackiest thinking and the most anxiety, were you able to make good decisions to address whatever problem or situation was associated with the emotional upset, or did the wacky thinking and anxiety seem to get in the way?

Ashley: That's a really interesting question. I think the times when I am most anxious, and my thinking is the most "off" are the times that I am completely paralyzed and almost unable to decide what to do next.

Dr. Amy: So, do you see an association between your thinking, your anxiety, and your subsequent behavior, or how you handle the problems you are facing?

Ashley: Oh, definitely. This is exactly why I thought CBT would be helpful for me.

Dr. Amy: Oh, that's great, Ashley. I'm so glad that this approach seems like such a good match for you. [pausing] Why don't you select the most upsetting or anxiety-provoking situation that you experienced in the past week and share your thoughts and your associated anxiety level?

In this dialogue, Ashley clearly reported that she had completed her homework and that she had much to discuss. Before jumping into specific details, I asked her what she learned from the homework in order to allow her the opportunity to describe the way in which the homework illustrated the interrelations between thinking, mood, and behavior. Fortunately, Ashley clearly saw these associations at work in her own life, so she readily pulled together these insights in a thoughtful, articulate manner. After discussion of the general conclusions that she drew from the exercise, I asked her to select one specific example from her homework that would provide the most compelling specific example of the cognitive behavioral model at work in her life.

In contrast, homework review did not go as planned with our relatively difficult client, Marilyn. As with Ashley, I encouraged Marilyn to complete the same exercise—the *thought record* to introduce the notion of cognitive restructuring and to illustrate the way in which the cognitive behavioral model is applicable to her life. However, as is captured in the dialogue below, she had a decidedly negative reaction to it.

Dr. Amy: [welcoming Marilyn to the session and initiating the brief mood check] It's good to see you back, Marilyn. I've really been looking forward to our session today as we are moving into our therapeutic work together. Is it okay if I check in on your mood using our mood scales?

Marilyn: [ignoring the question about the mood check] God, that homework that you had me do! All it did is make me feel worse! I just really don't at all see how it is going to help.

Dr. Amy: [leaning in and demonstrating genuine concern] Oh goodness, Marilyn, I'm sorry to hear this. The last thing I want to do is to have people do something in between sessions that would make them feel worse, although there are definitely times in any type of psychotherapy in which people experience emotional upset when they are facing difficult aspects of their lives that they wish were different.

Marilyn: I mean, I could be writing all day, non-stop, 24/7, because almost every aspect of my existence is so awful. I know you said that that doing this, this. . . [forgetting the name of the homework exercise]

Dr. Amy: [speaking gently] The *thought record.*

Marilyn: [frowning] Yes, yes the *thought record*, whatever it is called. There's just too much to write. It's overwhelming. One of my previous therapists tried to do something like this with me, and it failed miserably. I just *knew* this wouldn't work. [looking forlorn]

Dr. Amy: [continuing to express empathy, interest, and concern, as well as moving toward developing an agenda] Why don't we talk more about the homework, focusing on your experience with it, but also what I was hoping you'd get out of it. And we can put our heads together and see if there is a way to adapt it to be a better fit for you. Does that sound okay to you?

Marilyn: I don't know. I just really think this isn't for me.

Dr. Amy: Let's definitely take a closer look, then. I believe that I have plenty to offer you, even if we don't go in the direction of examining the thoughts that are associated with emotional upset.

In this dialogue, Marilyn clearly expresses displeasure with the homework and continues to question whether that intervention, and perhaps CBT more generally, is right for her. I was cognizant of balancing statements that communicated that I clearly heard and was open to what she was saying with an attempt to examine her experience more closely to ensure that we do not immediately abandon the intervention (which is a principle of strategy in CBT; see Chapter 1 of this volume). Thus, I suggested that we continue to talk about the homework to ensure that she understood the rationale for the homework, as well as to collaborate and reshape the homework so that it was more consistent with her strengths and preferences. Below, in the homework development section, I resume dialogue with Marilyn, after she expressed a willingness to try the homework again if it was modified to be more manageable for her.

Homework development. In addition to review of previous homework, cognitive behavioral therapists work with their clients to develop new homework that is designed to continue to advance clients to their treatment goals. Although homework development is placed toward the end of this chapter, it is important to recognize that *homework can be developed at any point in the session in which it is indicated and logical to do so.* For example, if you and your client have identified three items for the agenda, and a homework exercise logically emerges after discussion of the first agenda item, then homework can be developed at that point. In fact, I would argue that homework development is *most* effective when it is developed before the last few minutes of the session, such that there is enough time to ensure that the client understands the rationale for the exercise, so that the client is able to collaborate and help shape the exercise, and so that there is time for practice. Table 4.3 summarizes these and other tips for maximizing the effectiveness of homework development.

Allow me to comment on terminology. Throughout this discussion, I have been taking care to refer to homework as an "exercise" rather than as an assignment. This is a deliberate choice of language, as the word "assignment" connotates a power differential in which the therapist is a teacher who requires the client, as a student, to complete the homework that he or she chooses. In actuality, homework is developed collaboratively between the therapist and client.

Table 4.3 Tips to Maximize the Effectiveness of Homework Development

- Develop homework when it logically flows from discussion in session, preferably before the last few minutes of the session.
- Ensure that the homework makes logical sense on the basis of the content of the discussion.
- Be sure to collaborate with the client and customize the homework exercise on the basis of the client's preferences and strengths.
- Begin the homework exercise in session, so that the client has an opportunity to practice, providing a "template" to follow when he or she attempts homework outside of session.
- Make sure that the homework exercise is written on a piece of paper or stored in the client's smartphone, so that he or she remembers what the exercise is.
- Discuss with the client when he or she will do the homework and where he or she will keep the homework (if it is on a written sheet of paper).
- Ask the client whether he or she anticipates any obstacles to completing homework, and brainstorm solutions to overcome those obstacles.
- Obtain a rating that captures the likelihood of completing the homework (0% - 100%). If it is anything less than 90%, modify the homework to increase the likelihood of completion.
- In most instances, keep the homework to one specific exercise for the client to complete (versus multiple exercises). At times, multiple exercises are indicated, but in these cases, it is especially important to discuss the obstacles that could interfere with homework completion.

From my clinical experience, the more the client has input into the development of the homework, and the more the exercise is customized to the client's preferences, the more the client takes ownership over the homework and thereby is motivated to complete it. In addition, some clients have a negative reaction to the word "homework," itself.

In the rest of this section, I illustrate the development of homework with the clients we have been following in the book thus far. Recall that Ashley was responding well to the cognitive restructuring intervention and found it helpful; thus, I continued on with cognitive restructuring, helping her to acquire skills in evaluating her unhelpful thinking. In the following dialogue, we work together to develop a new homework exercise that extended the homework from the previous session, and incorporated the new learning that she had acquired.

Dr. Amy: Ashley, you've done such a nice job of taking the automatic thoughts that you had identified in your homework and beginning to take a good, hard look at them to evaluate the degree to which they are accurate and helpful.

Ashley: Thank you! I can't believe where my mind goes sometimes!

Dr. Amy: I wonder if we can take what we have done today and translate it into some more homework that you can practice in between our sessions?

Ashley: Yes, that would be great.

Dr. Amy: What resonated most with you today, during this discussion of reshaping your automatic thoughts?

Ashley: I really liked looking at the evidence that does and does not support the thought. Because there are so many times when I know there is very little basis to the way I'm seeing a situation, but my mind goes there anyway. Not only goes there, but also runs with it. And gets me into trouble.

Dr. Amy: [contemplating Ashley's observations] This gives me an idea. Would you like to hear what I think could be a possible extension to your homework?

Ashley: Yes, absolutely!

Dr. Amy: What if we were to modify the *thought record*, so that it has five columns? You can continue to jot down observations about situations that are upsetting, thoughts, and associated emotions. But then, you can also jot down evidence that supports the thought along with evidence that refutes the thought, so that you can get some practice with evidence gathering. What do you think?

Ashley: I think that sounds perfect!

Dr. Amy: Okay, great. Let's go to my computer and modify the *thought record*, so that you have a template to guide you over the next week in between sessions.

Ashley continued to express great enthusiasm for CBT and was diligent in completing her homework. As we moved from the identification of unhelpful thinking to the modification of unhelpful thinking, I asked Ashley what resonated most with her in session and used her response to make a suggestion for continued homework. Together, we collaboratively developed a homework exercise in which we modified her *thought record* to include space to record that evidence that did and did not support her automatic thoughts. This is an example of adapting and extending the homework exercises on the basis of client feedback and preferences.

Marilyn, on the other hand, gave me the feedback that the homework was overwhelming for her. On the basis of this feedback, as well as my observations of the way in which therapy had proceeded to this point, I hypothesized that continuing to pursue cognitive restructuring in this manner would push Marilyn even further away, possibly disrupting any therapeutic alliance that we had established. In the excerpt below, I worked with Marilyn to identify what, specifically, was overwhelming about the homework, consider ways to modify the homework, and move toward a commitment to attempting homework again.

Dr. Amy: Let's choose one specific instance when you attempted the homework, and it was too much for you. Walk me through what happened.

Marilyn: Well, I woke up in the morning, and I was just flooded with all sorts of negative thoughts. Like about how awful I knew the day was going to be. How I'm the scapegoat at work once again. How I have no one to come home to after a terrible day at work. . .

Dr. Amy: [taking the first opportunity to jump in before Marilyn becomes agitated] Oh goodness, Marilyn, it sounds like mornings are really tough for you.

Marilyn: [looking dejected] They are. They really are. I psych myself out before the day even starts.

Dr. Amy: I appreciate that it can be tough to identify one particular thought to work with, especially first thing in the morning when you are flooded with lots of thoughts and emotions.

Marilyn: [looking more relaxed, as if she realized that I was understanding what she was experiencing] It's just overwhelming. I don't know where to start.

Dr. Amy: I have an idea. What if you were to choose one *particular* instance each day that is upsetting, and you practice catching unhelpful thinking. In my experience, I find that working with *specific* situations can be a bit more straightforward than sorting through the barrage of thoughts that we have when we get stuck in our heads.

Marilyn: Okay. How do I do that?

Dr. Amy: Let's practice together. Why don't we consider the past 24 hours? Was there a specific time in the past 24 hours that you found yourself in a situation that was upsetting to you?

Marilyn: Well, yes, I had a pretty bad interaction with my supervisor yesterday. She told me that my attitude was making other people in the office uncomfortable.

Dr. Amy: I'm sorry to hear that Marilyn. Tell me what ran through your mind when she gave you that feedback.

Marilyn: [tearing up] That everyone hates me! That I can't get along with anyone.

Dr. Amy: [balancing an emphasis on responding empathetically to Marilyn's emotion and continuing the strategic application of cognitive restructuring] Marilyn, I think any person in the world would find that to be upsetting. When you say that to yourself—that everyone hates you, and that you can't get along with anybody—how do you feel emotionally?

Marilyn: Horrible, of course!

Dr. Amy: This is a perfect example of the types of thoughts we can work with, Marilyn. We can start to gather a sampling of these types of thoughts, like everyone hating you, like not being able to get along with anybody, and I can help you to start to reshape these thoughts, so that you don't feel quite as horrible in these situations.

Marilyn: You mean I did it? This is the homework?

Dr. Amy: [smiling warmly] Yes, this is it. I think what might have been problematic is that we weren't emphasizing specific situations enough, and the task quickly became unwieldy. What if, instead, you just take one situation like this every day and identify the key thoughts associated with your emotional upset?

Marilyn: Rather than the random thoughts that just always float through my mind?

Dr. Amy: Yes, exactly.

Marilyn: [frowning] Well, I can try, but . . . I don't know, it just seems like such a burden to stop everything and write down my thoughts. Like if I'm in a meeting or something. What am I going to do? Tell everyone to stop everything, so that I can write on my *thought record*?

Dr. Amy: You're not the only one who has expressed this concern, Marilyn. Although we generally do like people to start learning how to catch thoughts as they are occurring, we also realize that these exercises must be adapted for your specific life circumstances. One thing that has worked for my other clients is to type quick notes in your smartphone, rather than writing on the sheet of paper. Might that me more convenient for you?

Marilyn: Definitely, yes, I think it would be. I thought you were saying that I had to write on the sheet of paper.

Dr. Amy: I apologize if I gave you that impression, Marilyn. In fact, I think CBT works best when my clients figure out creative ways to really make it work for their style. So, it sounds like recording notes about upsetting situations, thoughts, and associated emotions in your phone would work better for you?

Marilyn: Definitely.

Dr. Amy: Am I correct in assuming that you're willing to give it another try? This time working only with the most specific situations, and recording in your phone rather than on the sheet of paper I gave you?

Marilyn: Okay, I can do this.

In this example, I used my clinical experience to recognize that it would be helpful for Marilyn to focus on her thinking in specific situations, rather than at that very moment trying to tackle the more general berating thoughts that ran over and over in her mind. We practiced in session, so that Marilyn had a tangible idea of what it meant to focus on a specific situation. Once Marilyn experienced some success, she demonstrated a greater openness to trying the exercise. When she expressed concern about recording her work on a *thought record*, I offered her an alternative—recording notes in her phone. This suggestion demonstrates the flexibility inherent in CBT and the importance of modifying homework exercises, so that they fit with the client's style, thereby increasing the likelihood that they would be completed. At the end of the dialogue, I solicited Marilyn's comment to attempt the homework again, incorporating the modifications that we had identified. I also purposefully apologized for the impression that she took away from our discussion in the previous session—that she *must* record her work on the sheet of paper. I did this to model collaboration, openness, and a willingness to take responsibility for any role that I played in miscommunication or misunderstanding.

Experiential exercise. It is my motto that I do not ask my clients to do anything that I have not done myself. In this spirit, I invite you to engage in an experiential exercise in which you practice your own "homework" for seven consecutive days, as a client might in between weekly therapy sessions. To achieve this aim, consider the following steps.

Table 4.4 Seven-Day Homework Recording Form

DAY	*WHAT DID YOU DO?*
1	
2	
3	
4	
5	
6	
7	

1. Identify a task that you must accomplish that involves several steps (e.g., writing a 15-page paper for a course), or a good habit that you would like to hone (e.g., healthy eating).
2. In Table 4.4 track your success across the seven-day period.
3. In the box below, write about your experiences, including the degree of difficulty you encountered in sticking with the plan, and what you learned from the exercise.

BOX 5 **REFLECTIONS ON HOMEWORK EXPERIENTIAL EXERCISE**

How easy or difficult was it for you to stick with the plan? What made it that way? What did you learn that might make it easier to comply with homework that you set for yourself in the future?

What do you learn from the tasks that you selected? For example, if you chose to gear your homework toward writing a paper for a class, what did you learn about researching and writing papers?

(continued)

(continued)

How will completion of this exercise affect the way in which you approach multi-step tasks or the establishment of new habits in the future?

Reflection. Take some time, now, to reflect on this discussion of homework. What do you see as the value of homework? What, if any, drawbacks or obstacles do you see associated with homework? In your own life, when have you completed tasks, such as homework, how did doing so help you to reach your goals? In the following exercise, please write about these experiences. Then, indicate the ways in which you plan to implement homework with your clients.

BOX 6 **REFLECTIONS ON HOMEWORK**

Think about a time in your life when you were trying to acquire or practice a skill or accomplish a goal. Did you complete tasks such as the homework exercises described in this section to meet your goals? If so, how effective were such homework tasks in helping you to refine skills or meet goals? If not, would it have been helpful to design homework tasks along the way to facilitate the process? Why so?

What do you see as advantages of working with your clients to develop and practice homework in between sessions? What, if any, disadvantages do you see?

How, exactly, will you implement homework with your clients?

Final Summary and Feedback

The end of the session allows the opportunity to summarize what has transpired, consolidate the main "nuggets" for the client to take away from the session, provide the client with the opportunity to put into his or her own words the learning that is being acquired, and be reminded of the homework to be completed between sessions. Similarly to what I expressed when I described the bridge from the previous session (and is captured in Table 4.1), open-ended questions (versus closed-ended questions) are most helpful during the final summary and feedback to allow clients to elaborate on and talk freely about what they have learned. This allows clients to put key concepts together and consider ways they can generalize to their lives outside of session. In addition (again, much like the bridge from the previous session), an opportunity is provided for clients to provide feedback to the therapist regarding any issues that might have arisen within the therapeutic relationship, such as the client feeling judged, dismissed, or misunderstood by the therapist. The following dialogue with Ashley exemplifies a straightforward final summary and feedback.

Dr. Amy: We're about at the end of our time here today, Ashley. What are you taking away from today's visit?

Ashley: Oh, this has been really helpful. It's another good reminder that my thinking can get me in trouble. But now I'm starting to develop the tools to get a handle on it.

Dr. Amy: And what would you say is the most important tool that you're taking away today?

Ashley: Looking at the evidence, for sure. But I really think a lot of what we covered today is going to be helpful. You know, looking at the probability of the worst that can happen, seeing that it is low, and also seeing that I can handle it if it occurs. Thinking about what I would say to a friend who is in the same situation, because I just *know* I would be way more helpful to a friend than I am to myself.

Dr. Amy: That's terrific Ashley, I'll so glad that you have learned so much today. How likely is it that you'll follow through with the homework that we have developed?

Ashley: Oh, for sure 100%.

Dr. Amy: Is there anything that you thought I got wrong today, or did I say anything that rubbed you the wrong way?

Ashley: No, not at all. If anything, this is a relief. I think I am finally getting the help that I have needed.

Not only did Ashley indicate specific pieces of the session that were helpful for her, she continued to express positive sentiments and gratitude toward her experience in CBT to this point. Notice that I asked her what she was taking away from the session; this is a question that I ask of most of my clients in the final summary and feedback, so that they can use their own words to express CBT principles of change. However, I also asked her a question about the homework, as well as whether anything in session bothered her, to ensure that I had enough information to conclude that she was leaving on a positive note. In contrast, Marilyn was a bit more mixed in the final summary and feedback.

Dr. Amy: Marilyn, from my perspective, we've had a productive session. What about today's session are you taking away, or do you have the sense will make a difference in your life?

Marilyn: I'm still not sure, to be honest.

Dr. Amy: [asking for permission] Is it okay to share something that I thought was especially helpful about today's session?

Marilyn: Okay, sure.

Dr. Amy: I found it interesting that, at first the homework wasn't resonating with you, but then after we took a closer look, it, indeed, was relevant, and we also figured out a way to make it work in your life. That's my favorite kind of CBT, when I work together with someone to really make it come alive for them.

Marilyn: Yeah, well, we'll see. I'm not sure that it will translate to my real life.

Dr. Amy: [reinforcing the homework] Fair enough. But how likely are you to give it a try?

Marilyn: Oh, I'll try it. A phone recording is much better than writing it down on that sheet of paper.

Dr. Amy: I want to acknowledge that, in our work to this point, you have expressed some skepticism. Where do you stand on that degree of skepticism now after today?

Marilyn: I don't really know. I guess we figured some things out today. But there's still so much to handle. I don't really know if one approach to therapy can do it.

Dr. Amy: Fair enough, I certainly don't want to be overly optimistic. But is it also fair to say that we were able to make some progress today, such that we figured out a more effective way to work with some of your thoughts?

Marilyn: Yes, yes, I think we did.

Dr. Amy: Great. [smiling warmly] I'll take that, Marilyn. [pausing] Is there anything you didn't like about today's session—anything that I got wrong or rubbed you the wrong way?

Marilyn: [hesitating] No . . . not specifically. [pausing] But I don't know, you're so optimistic.

Dr. Amy: I get the impression that my optimism can be a bit too much, Marilyn. But it is true that I do carry some hope that CBT has much to offer you.

When clients are hesitant to identify something they find helpful in session, it can be useful to ask permission to share your own view, as I did here with Marilyn. When you do this, it is important follow up to determine the degree to which your view resonates with them if they do not supply their own commentary, as Marilyn did. The final summary and feedback is also an appropriate time to check out the subjective "feel" of the client if you are detecting that there might be skepticism or disdain, as I did with Marilyn. When you do this, it is helpful to demonstrate openness to negative feedback, respond as warmly and genuinely as you do when clients provide positive feedback, and indicate a willingness to alter your behavior on the basis of the client's reaction.

As you have done with the other session structure components, take some time, now, to reflect on the final summary and feedback. What do you see as the value of the final summary and feedback? What, if any drawbacks or obstacles do you see associated with the final summary and feedback? In your own life, when have you completed an important task, did it help you to summarize what you did, and reflect upon your accomplishments? In the following exercise, please write about these experiences. Then, indicate the ways in which you plan to implement homework with your clients.

BOX 7 REFLECTIONS ON THE FINAL SUMMARY AND FEEDBACK

Think about a time in your life when you accomplished an important task. Did you summarize what you did to achieve what you did, and did you take the time to reflect upon your experience? If so, what value did you gain from doing so? If not, how might it have been helpful to do so?

What do you see as advantages of doing a final summary and feedback? What, if any, disadvantages do you see?

How, exactly, will you implement the final summary and feedback with your clients?

Experiential Exercise: Application to Clients

Now is another opportunity to do what you did in Chapter 3 of this volume—to apply the principles that you have just read in an experimental manner to your clients. As you did when you practiced the features of the therapeutic relationship that were most important to you, I would like you to implement systematically the session structure components described in this chapter, so that you can "live" them, rather than simply read about them. Use the following steps as a guideline:

1. Choose a client with whom you are working on a regular basis with whom you can implement CBT session structure components.
2. Implement each session structure component across the course of several sessions, one component at a time. For example, in your next session implement the brief mood check. If that runs smoothly, in the subsequent session, add the implementation of the bridge from the previous session. If it does not run smoothly, feel free to spend a second session mastering the brief mood check before moving onto adding the bridge from the previous session. Then add the implementation of the agenda, then add the implementation of homework development, then add the implementation of homework review (i.e., review of the homework developed in the previous session), and finally, add the implementation of the final summary and feedback. The idea is to achieve some sort of comfort or mastery (although, do not worry, you need not achieve *complete* mastery at this point!) before implementing another component. When you move onto implementing another component, continue with the implementation of the components you have already practiced, so that you are delivering the full scope of CBT session structure.
3. In the box below, record your reflections on the exercise.

BOX 8 REFLECTION ON YOUR EXPERIENTIAL EXERCISE

What, in general, do you conclude from your experiential exercise?

What, specifically, do you conclude about the individual session structure components?

Were they easier to implement than you had expected them to be? More difficult?

Why? If a specific issue arose with one or more session structure components, be sure to record it below.

Brief Mood Check

Bridge from the Previous Session

Agenda Setting

Homework Review

Homework Development

Final Summary and Feedback

What, specifically, will you do differently in the future to implement CBT session structure?

How has your view about CBT session structure changed after participating in this experiential exercise?

As you did in Chapter 3 of this volume on the therapeutic relationship, you have just conducted another important exercise as a practitioner-scientist! You carefully implemented important practices associated with evidence-based psychotherapy, and you developed some comfort with them, building from one to the other. This experience will allow you to continue to hone your session structure skills, observe your strengths and weaknesses, and identify areas for further attention.

CHAPTER 5 COGNITIVE RESTRUCTURING

Cognitive Restructuring

CHAPTER 5

It is human nature, when faced with stress, challenges, and disappointments, to focus on the negative, such as the worst-case scenario, how awful the situation feels, and/or doubts about our ability to persevere. Although there may be a grain of truth to this style of thinking (or, in some cases, several grains of truth), when it is excessive or overstated, it can easily bring on or exacerbate a negative mood state. Not only does a negative mood state perpetuate many mental health problems, such as depressive or anxiety disorders, it can also interfere with taking effective action and engaging in proper self-care. You may have recognized this sequence at work when you applied the basic cognitive behavioral theory to a situation in your own life in Chapter 2 of this volume. Thus, a central intervention in CBT called *cognitive restructuring* was developed to address faulty and otherwise unhelpful patterns in thinking.

I define cognitive restructuring as the process by which therapists help their clients to acquire skill in (a) recognizing unhelpful thinking that is exacerbating negative mood states, (b) evaluating the accuracy and usefulness of that thinking, and (c) if necessary, modifying that thinking to be more balanced and adaptive. Notice that I am *not* saying that cognitive restructuring is simply changing one's thinking or thinking positively. Although the results of cognitive restructuring might very well be that thinking is changed in some way, it does not presuppose that a client's thinking is abnormal and dysfunctional. In the spirit of collaborative empiricism, which I defined in Chapter 1 of this volume, the therapist and client, together, function as co-detectives, examining the accuracy and usefulness of all pieces of information that contribute to a particular way that the client is thinking about a situation. It is only if they conclude that the thinking is somehow inaccurate or not useful that they move toward changing it. Even when it is determined that change is in order, it is not simply thinking positively or thinking in a manner that is diametrically opposed to the original thought. Rather, the aim of cognitive restructuring is to achieve *balanced* thinking, such that the client objectively acknowledges the positive, neutral, and negative aspects of the situation. To achieve this aim, I often use the phrase "softening" negative thoughts rather than outright "changing" them, in order to respect the fact that many, if not most, clients are experiencing difficulties in their lives that would be upsetting or challenging for almost anyone.

In this chapter, I outline the cognitive restructuring process in the three steps that I typically share and practice with my clients. I also discuss tools to aid in cognitive restructuring. Next, I invite you to participate in an experiential exercise, in which you apply cognitive restructuring in your own life. Then, I illustrate the application of cognitive restructuring with the relatively straightforward and relatively difficult cases that we have followed throughout the volume thus far, and I invite you to apply cognitive restructuring to one of your own clients. Finally, I share tips for maximizing the effectiveness of cognitive restructuring and overcoming obstacles that you might encounter during the process.

Cognitive Restructuring: Three Steps

In this section, I outline the way in which I deliver cognitive restructuring with my own clients, which I have described previously in some of my other written works (Wenzel, 2013, 2017). Please keep in mind that there is no one "right" way to deliver cognitive restructuring (or, really, any cognitive behavioral intervention). Herein lies the "art" of CBT. Although it is true that therapists are advised to deliver interventions that are consistent with those that have been deemed as efficacious in the scientific literature, in most cases, there is no step-by-step recipe that therapists absolutely must follow. Thus, therapists can implement the "spirit" of the intervention in a strategic manner, while at the same time using their own unique style, personality, and sense of creativity to bring the intervention to life for the individual client. As stated previously, all the while, cognitive behavioral therapists conduct themselves as practitioner-scientists, collecting self-report and observational "data" from their clients to verify the degree to which the intervention is achieving its desired aims.

One caveat is in order before I proceed with discussion. This chapter is mainly focused on the restructuring of situation-specific thoughts, or thoughts that emerge when a person is faced with a particular instance that is upsetting. Another term for these situation-specific thoughts is *automatic thoughts*, which captures the fact that these thoughts often arise so quickly that we simply conclude that a situation made us feel a certain way, when in fact a thought about or interpretation of the situation arose so quickly that we did not even fully recognize its presence. I contrast the cognitive restructuring of automatic thoughts with the cognitive restructuring of underlying beliefs, or the cognitions described in Chapter 2 of this volume that are formed over time as a result of key formative life experiences. All of the cognitive restructuring techniques described in this section can apply to both the reframing of automatic thoughts, as well as the reframing of underlying beliefs, although all of the examples I provide are of the reframing of automatic thoughts. However, in a section toward the end of this chapter, I share some additional insights about the reframing of underlying beliefs that go beyond the more straightforward techniques that I describe in the following pages.

Step 1: Identifying Unhelpful Thinking

Thinking that is inaccurate and/or otherwise unhelpful can only be modified if we recognize that it has been activated. Thus, an important step in cognitive restructuring—one that is not to be underestimated—is helping clients to acquire skill in simply recognizing the presence of unhelpful thinking. The most fundamental question that therapists ask clients to identify unhelpful thinking is: "What was running through your mind in that situation?"

In my experience, less than 50% of clients are able to identify the *key* thought that is associated with their emotional distress. Notice that I have italicized the word "key." Most clients can identify something that might have been running through their minds, but that "something" might not necessarily be the issue that can explain his or her emotional distress. This makes sense, as we do not typically learn to do this in our everyday academic or personal lives. Thus, it is your job as the therapist to develop a sense of the types of thoughts that are fruitful to subject to cognitive restructuring and the types of thoughts that are associated with greater meaning. Cognitive behavioural therapists do this with the idea that the greater meaning accounts for a much greater percentage of the variance in the client's emotional distress and would, therefore, yield much more benefit if it were to be identified as the thought to be subjected to cognitive restructuring. The renowned cognitive behavioral therapist, Christine Padesky, calls these "hot" thoughts (Greenberger & Padesky, 2016). In the following dialogue with my client, Rachel, last mentioned in Chapter 3 of this volume, I further illustrate the distinction between hot thoughts and thoughts that, on their own, are less fruitful to subject to cognitive restructuring, and would benefit from additional examination.

SCENARIO #1

Dr. Amy: Can we talk more about the family gathering on Saturday night? It sounds like it was quite upsetting for you.

Rachel: Sure, I think I need to get some closure on that one.

Dr. Amy: [examining Rachel's homework] I see here you were faced with a situation, in which your aunt made a comment about your appearance. Tell me what ran through your mind in that situation.

Rachel: [becoming tearful] That I'm fat and ugly, and I will never be as good as any of my cousins.

Dr. Amy: [demonstrating empathy through tone of voice] Oh goodness, those are powerful thoughts, Rachel. When you notice those ideas—that you are fat, ugly, and not as good as your cousins, how does that make you feel?

Rachel: Horrible. Depressed and down.

Dr. Amy: And on our scale of 0–10 with 0 being the absence of being depressed or down, and 10 being the most depressed or down you can imagine being, what number would you assign to the intensity of that emotion?

Rachel: [sniffing] Like a 9 or a 10. It was really awful.

In this dialogue, I recognized that the automatic thoughts of being fat ugly, and not as good as her cousins were key hot thoughts that could explain the intense emotional distress that Rachel was experiencing. In other words, the power of the cognition matched the intensity of the emotion that she was experiencing. In the next dialogue, this is not the case. Notice the way in which I clarify the thoughts that were running through Rachel's mind, as well as the way I "dug" just a little deeper after Rachel identified a thought that was relevant, but probably not as "hot" as the ones identified in the first dialogue.

Dr. Amy: Can we talk more about the family gathering on Saturday night? It sounds like it was quite upsetting for you.

Rachel: Sure, I think I need to get some closure on that one.

Dr. Amy: [examining Rachel's homework] I see here you were faced with a situation in which your aunt made a comment about your appearance. Tell me what ran through your mind in that situation.

Rachel: I was like, "What is wrong with you?"

Dr. Amy: [recognizing that this is a vague, hypothetical question for which there is no true answer] So, your first reaction was, "What is wrong with you?" Tell me, what does it mean to you that your aunt made a comment on your appearance?

Rachel: That she's clueless! That she has no semblance of social grace!

Dr. Amy: Fair enough, Rachel. [pausing] However, I'm curious about one aspect of this. In the emotion column, you wrote that you were depressed or down at a level of 9 to 10. I would have expected something different from the thoughts you just shared. Maybe a level of anger?

Rachel: Well, yeah, I was angry too.

Dr. Amy: Okay, so there was definitely anger. But tell me what accounts for those very high ratings of being depressed and down. [hypothesizing that there is a more fundamental hot thought that is even more powerful than Rachel's judgment that her aunt is clueless and lacks social graces]

Rachel: [pausing, and averting eye contact] I'm fat! I'm ugly! I'm never going to be as good as my cousins, who are all so beautiful and have it together.

Dr. Amy: Ah, I think we've stumbled onto something here. What powerful ideas those are, Rachel. Do you think that those thoughts—of being fat, of being ugly, and of not being as good as your cousins—are the most central thoughts in understanding the intensity of how you were feeling?

Rachel: [looking forlorn] Yes, yes, I definitely think so.

Two aspects of this second dialogue deserve note. First, when clients ask vague questions, such as "What is wrong with you?", they are usually thinking in hypotheticals, and there is no factual answer to the question. In this case, I chose to encourage Rachel to identify the meaning associated with that initial reaction. In fact, I find that the question, "What did the situation mean to you (or mean about you)?", is perhaps the most effective question that truly gets at the hot thought that can best explain the intensity of the client's emotional distress. Thus, when clients pose automatic thoughts as questions, I either (a) encourage them to rephrase it as a statement (e.g., "There is something wrong with her" or "She lacks social graces"), and (b) if I suspect that there is a more significant underlying meaning that can better account for the client's emotional distress, I will ask about the meaning of the situation, or his or her interpretation of the situation.

Second, I pay close attention to the degree to which the identified thought matches with the identified emotion and/or with the intensity of the emotion. As exemplified in the dialogue, I would have expected "She's clueless" and "She has no social grace" to be associated more with anger than the profound level of depression that Rachel indicated. It was only upon acknowledgement of this discrepancy and subsequent questioning that Rachel identified thoughts that were even "hotter"—that she viewed herself as fat, ugly, and not as good as her cousins. The combination of recognizing that depression and being down did not exactly match the identified thoughts, along with the discrepancy between the intensity that I would have expected from those identified thoughts and the higher level of intensity that she had written down, led me to point out my reaction and question further about the key thoughts that she was experiencing.

Over time, you will develop a sense of the types of thoughts that are the most "loaded" (i.e., that are the "hottest")—if it seems daunting to you right now, as a beginner, know that you will have rich clinical experiences that will help you to home in on the most powerful thoughts as your CBT career progresses. If, as you are in the process of implementing cognitive restructuring with your client, you realize that there may be a more fundamental or loaded thought that would benefit from cognitive restructuring, do not despair. Your client will still gain a valuable experience by applying cognitive restructuring skills, and you can always recognize that there is a more fundamental thought midway through, finish the task at hand, and then move toward the evaluation of that second thought.

Step 2: Evaluating Unhelpful Thinking

Notice the word that I used in this heading—*evaluating* unhelpful thinking. Too often, I encounter cognitive behavioral therapists (and even authoritative texts that describe CBT) who refer to this step as "challenging" unhelpful thinking. I, myself, fell into this category when I started to work with Dr. Aaron T. Beck in 2004. He had been supervising me as I delivered CBT, and I boldly began to talk to him about the way in which I helped the client to "challenge" his negative thinking. Dr. Beck paused for a moment, and he indicated to me that he did not develop cognitive restructuring as a way to "challenge" thoughts. Again, in the spirit of collaborative empiricism—you as the therapist and your client being co-detectives examining the evidence before drawing a conclusion—we do not presuppose that a client's thinking needs challenging, but instead, we take a more neutral, curious evaluative stance, and we only decide that thinking is not adaptive or helpful if the results from our evaluation support that.

Thus, when therapists work with their clients to evaluate (potentially) unhelpful thinking, they pose, and they teach their clients to pose, critical thinking questions that allow their clients to grapple with many sides of their thinking. This type of questioning is called *Socratic questioning*, named after the Greek philosopher, Socrates. Socrates was quite the innovative teacher in his time, as he encouraged his students to argue multiple sides of an issue, in order to draw their own conclusions, rather than simply being told what to think. Cognitive behavioral therapists adopt the same type of stance with their clients surrounding unhelpful thinking.

Table 5.1 is a list of common Socratic questions that therapists ask their clients in the spirit of evaluating unhelpful thinking. Clients are encouraged to ask these types of questions on their own, so that they can begin to evaluate their thinking without the aid of a therapist. The idea is for one or more of these questions to be posed in response to the identification of unhelpful thinking and for the client to give honest answers to the questions, in order to arrive upon a more balanced way of viewing the situation. Many therapists-in-training believe that they have to ask Socratic questions exactly as they are posed in Table 5.1, when in actuality, some of the most effective CBT is done when the therapist and client, together, pose unique questions that fit the style of the conversation and the demands of the issue at hand. Thus, the questions listed in Table 5.1 are simply examples of effective questions, and you are encouraged to ask whatever unique questions are appropriate for your particular client.

Table 5.1 Socratic Questions to Facilitate the Evaluation of Unhelpful Thinking

QUESTIONS TO EXAMINE THE ACCURACY OF THINKING

- What evidence supports that thought? Is that evidence factual? What evidence is inconsistent with that thought?
- Is there any research, or are there any data that speak to this issue? If so, what does the research or data say?
- What are some other explanations for the situation being as it is?
- What is the worst that can happen? The best? The most realistic? Is the most realistic scenario closer to the worst-case scenario or the best-case scenario?
- What is the likelihood of the worst-case scenario?
- If the worst happens, how bad would that, realistically, be? How would I cope?
- Does _____ have to lead to or equal to _____?
- Is _____ really so important or consequential?
- What would I tell a friend in this situation? [if different than what the client would tell him- or herself] What accounts for the difference?

QUESTIONS TO EXAMINING THE HELPFULNESS OF THINKING

- What is the effect of believing my thinking? What is the effect of changing my thinking?
- What are the advantages and disadvantages of thinking in this way?
- How useful is it to be thinking in this way?
- If I have to be in this upsetting situation, how can I attain wisdom or achieve personal growth?

Note: Many of these questions can be found in J. S. Beck (2011), Wenzel (2013), and Wenzel (2017).

Step 3: Modifying Unhelpful Thinking

If, as a result of this evaluation, it is determined that the client's thinking is inaccurate and/or unhelpful, then the therapist works with the client to develop an alternative way of viewing the situation. Here I call this alternative viewpoint an *adaptive response*—other terms that have been used in the literature include *alternative response*, *balanced response*, and *rational response*. As stated previously, *an adaptive response is not simply a more positive way of thinking.* Rather, it is a compelling, believable alternative viewpoint that takes into account many of the pieces of factual information that contribute to the way in which a person makes sense of a situation with which he or she is faced. Whereas automatic thoughts tend to be quick, specific, evaluative statements, adaptive responses tend to be lengthier, addressing many features associated with the unhelpful way of viewing the situation. Typically, simplistic adaptive responses, such as "Don't worry, everything will be okay" or "Just get over it" are associated with minimal, if any relief, and usually are not helpful the next time a similar thought is activated. Table 5.2 provides examples of the types of automatic thoughts that are elicited in CBT, with a corresponding adaptive response.

How can one gauge the degree to which cognitive restructuring is efficacious? I encourage my clients to identify the emotional reaction associated with the original automatic thought (e.g., sad, nervous, angry) and rate its degree of intensity on a Likert-type scale (e.g., 0 = none; 10 = the most intense one can imagine experiencing). After crafting the adaptive response, I ask my clients to re-rate the degree of emotional intensity. I define "no more than mild emotional distress" as ratings anywhere between a "0" and a "3" on a 10-point scale. When clients

Table 5.2 Examples of Typical Automatic Thoughts and Corresponding Adaptive Responses

AUTOMATIC THOUGHT	*ADAPTIVE RESPONSE*
My friends don't want me around.	None of my friends have ever given me the feedback that they don't want me around. Just the other day, Taylor invited me to lunch. I have offered a great deal to my friends over the years, such as loyalty and a trustworthy ear to listen to their problems.
I'm going to get fired.	It is true that my company is facing layoffs. However, I received stellar feedback in my most recent reviews, and I have never received a reprimand. I play an important role in the company, and in the event that I am laid off, there are many other companies where I can look for employment.
I'm going to get sick with a horrible disease.	I recently had a physical, and I received a clean bill of health. In general, I practice healthy habits, like following a clean eating diet and exercising three times a week. It is true that no one can say with certainty that they will not get a horrible disease. However, the likelihood of that is low, and if it happens, there are many highly-regarded doctors and hospitals in the area.
I'm a bad parent.	I can list many, many things that I do for my children, such as cooking for them, helping them with their homework, and taking them to their activities. They are always happy to see me when I pick them up from school, and I am the first one they seek out when they are hurt. No parent is perfect, but even when I am not perfect, there is no evidence that I am doing any damage to them.
My girlfriend is going to leave me.	If the relationship feels more distant right now, it is because she told me that she is coming down with something and feels sick and worn down. I cannot forget all the expressions of love that she has shown me recently, such as surprising me with a gift for no reason and really being there for me when I was going through stress.

arrive upon a rating of a "3" or lower, I ask them whether they would behave any differently, such as making sounder choices, taking care of themselves better, or approaching (rather than avoiding) an aversive situation. Such questioning allows clients to see that cognitive restructuring can help them not only to manage their emotion, but to respond more adaptively in the situation. When clients rate the emotional intensity associated with the adaptive response as a "4" or higher, I subsequently ask them to consider what piece of the original automatic thought that the adaptive response does not address, and I encourage them to engage in additional Socratic questioning and expand the adaptive response. Take, for instance, the first example listed in Table 5.2. The original automatic thought was "My friends don't want me around," and the adaptive response was "None of my friends have ever given me the feedback that they don't want me around. Just the other day, Taylor invited me to lunch. I have offered a great deal to my friends over the years, such as loyalty and a trustworthy ear to listen to their problems." Suppose the client who supplied this adaptive response continued to rate her level of emotional distress as a "4" or higher after developing it. She then might add additional pieces of information, such as more specific incidents, in which friends asked her to go on outings, specific feedback friends have given her suggesting that they value the friendship, and so on, until her self-reported level of emotional distress decreases.

Modalities for Cognitive Restructuring

Cognitive restructuring often occurs naturally in conversation between the therapist and client during the session. When this is the case, I ask strategic questions to facilitate the consolidation of learning, such as "What did we just do here?" and "How will you take the principles of what we just did and apply them to your life when you leave here?"

Because cognitive restructuring is a relatively sophisticated skill to acquire, most clients need some sort of a prescribed format for organizing their work and continuing it outside of session. A traditional tool for achieving this aim, referenced in some of the previous chapters of this volume, is the *thought record*. A *thought record* is a sheet of paper that contains a grid with columns, in which clients record information about upsetting situations, key thoughts, emotional responses (and their intensity), and in many instances, the adaptive response, and a re-rating of the emotional intensity associated with the new adaptive response. Worksheet 5.1 provides an example of a common *thought record*. Clients are asked to keep the *thought record* with them in a convenient place, and when they experience an upsetting situation, or notice a negative shift in their mood (even in the absence of a specific situation), they work through the columns to identify the key thought associated with emotional distress, the intensity of that emotional distress, a compelling adaptive response, and a re-rating of their emotional intensity associated with the newly-crafted adaptive response. The accumulated work can be reviewed at the time of the subsequent session, and in fact, the list of upsetting situations identified on the *thought record* can also serve as an agenda for the session, so that the therapist and client simultaneously review the homework and address the items of interest to the client as the session progresses.

Worksheet 5.1

Sample Thought Record

Situation	**Key Thought**	**Emotion (0 = none; 10 = most I can imagine experiencing)**	**Adaptive Response**	**Re-Rate Emotion (0 = none; 10 = most I can imagine experiencing)**

Although the *thought record* is, perhaps, the most standard tool that facilitates cognitive restructuring, it is not the only one. Some clients report that they find the *thought record* format to be helpful, but others report that they do not like the columns and could use more space to work out their adaptive response. One alternative is the *Automatic Thought Worksheet* (see Worksheet 5.2), a document in which clients can record automatic thoughts associated with upsetting situations, answer key questions to evaluate the accuracy and usefulness of their thoughts, and pull together their evaluation into a compelling adaptive response. Currently, I have a slightly higher percentage of clients who prefer the Automatic Thought Worksheet, relative to the traditional *thought record*.

Worksheet 5.2

Automatic Thought Worksheet

AUTOMATIC THOUGHT WORKSHEET

SITUATION: Describe the upsetting situation that you experienced.

____

____

____

THOUGHT: Indicate the key thought, interpretation, or meaning that is most associated with your emotional distress.

____

____

EMOTION: What feeling(s) did you experience? ____________________

Rate the intensity of the feeling on a scale from none to the most extreme you have ever experienced:

0	1	2	3	4	5	6	7	8	9	10
None										Most Extreme

EVIDENCE:

List the factual evidence that supports your thinking.

____________________ ____________________

____________________ ____________________

____________________ ____________________

List the factual evidence that is inconsistent with your thinking.

____________________ ____________________

____________________ ____________________

____________________ ____________________

OTHER EXPLANATIONS: What are some other, more benign explanations for this situation?

____________________ ____________________

____________________ ____________________

OUTCOME EXPECTANCY:

What is the worst thing that could happen in this situation?

____

____

What is the best thing that could happen in this situation?

What is the most realistic thing that could happen in this situation?

If the worst were to happen, how bad would it be, and how would you cope?

USEFULNESS OF THINKING:

What are the advantages of your thinking?

What are the disadvantages of your thinking?

ADDITIONAL EVALUATION: Write down and answer another question that will help you to evaluate the accuracy and/or usefulness of your thinking?

Question:

Answer:

ADAPTIVE RESPONSE: Consider the answers to all of the questions posed on this worksheet, and develop a compelling, believable, and balanced alternative way of viewing the situation. It is okay to repeat some of the information that you included in your previous responses.

RE-RATING OF EMOTION: Re-rate the intensity of the feeling that you had identified above on a scale from none to the most extreme you have ever experienced. If the rating is a "4" or higher, go back and add to your adaptive response to see if you can reduce your emotional distress even further.

0	1	2	3	4	5	6	7	8	9	10
None										Most Extreme

BEHAVIORAL CHANGES: What will you now do differently as a result of constructing the adaptive response?

Moreover, many clients prefer to avoid writing on sheets of paper altogether to be cumbersome and inconsistent with the way they keep reports in the age of technology. Several mobile phone applications have been designed for the purpose of facilitating many CBT interventions, including cognitive restructuring, such as MoodKit for iPhone, iPromptU for iPhone and Android, and Pacifica for iOS, Android, and Internet. At times, clients like to develop their own format for recording their cognitive restructuring work, such as by dictating it into voice memo files, creating a Microsoft Excel spreadsheet, or keeping a fancy journal that is devoted to their CBT work.

A unique vehicle for cognitive restructuring is the *behavioral experiment*, which is an especially useful tool for clients who report that they believe their adaptive responses intellectually but not emotionally. Behavioral experiments provide a context for clients to test their negative thoughts (especially negative predictions about things that will happen in the future) prospectively and experimentally in their own lives, rather than through a solely verbal or intellectual cognitive restructuring exercise. Table 5.3 displays typical steps for conducting behavioral experiments, along with a specific example with a client.

Table 5.3 Typical Sequence of a Behavioral Experiment

STEP	*EXAMPLE*
Client expresses a negative prediction describing something that she expects to happen in her life (i.e., an automatic thought).	"I will be rejected when I ask my acquaintance out for a lunch date."
Client works with the therapist to develop a way to test out the prediction.	Client acknowledges that he will encounter the acquaintance at class later in the week, and he agrees to ask the acquaintance out for a lunch date.
Client works with the therapist to hone his approach to the experiment to maximize the likelihood of success (and, therefore, the refutation of the automatic thought).	Client practices social skills to ask the acquaintance on the lunch date in an effective manner (e.g., making appropriate eye contact).
Client works with the therapist to develop a coping plan if the experiment is not successful.	Client decides to (a) ask her best friend out to lunch on the same day , and (b) construct an adaptive response emphasizing her ability to cope with adversity, in the event that the acquaintance declines.
Client implements the "experiment" for homework, taking care to adopt a "win-win" mentality (i.e., "Either I show myself that the worst-case scenario will likely not happen, or if it does happen, I show myself that I can cope with it.")	Client asks the acquaintance out on the lunch date.
At the time of the subsequent session, the results of the experiment are discussed, and the client develops an adaptive response on the basis of the experience.	The client indicates whether the acquaintance agreed to the lunch date, what happened on the lunch date (if it occurred), and a new, adaptive response based on the experience (e.g., "If I put my best foot forward, it is likely that most people will not decline a lunch date, because I am a likeable person.")
Therapist encourages client to generalize his learning to similar automatic thoughts that might be experienced in the future.	"If I'm hesitant to extend a social invitation in the future, I must remember my success with this experiment, as well as the fact that people say I'm a likeable person."

Notice in Table 5.3 that I indicate that the behavioral experiment should be set up as a "win-win" standpoint. *Either* clients show themselves that their negative predictions are unlikely to be realized, or if a "worst-case scenario" occurs, then clients show themselves that they can tolerate it and cope effectively. This set-up ensures that clients will have a valuable learning experience no matter what happens. In addition, it is often helpful to coach clients on problem solving and social skills to maximize the likelihood that their experiment is successful, allowing them important behavioral practice to supplement the valuable learning experience that is being crafted for them. An example of the behavioral experiment is presented in the next section where I illustrate additional cognitive restructuring dialogue with our relative straightforward client, Ashley.

It truly does not matter which format clients choose to record their cognitive restructuring work—it is more important that they settle upon a modality that is comfortable for them and that maximizes the likelihood that they will engage in practice between sessions. From a collaborative stance, you can present various options with which you have acquired familiarity, experiment with them in session with your client, and allow the client to choose the modality that he or she likes best.

Experiential Exercise

Continuing in the spirit of not asking our clients to do anything that we, as therapists, would not do, I invite you to practice cognitive restructuring on your own. Not only will this exercise hone your skill in cognitive restructuring, which will allow you to communicate tips and insights to your clients, I am also hopeful that you will experience its benefit firsthand. For the next week, I encourage you to recognize at least one situation each day, in which you notice a negative shift in your mood state and take the time to complete a cognitive restructuring exercise to restructure the unhelpful thinking associated with it. You might consider trying out different modalities—the *thought record*, the Automatic Thought Worksheet, one or more of the recommended mobile phone applications, or your own format—so that you get a feel of how each of them uniquely facilitates the cognitive restructuring process. Then, in the box below, please reflect on your experience.

BOX 1 REFLECTIONS ON THE EXPERIENTIAL COGNITIVE RESTRUCTURING EXERCISE

What insights did you develop from this exercise?

Which modalities did you try? What did you like about each one? What drawbacks did you see about each one?

How will you continue to implement cognitive restructuring in your own life?

How easy or difficult was it for you to stick with the plan of completing at least one cognitive restructuring exercise each day?

What did you learn that has relevance to implementing cognitive restructuring with your clients?

Case Examples

In the following section, I illustrate the application of cognitive restructuring with our relatively straightforward case, Ashley, as well as with our relatively difficult case, Marilyn. Recall that both of these clients were engaged in cognitive restructuring in Chapter 4 of this volume, when they were reviewing their homework and developing new homework to extend their learning. After each dialogue, I invite you to reflect on your observations and consider the manner in which you would continue to implement cognitive restructuring or other interventions with them.

Straightforward Case

In Chapter 4 of this volume, Ashley had readily identified the automatic thoughts that were associated with her anxiety, and she responded well to the notion of examining the evidence that supported and was inconsistent with them. This dialogue took place in the subsequent session, when Ashley and I were reviewing her homework and expanding the repertoire of tools to evaluate, and respond to unhelpful thinking. We ultimately set up a behavioral experiment for her to implement between sessions.

Dr. Amy: [reviewing Ashley's written homework] Is it okay if we take a look at this situation here? [Ashley nods her head] It looks like you experienced the most emotional upset in this situation than you did all week. You had a disagreement with another mom in your mothers' group?

Ashley: Yeah, it was awful. I'm so mortified. My son Dylan was playing with her son, and they started to get cranky with each other and not sharing this toy truck they were playing with. She jumped in and told my son that he wasn't being very nice, and that he should share. Even though it really seemed like it was her son who was kind of being a bully. This isn't the first time this has happened either. I can't go back there!

Dr. Amy: [making a reflection] So you believe that you can't go back. What's the reasoning behind that?

Ashley: She's turning all the other mothers against me! They probably think *I'm* the one who is a problem. I'm sure if I go back there, they'll just snub me and act like I don't belong.

Dr. Amy: [recognizing that Ashley is making some substantial assumptions that very well might be inaccurate but that will have the potential to make her decide that she will leave the mothers' group] Those are very powerful thoughts, Ashley. Is it okay if we take a closer look at those?

Ashley: Yes, okay.

Dr. Amy: [reinforcing the cognitive restructuring skills that Ashley has already acquired in previous sessions] Ashley, you've done such a nice job of examining the evidence that is and is not consistent with the thoughts that you had identified. How do you apply that line of reasoning here, to the ideas that the mothers are against you, believe that you are the problem, and will likely snub you if you go back?

Ashley: [sniffing] I don't know. It's just that this other mother is so domineering. And persuasive. Like she always gets her way in the group.

Dr. Amy: Okay, so on the one hand, you have observed others following her lead. How do you know that this is going to happen in this situation?

Ashley: I don't; it's just how it usually goes.

Dr. Amy: Fair enough. You certainly have experience with the mothers' group. [expanding the scope of cognitive restructuring] I'm wondering if we can test out the idea that the other mothers will snub you and act like you don't belong?

Ashley: How would we do that?

Dr. Amy: I'm thinking of something that we call a behavioral experiment. This involves you going back to the group, putting your best foot forward, and seeing for yourself whether this actually happens—whether the other mothers give you the message that they don't want you there.

Ashley: [looking sheepish] Oh gosh, I don't know if I could do that. It sounds so scary!

Dr. Amy: It *is* true that there is always a risk with experiments such as these—that the other mothers might respond to you exactly as you are predicting. But I wonder what the "up side" of such an experiment might be?

Ashley: [looking thoughtful] Well, if I'm wrong, then I'll be able to see that, and I won't be so anxious about going to other meetings in the future.

Dr. Amy: Exactly! On the one hand, there is a risk that the other mothers will snub you, which wouldn't feel good at all. But on the other hand, you might see, first-hand, that your fears might not be confirmed, and that might help you to feel better about the group.

Ashley: [taking a deep breath] I see what you mean. [expressing hesitation] But, gee, I don't know. I'm not sure I can handle all the stress.

Dr. Amy: [providing empathy] I appreciate how daunting this might feel to you. I think it could be helpful to work for the remainder of the session to create a "win-win" situation for you. I help you to figure out how to put your "best foot forward," you know, by deciding which mothers might be most inviting to sit by next time, who you can chat with, and things like that. I can also help you prepare for the worst-case scenario, so that you have a plan for coping, if the other mothers act coolly toward you.

Ashley: And then I guess preparing for the experiment and actually doing it would be the homework?

Dr. Amy: [smiling] You got it!

Ashley and I spent the remainder of the session planning the experiment. We identified the two mothers with which she was the friendliest in the group—and these also happened to be mothers who had made comments suggesting that they recognize that the mother with whom Ashley had a problem is, indeed, a bit domineering. We considered neutral and child-centered conversation topics that she could initiate with these women, and we role-played, so that Ashley could practice effective social skills for maintaining these conversations. We then turned our attention to the worst-case scenario of the other mothers treating her in a manner suggesting that she is no longer welcome in the group. We developed operational definitions of what those indications might be (e.g., the other mothers giving her short answers and not extending the conversation if she asked them a question), and we developed a plan for tolerating emotional upset should this be the case (e.g., an adaptive response reminding herself that she made a tremendous therapeutic gain by facing the daunting situation). At the time of the next session, Ashley had good news to report.

Ashley: [enters room smiling] Hi Dr. Amy!

Dr. Amy: Well, hello, Ashley. It's great to see you again. And to see that smile on your face as well.

Ashley: [beaming] I have really good news to report!

Dr. Amy: That's terrific. I've been looking forward to hearing the results of your experiment. [I conducted a brief mood check and worked with Ashley to set a session agenda. Debriefing from the behavioral experiment was the first order of business.]

Dr. Amy: Start form the beginning. Tell me what you practiced leading up to the experiment, what happened, and what you learned.

Ashley: Well, you know how nervous I was to go to the next meeting. So, each day before the meeting, I reviewed the notes I took of ways to start conversations with some of the nicer mothers. On the day of the meeting, I kept telling myself that the tiff with the other mom didn't have to be a regular thing, that it could have been an isolated incident, and that I could avoid another incident if I stayed away from her. I won't lie to you—I almost didn't go, because I was so nervous. But I did, and guess what? That mother wasn't even there. She was away for a long weekend with her family! So, it gave me a really nice opportunity to get to know some of the other moms, without her watching everyone like a hawk and directing the conversation.

Dr. Amy: You're kidding! The mother you were worried about wasn't there, and you got to connect more closely with the other moms.

Ashley: Yes! And that's not all. A lot of the other moms commented how much they liked the meeting when she wasn't there. And two of them even mentioned that they noticed how she treated me, and that they didn't agree. I mean, we were all trying to be polite and not gossip about her behind her back, but it was clear that the other moms feel the same way that I do.

Dr. Amy: What an experience, Ashley! What conclusions do you draw from this?

Ashley: [pausing to think] Well . . . it showed me that I'm a person who immediately goes to the worst and assumes that *I* am the problem, and that *I* am the one people will turn against, when that hasn't ever happened. I'm not sure I'd truly believe that without having this experience.

Dr. Amy: Great, Ashley. And what does this experience do to the likelihood of attending future meetings?

Ashley: [speaking with confidence] Oh, I'll keep going. I feel like this took the whole group to a new level for me, that I really started to develop some friendships. [furrowing her brow] I'm still worried about another confrontation with that mother, though, because she really seems to pick on the quiet ones.

Clearly, the behavioral experiment was successful, in that it showed Ashley that she was still welcome in the group, that the other mothers did not think negatively of her, and, in fact, that the other mothers were closely aligned with her in her view of the mother with whom she had the issue. Notice how I took care to consolidate Ashley's learning by asking her to state the conclusion that she drew from the experiment and reflect on the likelihood that the results of the experiment would influence her participation in the mothers' group in the future. Interestingly, although this particular cognitive restructuring exercise was quite helpful in reducing one important manifestation of Ashley's anxiety, it appeared that her attention had turned to trepidation about encountering the difficult mother at a subsequent meeting. This scenario demonstrates the ebb and flow of emotional distress in clients' lives and the continual manner in which cognitive behavioral strategies can be applied to meet life's demands. In the box below, please reflect on the dialogue that you read above, including the way in which you would have applied cognitive restructuring with Ashley thus far, how you might apply it to the new concern that she introduced, and what else you might do with her to fully address her anxiety.

BOX 2 REFLECTIONS ON COGNITIVE RESTRUCTURING WORK WITH ASHLEY

What did you find effective about this dialogue?

What did you find surprising about this dialogue? What might you do differently?

How would you apply cognitive restructuring to address Ashley's concern that there will be a later confrontation with the woman in her mothers' group? What types of Socratic questions might you pose?

Did you feel a pull to implement any other interventions either during the dialogue, or at the end, when Ashley introduced the new concern? If so, what intervention did you see as indicated, and how would you implement it?

Difficult Case

Recall that, at the end of Chapter 4 of this volume, Marilyn had agreed to identify key thoughts associated with specific situations in a way that suited her personal preferences—once per day rather than continuously during the day, and using the notes function on her phone, rather than on the *thought record* that I had given her. When Marilyn returned for her next session, I attempted to move toward the Socratic questioning of her key thoughts, in order to begin to coach her in constructing adaptive responses. However, we faced some "bumps" along the way, as captured in the following dialogue.

Dr. Amy: I'm so glad that this approach to recording your homework worked better than using the *thought record*, Marilyn.

Marilyn: Yes, that was a good suggestion. I thought it would be too much, but this made it more manageable.

Dr. Amy: [catching Marilyn's positive feedback and emphasizing our therapeutic relationship] Marilyn, I honestly think that we are starting to make a great team together. You've had a lot of experience in therapy, and you have a strong sense of what works and doesn't work for you. I think we should continue to capitalize on that, so that we can keep refining our work and ensuring that these CBT strategies make a difference in your life.

Marilyn: [still looking skeptical, as she had in previous sessions, but to a lesser degree] Well, I did it. That's more than I can say for most of the other times I've been in therapy.

Dr. Amy: Is it okay if we take a look at what you recorded in your phone and move toward finding an effective way to work with these thoughts?

Marilyn: Um, sure okay. What should I do, just read them to you?

Here, I will point out that review of homework can take place in a number of ways, and as with all aspects of CBT, there is no one "right" way to review cognitive restructuring homework. Rather, cognitive behavioral therapists collaborate with their clients to decide on the most comfortable and effective way to review homework. Some clients prefer to read verbally through the material that they recorded; other clients prefer that the therapist either read it silently or out loud; still other clients will email it in advance to their therapist, so that their therapist can print it out and have it readily available in session. In this case, I asked Marilyn what she thought would be best, and she astutely suggested that we focus on the situation that was most upsetting to her (which is a suggestion that I often make to clients if they ask for my input).

Marilyn: They asked me to make a small presentation to the board of directors at work. But every time I'm asked to do something like this, they throw me under the bus.

Dr. Amy: [providing reflection and clarification, while at the same time reinforcing the cognitive restructuring model] So, the situation is that you've been asked to make a presentation to the board of directors, and your thought is "They will throw me under the bus?"

Marilyn: Yes. And I also wrote down as a thought, "This will be a disaster."

Dr. Amy: [reinforcing Marilyn's newfound ability to recognize key thoughts associated with upsetting situations] And when you have those ideas that you'll be thrown under the bus and that it will be a disaster, how do you feel emotionally?

Marilyn: [beginning to become irritated] What do you think? It's awful! I've been having trouble sleeping. I can't eat. I'm totally on edge!

Dr. Amy: [communicating empathy and continuing to reinforce the cognitive behavioral model] I would expect that, Marilyn, on the basis of just how powerful those two ideas are. [moving toward the restructuring of those thoughts] I wonder if we can do some work to examine those ideas to see if we can come up with a softer way of viewing the situation?

Marilyn: [becoming defensive] Softer? Are you saying I shouldn't think like this? Because it's happened to me every time. Every. Single. Time.

Dr. Amy: [realizing that it would likely be more effective to ask Marilyn Socratic questions that would help her buy further into the process, rather than restructuring the thought, itself, and also providing empathy and validation] I believe you, that you've had so many negative experiences. Let me ask you something from another perspective. When you go into the meeting with predictions that you will be thrown under the bus and that it will be a disaster, what effect does that have on you?

Marilyn: Well, I'm not at all looking forward to the meeting.

Dr. Amy: I wouldn't look forward to the meeting, either, if I expected to be thrown under the bus, and if I expected that it would be a disaster. I'm wondering, though, if there might be some subtle effects of that mindset that might make it even worse for you?

Marilyn: [continuing to be defensive] Like I bring all this on myself?

Dr. Amy: No, not that you bring it all on yourself. You've given me plenty of evidence suggesting that there are some strange dynamics in your workplace that seem to defy the conventional expectation for the way in which workplace relationships typically proceed. Would you like some examples of what I was wondering about?

Marilyn: [hesitating, but ultimately agreeing] I mean, I guess.

Dr. Amy: For example, I can imagine someone who has those thoughts really having a tough time sleeping before the meeting, so that the next day they go into work feeling groggy, sluggish, and generally not on top of their game.

Marilyn: Oh, well, sure, that has happened in the past, so I'm sure it will happen this time around, too.

Dr. Amy: And when you are focused on the ideas of being thrown under the bus and the presentation being a disaster—does that help you prepare more efficiently, or does it interfere with preparation?

Marilyn: [responding with irritation] I can still do my job, in case you're implying that I can't!

Dr. Amy: [using a soft tone of voice] No, that's not at all what I'm implying. You're quite articulate about your work, so I'd guess that you can do your job very well. I'm more wondering if preparation seems excruciating, and if the misery of it gets drawn out because these thoughts are so consuming and upsetting.

Marilyn: [looking mildly surprised] Well, yes, I guess that does happen. The meeting isn't for another two weeks, and I'm already dreading it. I can tell it's affecting my energy and appetite.

Dr. Amy: Ah, so it's possible, then, that you're experiencing some negative personal consequences by focusing on those thoughts?

Marilyn: Okay, I will grant you that. But this is really true! This has happened every time!

Dr. Amy: I propose a twofold plan. First, let's see if between the two of us, we can come up with a reframe to those thoughts that is not at all unrealistically positive, or denies your previous experience. And second, perhaps we can develop a plan to cope if it happens once again that you are thrown under the bus, and that it's a disaster.

Marilyn: Okay, I guess so. But what would be a reframe to those thoughts if they are true?

Dr. Amy: Here's a possibility off the top of my head, although I'm going to want you to, ultimately, use your own voice to craft an alternative that feels right to you. Something like: "In the past, these situations have been uncomfortable and have not turned out the way I've wanted them to. I can take pride in knowing that I've done my very best, and if I receive negative feedback, it could very well be due to the strange work culture rather than anything that I truly did wrong." What do you think of that?

Marilyn: I mean, there's truth to it. But it doesn't address how awful it is when I get yelled at for giving them what they see as bad news, when I'm just the messenger.

Dr. Amy: Fair enough. We can also discuss how to cope and how to respond effectively if that happens. I'm curious though, if you were to come up with your own statement in the spirit of what I just shared with you, do you think it would help you to experience less dread in the days leading up to the meeting and perhaps even prepare a bit more efficiently?

Marilyn: Maybe.

Dr. Amy: Would you be willing to give it a shot?

Marilyn: [nodding head] Okay.

In this dialogue, Marilyn had a reaction when I suggested developing adaptive responses to the ideas that she was going to be thrown under the bus and that the meeting would be a disaster, claiming that these were facts based on previous experience. Cognitive behavioral therapists certainly do not want to invalidate clients' previous experiences; however, ultimately, I was hoping that Marilyn would evaluate the upcoming meeting on its own merit, rather than solely in the basis of her previous experience. In addition, I was also hoping that we could soften judgmental language, such as"being thrown under the bus" and "disaster," because such "loaded" language usually "fuels the fire" of negative emotional reactions unnecessarily. When Marilyn had this initial negative reaction, I realized that it would be prudent to back up and use Socratic questioning to illustrate the effects of her thinking on aspects of her experience associated with the board meeting, such as her sleep the night before and her cognitive resources that she could devote to preparation. Because she continued to express uncertainty as to how to restructure her thoughts in a way that would feel okay to her, I gave her an example. Moreover, I attempted to add additional rationale to the learning process by asking her if there was a possibility that such an adaptive response could help with the dread she experiences the day before these meetings and her ability to prepare for it.

In the following box, take some time to reflect on this demonstration of cognitive restructuring with Marilyn. In addition to evaluating your reaction to the written dialogue above, consider the way in which you would complete the cognitive restructuring process with the thoughts that she will be thrown under the bus and that the meeting will be a disaster. In addition, think about additional interventions from which Marilyn might benefit as she prepares for the board meeting.

BOX 3 REFLECTIONS ON COGNITIVE RESTRUCTURING WORK WITH MARILYN

What did you find effective about this dialogue?

What did you find surprising about this dialogue? What might you do differently?

How would you assist Marilyn in crafting an adaptive response using her own words? What Socratic questions might you pose?

Did you feel a pull to implement any other interventions either during the dialogue or toward the end, when coping with and responding to a negative outcome were introduced? If so, what intervention did you see as indicated, and how would you implement it?

Tips for Maximizing Effectiveness

Cognitive restructuring is viewed by many cognitive behavioral therapists as a central intervention in CBT. To this point, I have described three basic steps of cognitive restructuring and modalities for facilitating it, provided an opportunity to practice with it, and illustrated its application with our easy and difficult case. In this section, I comment on simple practices I have learned across the course of my career to help cognitive restructuring to run as smoothly as possible.

In some instances, when clients seem "lukewarm" about cognitive restructuring, it seems to be associated with the fact that its rationale is presented in a way that emphasizes theory but foregoes discussion about application. I have supervised many therapists-in-training who diligently draw out models, such as that depicted in Figure 2.1 of this volume, and provide an eloquent description of the theory that captures the ways in which a certain way of thinking is evoked in various situations, and the ways in which that thinking is associated with emotional and behavioral reactions. There is nothing inherently ineffective about this; in fact, in the spirit of encouraging our clients to become their own cognitive behavioral therapists, it is ideal when they truly grasp the underlying principles. However, my experience is that CBT is still new enough to clients that they are getting accustomed to many of CBT's features—the structure, the homework, and so on—that it can be difficult for them to grasp the significance of an abstract model because they are processing so much information simultaneously. Thus, I strongly encourage you to take the time to illustrate applications of the theoretical model in a compelling manner, so that clients can see, vividly, the way in which their thinking can be exacerbating their emotional disturbance and how adjusting their thinking can bring relief and a clearer mind to enact effective problem solving. You can do this with a hypothetical example, an example of your work with a previous client (with identifying information and details changed, of course), or from your own life. I also encourage you to ask clients to think about a time in their recent past when they were thinking in one way, only to learn that their thinking was somehow inaccurate or unhelpful that they could have saved themselves emotional distress had they been thinking in a more balanced manner.

In the previous section on Modalities for Cognitive Restructuring, I emphasized the importance of allowing clients to decide upon the modality of cognitive restructuring that best suits their lifestyle and preferences, and I supplied many alternatives from which you and your clients can choose. Please be mindful of the fact that those are not the only options—cognitive restructuring can be done in an endless number of creative ways depending on the circumstances. It is much more important that the intervention is tailored to the needs, preferences, and proclivities of the client than it is to be using a "standard" CBT intervention. I recall one instance in which I was working with a mechanic of heavy machinery, and many of the upsetting situations he experienced concerned the way in which his supervisor treated him. He was worried that his supervisor would further berate him if he saw him completing his cognitive restructuring homework in the break room. To circumvent this concern my client bought a 3½ × 5 inch flippad of paper, stored it in the pocket of his carpenter pants, and completed cognitive restructuring exercises while laying on his back when he was working underneath the machinery!

The *thought record* and the Automatic Thought Worksheet, depicted in Worksheets 5.1 and 5.2, need not be presented in these formats. You can modify them, or create new ones, with your clients to capture any relevant cognitive restructuring dimensions from which your client would benefit. For example, in Chapter 4 of this volume, when Ashley indicated that she found it helpful to examine the evidence for and against her thoughts, I developed a *thought record* with six columns—(a) situation, (b) key thought, (c) emotion and its intensity, (d) evidence supporting the thought, (e) evidence inconsistent with the thought, and (f) a conclusion drawn from the examination of the evidence. Recently, I had a client express overwhelm with the cognitive restructuring process and request that we pare it down. She decided that the most useful Socratic question was, "Can there be any other explanations?" She wrote that question on a sheet of paper, and as upsetting situations happened between sessions, she made note of them, identified the key thought associated with them, and wrote down possible other explanations.

The timing of when clients complete cognitive restructuring exercises can also make a difference. Every once in awhile, I see my clients quickly completing their cognitive restructuring homework in the waiting room before appointments. Although it is certainly better that they complete their homework at that time, rather than not completing it at all (!), saving it up and completing it at the end of the week partially defeats the purpose of the exercise. The idea is to attain practice in catching our thoughts in the moment when they occur, so that we can apply our cognitive restructuring skills and craft an adaptive response before our emotional reactions become overwhelming. Although it is often not possible for clients who are acquiring skill in cognitive restructuring to complete a homework exercise immediately at the time they have found themselves in an upsetting situation, they are encouraged to do so as soon as possible when they are able. Not only is it expected that doing so will help them to get a timely benefit from a balanced way of thinking about the situation, the thoughts and emotions that they record will be more accurate than they would be if the exercise were completed several days later, after the upsetting situation very well might have come to some sort of resolution. As they get practice, the expectation is that clients will be able to apply cognitive restructuring in the moment when they find themselves in an upsetting situation, without necessarily having to work through the exercise in written format.

Another tendency I have noticed in my clients over the years is for them to observe that there is a general pattern to the upsetting situations in which they find themselves, and, consequently, to complete one or two "representative" cognitive restructuring exercises for homework. However, approaching cognitive restructuring homework in this manner does not allow clients to achieve the aim that I described in the previous paragraph—to practice the application of cognitive restructuring in a particular moment or close to the moment in which an upsetting situation occurs. Moreover, something else uncanny happens when clients take this approach. They tend to describe the situation in very general terms (e.g., "when my husband doesn't help out more"). In turn, they tend to report their thoughts in very general terms (e.g., "He's lazy"). However, it is often the case that this general thought has never been activated in any specific situation, and in reality, that there is a range of cognitive and emotional responses that would have been detected had the client recorded each specific instance. For example, at times a client might have a depressive response (e.g., "I'm stuck in this situation with no way out"). At other times she might have an anxious reaction (e.g., "I won't be able to get everything done before company arrives, and the house will look like a mess"). At still other times, she might have an angry response (e.g., "He is taking advantage of me."). All of those nuances are lost when clients report in generalities, and they lose a valuable opportunity to develop adaptive responses that will be helpful when they have similar emotional reactions in the future.

Although most clients report a reduction in emotional distress after applying cognitive restructuring skills, in many instances, the intensity of their emotional distress does not decrease to a level of "3" or lower—defined as no-to-mild emotional distress. When this happens with my clients, I pose the question, "Which piece of your thought does this adaptive response not address?" In almost every instance, there is some sort of unacknowledged association or implication, and once these pieces are accounted for in the adaptive response, the client usually reports an even further decreased intensity of emotional response. In addition, be alert for secondary cognitive and emotional reactions to the cognitive restructuring exercise itself. I once had a severely depressed female client who did a beautiful job developing a compelling adaptive response to the automatic thought: "My husband will get sick of my depression and leave me." He was an extremely supportive spouse, and there was no evidence that he was unhappy with the relationship; if anything, he repeatedly communicated the message that he was with her through "thick and thin." At the end of the exercise, when I asked her to re-rate her level of emotional distress, she had only dropped one point—from a "10" to a "9." When I asked her to help me understand why her rating of emotional distress did not decrease further, she said with such despondency in her voice: "Because there's something wrong with me. I'm the only one in the world who needs these remedial CBT skills." Clearly, more cognitive restructuring targeting those self-deprecating thoughts was in order.

Finally, be aware of situations when clients are thinking about their life circumstances in a fairly accurate manner, and they are experiencing emotional distress at a level that almost anyone would experience in their situation. I recall an instance in which I was supervising a therapist whose client was very angry when he perceived that a person to whom he lent a sizable sum of money was avoiding him. When the therapist questioned the client about the evidence, the client provided an abundance of observations to support this notion, such as the fact that the person was not responding to text messages and voicemail messages, the person did not answer the door despite the car being in the driveway, and, on one occasion, the person turned around and walked in another direction when he saw the client approaching him. The therapist, new to CBT, continued to venture down the path of changing the thought, so that the client would experience a reduction in anger, almost as if to suggest that the idea that this person was avoiding him was inaccurate. However, the client was not responsive to the intervention and began to express frustration to the therapist, perceiving that she was trying to convince him not to be angry when it truly appeared that the person to whom he lent money was avoiding paying him back.

The important message from this anecdote is that not all of our clients' thoughts are distorted. Not only do many of their thoughts have a grain of truth in them, in some instances, such as this one, the preponderance of evidence suggests that they are accurate. Thus, an important rule of thumb about cognitive restructuring is "don't beat a dead horse." If the client is not responsive, and you continue to push the agenda of cognitive restructuring, you run the risk of being in a position in which you are trying to convince your client of something that does not feel right to him or her, or even finding yourself in a position in which it feels as if you are arguing with the client. In both instances, the therapeutic relationship could be compromised. When it becomes evident that there is much factual information in support of the way in which the client is viewing the situation, often turn to an acceptance technique called cognitive defusion. I write more about cognitive defusion in Chapter 7 of this volume.

Application to a Client

Take the opportunity now to practice cognitive restructuring with one of your own clients. Think of a client on your caseload who struggles with negative or unhelpful thinking even when he or she sees that there is evidence to the contrary. Over the course of as many sessions that are needed, systematically implement cognitive restructuring according to the sequence described earlier in the chapter. If your client's unique circumstances lend themselves well to an innovative approach to cognitive restructuring, such as a behavioral experiment or something else that you devise from your own creativity, please feel free to implement it. Use the following steps as a guide.

1. Educate your client about the association between thinking and mood, and ask him or her to reflect upon the way in which it applies to his or her life.
2. Teach your client to identify automatic thoughts that emerge in situations in which he or she experiences a negative shift in mood. Encourage your client to record situation-specific automatic thoughts for homework between sessions.
3. After your client has become adept at recognizing key automatic thoughts (which could take more than one session), help your client to acquire skills in evaluating his or her automatic thoughts. This could involve the application of Socratic questions, the implementation of a behavioral experiment, or some other creative method to do so. Encourage your client to practice evaluating the accuracy and usefulness of his or her thoughts for homework between sessions.
4. At the time of the subsequent session, help your client to acquire skills in developing compelling adaptive responses on the basis of the methods of evaluation. Be sure to have your client rate the intensity of his or her emotional distress associated with the original automatic thought and the new adaptive response.
5. Discuss with the client ways to continue implementing cognitive restructuring and incorporating its principles into the way he or she lives his or her life.
6. In the box below, reflect on your cognitive restructuring work with your client.

BOX 4 **REFLECTIONS ON COGNITIVE RESTRUCTURING WORK WITH YOUR CLIENT**

What do you conclude from this experiential exercise? How effective was your cognitive restructuring intervention?

Was cognitive restructuring easier or more difficult to implement than you had expected? Why?

What, specifically, will you do differently in the future to implement cognitive restructuring?

How has your view about cognitive restructuring changed after participating in this experiential exercise?

Caveat: Cognitive Restructuring of Thoughts Versus Underlying Beliefs

As mentioned in Chapter 2 of this volume, underlying beliefs consist of core beliefs about the self, others, world, and future, and intermediate beliefs representing strict rules and assumptions by which people live their lives. I refer to them as underlying beliefs because they are often present across situations, rather than being activated in individual situations, as are automatic thoughts. Moreover, they often explain the nature of the automatic thoughts that are experienced in times of emotional upset. Many clients learn to restructure automatic thoughts and are satisfied with the course of treatment, believing that they got what they wanted out of CBT and could leave with the confidence that they can handle stressors and challenges in their lives differently than they had when they first entered therapy. Other clients, however, recognize that there is a strong pattern that links the particular automatic thoughts elicited situationally and believe that even greater change can occur when they shift negative, unhelpful underlying beliefs into underlying beliefs that are more adaptive and helpful. When the therapist and client work toward belief modification, the tone of work done in session is usually very "deep" and fundamental (although this is not to say that work at the automatic thought level cannot be deep and fundamental!).

It is beyond the scope of this chapter to describe at length the process of belief modification. Good resources on belief modification include Judith S. Beck's seminal book, *Cognitive Behavior Therapy: Basics and Beyond (2nd Ed.)* (2011), Jeffrey Young's writing on schema therapy (e.g., Young, Klosko, & Weishaar, 2003), or a chapter I wrote on the topic that is freely available in open-access format on the Internet (Wenzel, 2012). However, in this section I include a few general pieces of information on belief modification that provides context to readers as they take their cognitive behavioral practice to this next level. First, it is important to recognize that belief modification does not happen in a single setting. Underlying beliefs are formed across years of personal experiences and interactions with others, so they are deeply entrenched, sometimes painful to face head-on, and are even regarded at times as part of a person's identity. In fact, some clients endure a bit of a grieving process when they begin to soften old, unhelpful core beliefs, feeling as if a replacement is unnatural and awkwardly trying to negotiate a new way of being.

A second recommendation for belief modification is that it is important to work carefully with the client to operationally define the specific components of an old, unhelpful underlying belief and identify a realistic and compelling new, more adaptive underlying belief toward which the client will work. Many clients report self-deprecating, extreme beliefs, such as "I'm a failure" or "I'm worthless," but when these beliefs are considered more specifically, it appears that they are basing their judgment on one or two major areas of their lives with which they are not happy, and they are dismissing areas that are going at least okay. I once worked with a male client with the core belief "I'm not good enough," who was especially unhappy with his career advancement and the wealth (or lack thereof) that he had accumulated in his life. When I asked him to consider what makes a person "good enough," he identified career and financial success, but also a nice home, a strong marriage, strong relationships with his children, strong friendships, health and wellness, and involvement in hobbies and interests. Then, I asked him to rate where he stood in each of these dimensions, and it turned out that he viewed himself as doing fairly well in all areas, except career and financial success. That, in and of itself, was a powerful intervention that prompted him to rethink the idea that he was altogether "not good enough."

We moved toward the development of a realistic and compelling new belief: "I'm just as good as the next guy." We chose this language carefully, as moving toward a core belief such as"I'm successful" might not have felt entirely "right" to him on the basis of a history of both positive and negative professional, academic, and personal experiences in his life. Thus, it is most helpful when clients word their new, healthier belief in ways that are balanced and realistic so that they remain compelling even of times of frustration or disappointment.

Third, all of the techniques that are used to modify situational automatic thoughts can also be applied to belief modification. For example, examining the evidence that supports and does not support underlying beliefs and examining the advantages and disadvantages of underlying beliefs are common interventions that are used in the spirit of belief modification. There are, of course, additional advanced techniques that are usually used in conjunction with these more standard cognitive restructuring techniques and that are described at length in the resources I referenced in this paragraph. However, my point is that even at this stage in your CBT training, you know a little bit about how to approach belief modification, and you can build on this knowledge with additional training.

Finally, the previous discussion notwithstanding, there are many advanced restructuring techniques that are uniquely suited to belief modification. For example, experiential techniques, such as role-plays, can bring clients back to the time in which negative beliefs were being formulated, activating the emotional experience and allowing them the opportunity to, in the moment, apply the cognitive restructuring skills they have learned as adults to shift the investment that they had in these beliefs (cf. J.S. Beck, 2011; Young et al., 2003). In one variation of this technique, the client plays two roles in a role-play, such that he plays himself as an adult participating in CBT who supplies advice and insight to his younger self who experienced aversive events that contributed to the development of unhelpful underlying beliefs. In another variant, the client can play the role of another person who delivered damaging messages to him or her during childhood, and the therapist can play the role of the client as a child, so that the client can see that other forces might have been at work when the person was delivering damaging messages (and that there was nothing inherently wrong with the client him- or herself).

Many cognitive behavioral therapists find that belief modification is some of the most rewarding work they do in CBT because it (a) incorporates creativity, ingenuity, and powerful emotional experiences in session, and (b) oftentimes results in a transformation of the client's self-concept or view of others or the world. Although I appreciate that belief modification likely seems to be a daunting prospect as you are just learning CBT's "basics," once you have gained some practice with the strategies described in this book, you will be ready for the advanced application of CBT strategy in the service of helping your client to shift his or her underlying beliefs.

CHAPTER 6 BEHAVIORAL INTERVENTIONS

Behavioral Interventions

CHAPTER 6

To this point, this volume has been heavily focused on the cognitive aspect of CBT, or how to adjust thinking about stressors, challenges, disappointments, and surprises that we experience in our lives. However, the "B" part of CBT is just as important as the cognitive piece, and in fact, some research shows that clients who receive only behavioral interventions only have outcomes that are just as good (if not even slightly better) as clients who receive a full package of CBT (that is, CBT that includes both cognitive and behavioral components). I will talk about some more about this research below in relevant sections. At this point, I will simply make the point that behavioral interventions are crucial to deliver to most of your clients. I often say that a client can do an eloquent job of cognitive restructuring, but if he is still avoiding threatening or difficult situations that he must face, or if she is still engaging in behaviors that are self-defeating and even harmful, then CBT is not fully successful.

In my experience, my therapists-in-training focus heavily and, at times, almost exclusively, on cognitive restructuring at the expense of behavioral interventions. Although I have not conducted research to elucidate the true reasons for this, I suspect it is because cognitive restructuring is seen as part and parcel with *cognitive therapy*, the precursor to CBT that is practiced in a contemporary manner today, so cognitive restructuring is almost the "default" CBT intervention. I hope that this chapter will demonstrate the vast potential that behavioral interventions hold and that the reader will begin to view them as "go to" interventions for indicated clinical conditions.

This chapter describes three standard behavioral interventions that are delivered in CBT: (a) behavioral activation for depression, (b) problem solving (which is often accompanied by some sort of skills training), and (c) exposure for anxiety-related disorders. However, before proceeding, I should point out that it is a bit of a false dichotomy to designate any intervention in CBT as one that is purely "cognitive" or purely "behavioral." As you will see as you work through this chapter, important cognitive change occurs when a client successfully enacts behavioral interventions. For example, when clients begin to re-engage in their lives after a period of isolation due to depression, they reclaim a sense of *self-efficacy*, or the belief that they can effect positive change in their lives. When clients begin to face situations or stimuli that they previously avoided due to fear and anxiety, they learn that they can tolerate risk and emotional distress, and they begin to see that the feared consequence that they dread is very unlikely to occur. The same thing happens with cognitive interventions going in the reverse direction. If clients approach stressors in their environment with a balanced, adaptive mindset, it is likely that they will make good choices, be able to enact solutions to their problems and engage in healthy self-care. Thus, the cognitive and behavioral nature of all the interventions described in this volume cannot be fully teased apart, even if an intervention is designated as one that is primary "cognitive" or "behavioral."

Behavioral Activation

Behavioral activation is an intervention that aims to help depressed clients become more activatly engaged in their environments, with the idea that they will obtain positive reinforcement from this active engagement, which will, in turn, exert an antidepressant effect (Dimidjian, Barrera Jr., Martell, Muñoz, & Lewinsohn, 2011; Martell, Dimidjian, & Herman-Dunn, 2010). Currently, behavioral activation is viewed as a stand-alone treatment for depression (Addis & Martell, 2004; Lejuez, Hopko, Acierno, Daughters, & Pagoto, 2011; Lejuez, Hopko, & Hopko, 2001; Martell, Addis, & Jacobson, 2001; Martell et al., 2010), as well as a mainstay intervention in the larger cognitive behavioral treatment package for depression (J. S. Beck, 2011; Wenzel, 2013; Wenzel, Brown, & Karlin, 2011).

Behavioral activation has a long and interesting history; behavioral approaches to the treatment of depression have their basis in behavioral theories of depression, such that the authors of which proposed that depression results from a lack of response-contingent positive reinforcement in one's environment (Ferster, 1973; Lewinsohn, 1974). Depression was characterized as a vicious cycle (see Figure 6.1), such that the more depression a person experienced, the most she would isolate and avoid engaging in activities that would give her a sense of pleasure of accomplishment. In other words, the depressed individual is characterized as living her life in a manner that is driven by negative reinforcement, or by experiencing the temporary rewards of avoidance, rather than by positive reinforcement. Although such "shutting down" might seem understandable in light of such an individual's depressed mood, the functional result is that she is depriving herself of the opportunity to obtain the benefits from joyful and meaningful

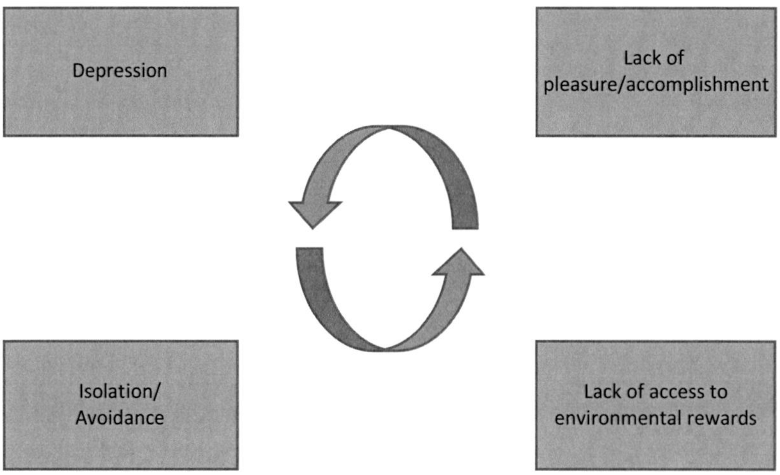

Figure 6.1 Vicious Cycle of Depression

activities, thereby worsening depression and entrenching her in this vicious cycle. Behavioral interventions for depression, then, were designed to help such a client break through this vicious cycle of depression by seeking out adaptive activities, minimizing engagement in activities that contribute to depression, and solve problems that interfere with both of these goals (Dimidjian et al., 2011).

None of this was actually called behavioral activation back in the 1970s. In fact, although the "father" of behavioral approaches to the treatment of depression, Peter Lewinsohn, and his colleagues developed a productive line of research through the 1980s; eventually, cognitive therapy (with a primary focus on cognitive restructuring) took "center stage," and stand-alone behavioral interventions for depression faded away to some degree. It was not until the 1990s, when Neil Jacobson of the University of Washington and his colleagues compared behavioral interventions on their own with a full package of CBT that the powerful nature of behavioral interventions was once again demonstrated. Unexpectedly, behavioral interventions alone were just as efficacious as a full package of CBT (including behavioral interventions, cognitive restructuring of automatic thoughts, and cognitive restructuring of beliefs) at the end of treatment (Jacobson et al., 1996), as well as at a two-year follow-up assessment (Gortner, Gollan, Dobson, & Jacobson, 1998). These studies were replicated, this time using manualized behavioral activation intervention, as compared to (a) a full package of CBT, (b) antidepressant medication, and (c) pill placebo. That is, behavioral activation was just as efficacious as CBT and antidepressant medications at the completion of treatment (Dimidjian et al., 2006), with gains largely maintained across a two-year follow-up period (Dobson et al., 2008).

Thus, behavioral activation is clearly a first-line intervention for depression. Think about the application of behavioral theory to your own life. Have you noticed an association between your mood and your activity level? Or between your mood and the kinds of activities in which you engage? In the box below, take some time to reflect on the application of behavioral theory to your own experience.

BOX 1 REFLECTIONS ON BEHAVIORAL THEORY

What have you noticed regarding the association between your mood and activity level?

What types of activities give you the greatest sense of accomplishment? The most pleasure? The most meaning? Do you find an association between engagement in these activities and your mood state?

(continued)

(continued)

Conversely, what kinds of activities do you find aversive? Do you find an association between engagement in these activities and your mood state?

Were the results from the studies comparing behavioral activation with a full package of CBT surprising to you? Why or why not?

Techniques

The two main techniques of behavioral activation are activity monitoring and activity scheduling. *Activity monitoring* is much as it sounds, such that between sessions, clients write down the activities in which they engage during waking hours. Although this task sounds daunting, it is important for clients to complete this exercise prospectively, as memory invariably becomes vague and fills in with inferences when people try to remember the specific way in which they spent their time several days prior. Worksheet 6.1 is an example of an *activity log*, which allows clients to record this information. Notice that there are two columns in addition to the columns depicting the time of day and the activity in which the client engaged. In these columns, clients provide a rating of the degree to which the activity provided them with a sense of accomplishment and the degree to which the activity provided them with a sense of pleasure. At the bottom of the form, clients indicate an overall depression rating for the day. It is expected that clients will see a pattern to their responses over time, such that the higher the ratings of accomplishment and pleasure associated with their activities, the lower will be their depression rating at the end of the day.

Worksheet 6.1

Activity Log

Activity Log: Date ______________________________

Hour	Activity	Accomplishment (0 = None; 10 = Most)	Pleasure (0 = None; 10 = Most)
5–6am			
6–7am			
7–8am			
8–9am			
9–10am			
10–11am			
11am–12pm			
12–1pm			
1–2pm			
2–3pm			
3–4pm			
4–5pm			
5–6pm			
6–7pm			
7–8pm			
8–9pm			
9–10pm			
10–11pm			
11pm–12am			

Overall Depression Rating (0–10): _____

Activity monitoring is meant to yield useful and practical information. It is hoped that clients see that they are getting less benefit from some activities that they might expect (e.g., taking a nap in the middle of the day) and that other activities are associated with substantial benefit. After completing a course of activity monitoring, clients work with their therapist on *activity scheduling* so that they schedule activities at key times during the subsequent week that are expected to yield an antidepressant benefit. Clients are not expected to *over*schedule activities associated with a sense of accomplishment or pleasure, but instead they are encouraged to choose a few activities that they can work in at key times that were shown in the activity monitoring exercise to be associated with particularly low levels of accomplishment and pleasure. It is hoped that clients begin to feel less depressed as the capitalize on activity scheduling, and as a result, that they generalize their learning and begin to adopt a more active lifestyle.

Experiential Exercise

Let's apply an aspect of behavioral activation in your own life. For the next three days, I encourage you to keep your own activity log by making three photocopies of Worksheet 6.1. Keep track of the activities in which you engage during waking hours, rate the amount of accomplishment and pleasure associated with them, and provide an overall depression rating at the end of the day. When I have encouraged workshop participants and supervisees to complete this exercise, I often receive the feedback that they are surprised how much work it involves. In the box below, please reflect on your own experience in keeping the activity log and the conclusions that you drew from it.

BOX 2 **REFLECTIONS ON THE ACTIVITY LOG EXERCISE**

What insights did you develop from this exercise?

Was it easy or difficult to complete this exercise? Why?

How will you continue to implement behavioral activation in your own life?

What did you learn that has relevance to implementing cognitive restructuring with your clients?

As you undoubtedly saw, this is an exercise that requires persistence and perseverance. It takes a lot of energy, planning, and follow through to remember to record the way in which one spends one's time every waking hour of the day. Imagine, then, if you are depressed and coping with anhedonia, fatigue, and foggy-headedness. Thus, it is important that you honor and respect the hard work that your clients put into the exercise. This means that it is important to spend adequate time in session evaluating the "data" supplied by the client, carefully examining the times in which the client experienced a sense of accomplishment and pleasure, as well as the times that he or she did not. Encourage the client to draw his or her own conclusion about activity level and the intensity of depressive symptoms. Help the client to think carefully and creatively about ways to implement the principles of behavioral activation in activity scheduling so that he or she can obtain the greatest benefit.

Case Example: Difficult Case

Behavioral activation was a logical intervention for Marilyn for two reasons: (a) she reported depression and isolation, two interrelated conditions for which behavioral activation is especially indicated; and (b) I had already illustrated the way in which I thought her work at the ice rink was consistent with the aims of behavioral activation. My hypothesis was that if Marilyn could observe, first hand, the benefits of behavioral activation, she would, in turn, feel more positively about treatment, and (per the research described in Chapter 3 of this volume), the therapeutic alliance would be strengthened.

The following is an update on the progression of Marilyn's course of treatment, so that you have a sense of where we were at when I introduced behavioral activation in earnest. After the dialogue presented in Chapter 5 of this volume, we spent another couple of sessions focusing on cognitive restructuring, crafting adaptive responses that were designed to curb the bitterness that she felt toward her co-workers, her mother, her ex-boyfriend, and a friend whom she believed had betrayed her. Marilyn had been emphatic that she was accurate in the way she was viewing the transgressions, and she continued to respond with irritation when she perceived any indication that I was questioning her view of these situations. However, she bought into the notion that her thinking could take on an especially harsh and bitter tone, which likely interfered with her ability to deal effectively with situations that involved these individuals. Although Marilyn continued to complain about cognitive restructuring and CBT in general, she had a couple of "victories" in which she admitted that by softening her thinking, she was able to handle a few difficult interpersonal situations more effectively than she had in the past. In all, I continued to view the therapeutic relationship as a bit tenuous, but I was encouraged by the fact that she remained in therapy for multiple sessions, as well as by the fact that she was able to see at least some benefit from cognitive restructuring.

At the time of her eighth CBT session, Marilyn presented in a particularly despondent mood. It was early March, a particularly dismal period of time in the Mid-Atlantic (where we live) when people begin to get "cabin fever" and wonder whether winter will ever end. A series of snow storms had forced Marilyn to cancel the few activities outside of work that she had planned, including meals with friends and even the skating classes that she was teaching. It was at this time that I asked permission to re-introduce the concept of behavioral activation, reasoning that (a) the rationale underlying the intervention would be particularly salient in light of the thwarted activities and her increased depression; (b) Marilyn would benefit from additional planning, so that she would have a "back-up plan" for the engagement in meaningful activities in light of obstacles like inclement weather; and (c) Marilyn would receive a different kind of benefit from behavioral activation than she did from cognitive restructuring, thereby further increasing her motivation for, and commitment to, treatment.

Marilyn: God, this is just the worst. I *hate* this time of year!

Dr. Amy: Believe me, Marilyn, I understand. I have a bit of cabin fever, too.

Marilyn: Just when it seemed that things are getting a little bit better, then back to square one. Argh! My life is so infuriating.

Dr. Amy: I know, this weather is a real drag. Many of the people I see in my practice have been talking about its effects on their mood. [pausing] Can I share with you what this reminds me of, Marilyn?

Marilyn: [looking surprised] Okay.

Dr. Amy: Do you remember, early on when we first met, I was talking with you about activity and its effect on mood? And I was pleasantly surprised to learn about your talent for ice skating, because it fits so nicely in with an aspect of CBT that we know to exert a powerful antidepressant effect?

Marilyn: Oh yeah, that's right.

Dr. Amy: I wonder if the principles of that approach to depression—which we call behavioral activation—can apply here?

Marilyn: Well, I think you said my skating can help make me feel good about life, right? And I got mad at you for it?

Dr. Amy: [pleasantly surprised that our relationship has gotten to the point that we can comment on previous sources of tension] Ha, something like that, Marilyn! The idea is that the more we do things that make us feel good—things that give us pleasure or joy, a sense of accomplishment, or meaning—the less depressed we feel. It's not surprising to me that the past week hasn't been great for you, in light of the fact that you weren't able to do the things that tend to give you the most joy.

Marilyn: Well, what can I do about it? I just have to ride out the weather. I can't control it.

Dr. Amy: You're right, we can't control the weather. But what we *can* do is to start to expand your repertoire of activities that give you a sense of pleasure and accomplishment—activities that really feed your soul. You have a couple of really good ones—the skating, and the time you spend with friends. But I'm wondering if we might take a look at how you're spending your time when you're at home and see what we might add, because I get the sense that this is the time at which you are most vulnerable to depression.

Marilyn: I think you're right. No, I *know* you're right.

Dr. Amy: I have an idea. When I go down this road with my other clients, I ask them to write down how they are spending their time, so that we have a very accurate view of what is happening and how much benefit they are getting from their activities. Then, we can use the information you collect to work in more enriching activities at the most key times.

Marilyn: Oh, I don't know, remember how I don't like writing things down?

Dr. Amy: [smiling] I remember, Marilyn. Fortunately, we can adapt this exercise in the exact same way we adapted our thought work. You can record your work in your phone. Might you consider that?

Marilyn: [hesitating only a little] I think so.

Marilyn expressed some hesitation to write down how she was spending her time every hour of the day, including work, so I modified the exercise for her to write down the way in which she was spending her time in the mornings before work, in the evenings after work, and on the weekend that intervened between sessions. She agreed to record what she was doing and rate the degree of pleasure and accomplishment she obtained from each activity, along with an overall depression rating at the end of the day. When she returned, and we reviewed her homework, the results were striking.

Dr. Amy: You really put a lot of effort into this, Marilyn. What do you conclude from the "data"?
Marilyn: The weekends. They are the absolute worst.
Dr. Amy: Why do you think that is?
Marilyn: Because, unless there is a tournament or a special event, there is no skating on the weekends. And the days tend to drag on and on if I have nothing planned.
Dr. Amy: Shall we start there, then? With the weekends?
Marilyn: Yes, I think we better.
Dr. Amy: [reviewing the information that Marilyn recorded about her weekends] It looks to me like the mornings are okay for you, as you get a decent sense of accomplishment from getting errands done like food shopping and dry cleaning. But the afternoons seem really tough for you. And it looks like, by 3 or 4 in the afternoon, you settle in and watch a movie with a cocktail.
Marilyn: [becoming tearful] Isn't that pathetic? I grab a drink just to pass the time. Because I'm so lonely.
Dr. Amy: Let's put our heads together and figure out some alternatives, Marilyn.
Marilyn: [nodding her head]

At first, Marilyn had difficulty identifying activities other than those that were chores around the house that she had been putting off. Although it likely would be the case that Marilyn would obtain a sense of accomplishment from completing them, it was equally as likely that she finds them aversive enough that she would have trouble getting started on them, and then become more, rather than less, discouraged. Thus, I often encourage clients to start with activities that are mainly associated with a sense of pleasure to increase the likelihood of follow through, allowing them to observe the benefits of behavioral activation first-hand. When I explained this to Marilyn, she became mildly agitated, claiming that she did not know what she could do at home that would bring her a sense of pleasure, and that if she did know, she would already be doing it. I asked for permission to supply some ideas from previously successful behavioral activation interventions, which helped Marilyn to consider possibilities that she had not previously acknowledged. By the end of the session, she had generated a small pool of two sets of activities that she could pursue on weekend afternoons. One set of activities involved things she could do outside the home, including area museums, lunch with friends who she did not see often, pottery at a local pottery studio, yoga classes, and services and activities at a Unitarian church. The other set of activities involved things she could do at home, either because the weather was bad, or because she did not feel like going out. These activities included reading a fiction series that she had been interested in checking out for several years (but never did), learning how to crochet, cooking meals of different cuisines than she was accustomed to preparing, redecorating her guest bedroom, and making phone dates with friends who had moved out of the area. Marilyn was hesitant to decide upon a specific activity on a specific day, but she agreed to choose one activity from the list on the intervening Saturday and Sunday, and implement an additional two activities from the list during the week.

Think about the previous dialogue that I had with Marilyn, as well as the course of activity scheduling described previously. Take some time to reflect on my work with Marilyn and consider what you found to be effective and what you might do differently.

BOX 3 **REFLECTIONS ON BEHAVIORAL ACTIVATION WORK WITH MARILYN**

What did you find effective about the dialogue and the subsequent description of the course of activity scheduling?

What did you find surprising about my work with Marilyn? What might you do differently?

If Marilyn were to return to session having been successful with her homework, what might you do next with her?

If Marilyn were to return to session having been *un*successful with her homework, what might you do next with her?

Did you feel a pull to implement any other interventions at this point in the course of treatment? If so, what intervention did you see as indicated, and how would you implement it?

Tips for Maximizing Effectiveness

As evidenced by the research described previously in this chapter, behavioral activation has the potential to be a powerful intervention in the treatment of depression. This intervention is a terrific match for depressed clients who report isolation, low motivation, and lack of interest and enjoyment in their lives. This being said, completion of the activity log can be a daunting task for a depressed client. Some clients become overwhelmed with recording the way in which they are spending their time, every hour of the day, as well as supplying the accompanying ratings. If your client completes the activity log in that way, be sure to respect the hard work that the client has put into the task by spending sufficient time reviewing it and drawing conclusions from it at the time of the subsequent session. If a client balks at completing the activity log every hour, you can work collaboratively with the client to determine the most reasonable alternative, as I did with Marilyn. For example, you could have the client complete the activity log for only a few days, such as two weekdays and one weekend day. Or, as I did with Marilyn, you can have the client complete the activity log at the most problematic times of the day or week. Another option is to create a different kind of recording form, such as a list of activities associated with a sense of accomplishment and pleasure that requires clients simply to check off the activities in which they engage and supply an overall depression rating at the end of the day.

In the original description of activity scheduling, the client and therapist would, together in session, decide on some activities to work in during the week and add them in specific slots on the activity log. However, in my clinical experience, this practice has not always been as effective as it is intended to be. Outside forces can interfere with the completion of an activity during one particular hour, and this can be especially discouraging for depressed clients who are prone to all-or-nothing thinking (e.g., "I missed the first activity I was supposed to do, so why bother doing the rest of activities?") and self-deprecating statements (e.g., "I'm a failure—I can't even follow through with a simple activity"). I encourage you to consider scheduling activities during broader time frames (e.g., Tuesday afternoon, Friday evening), have back-up plans for alternative activities to fill the same time period if the original activity falls through, and have alternative days and time frames in which the same activity can be implemented at a later time. I also normalize this approach to "flexible scheduling" with my clients, reassuring them that we all encounter times when we must adjust our schedule due to unforeseen circumstances. Relatedly, some depressed clients worry that they will not "feel like" engaging in an activity when the time comes due to depressed mood, anhedonia, or fatigue. Although one goal of behavioral activation is to teach clients that they can engage in activities even when they do not "feel like" doing so (Farmer & Chapman, 2016), until clients learn this for themselves, be sure to have an array of "quiet" activities that clients can do at home on their own in the event that they abandon more active pursuits for this reason.

Other depressed clients have difficulty identifying activities that they might find pleasurable. I commonly hear clients say that they have been depressed for so long that they just do not know what they are interested in and what will make them feel good. I liken this to a person who has blinders on the sides of her eyes, limiting the degree to which she can see using her peripheral vision. She can look straight ahead and take care of what is in front of her, but the blinders keep her from opening up her mind and "dreaming" about doing things beyond the tasks that must be completely on a daily or regular basis. One way to stimulate creative thinking about pleasurable activities is to give clients a *Pleasant Events Schedule*, a tool first developed by Lewinsohn and his colleagues to assess the degree to which clients were obtaining an adequate amount of response-contingent positive reinforcement (MacPhillamy & Lewinsohn, 1971). Over time, this tool has been used less for the purpose of assessment and more as a way to provide clients with ideas for behavioral activation. You can find many versions of the Pleasant Events Schedule simply by using a search engine, such as Google. During session, clients can review the activities that are listed on the Pleasant Events Schedule and circle a certain number of activities that seem attractive to them and that they would be willing to incorporate into activity scheduling.

Application to a Client

Now it is time for you to practice behavioral activation with one of your own clients. Think of a client on your caseload who struggles with depression and who seems especially isolated and inactive. Over the course of a couple of sessions, systematically implement behavioral activation via activity monitoring and scheduling. Use the following steps as a guide.

1. Educate your client about the behavioral model of depression, and ask him or her to reflect upon the way in which it applies to his or her life.
2. Introduce the activity log to your client, as well as the rationale for activity monitoring. Discuss with your client completing the activity monitoring forms (i.e., writing down how time is spent, supplying accompanying ratings), or modifying them to make them more palatable. Spend time in session completing the activity log for the time before the session, so that the client has a model to follow at home.
3. At the time of the next session, review the activity monitoring exercise with your client. Ask your client to draw conclusions about the associations among activity level, types of activities engaged in, and mood.
4. Brainstorm a few activities that the client can work into his or her schedule in the time between this session and the subsequent session. Be sure to identify "back-up plans," including alternative activities and times if a factor such as weather interferes with their completion.
5. Ask your client to complete the activity log for homework once again, paying special attention to ratings associated with the new activities that were scheduled.
6. At the time of the next session, review the activity scheduling exercise with your client. Ask your client to draw additional conclusions about the associations among activity level, types of activities engaged in, and mood.
7. Discuss with the client ways to continue implementing behavioral activation and incorporating its principles into the way he or she lives life.
8. In the box below, reflect on your behavioral activation work with your client.

BOX 4 **REFLECTIONS ON BEHAVIORAL ACTIVATION WORK WITH YOUR CLIENT**

What do you conclude from this experiential exercise? How effective was your behavioral activation intervention?

Was behavioral activation easier or more difficult to implement than you had expected? Why?

What, specifically, will you do differently in the future to implement behavioral activation?

How has your view about behavioral activation changed after participating in this experiential exercise?

Problem Solving

Even the best-laid cognitive behavioral interventions are met, at times, with obstacles. We encounter all sorts of "curve balls" as we live our lives, and to function adaptively, we must think clearly and implement problem solving to move forward and achieve our goals. Thus, problem solving goes hand-in-hand with all of the interventions described in this and other texts on CBT. According to D'Zurilla and Nezu (2007), *problem solving* is defined as "the self-directed cognitive-behavioral process by which a person attempts to identify or discover effective or adaptive solutions for specific problems encountered in everyday living" (p. 11). Problem solving involves a process by which clients (a) identify a specific problem that they are facing, (b) identify a solution or a combination of solutions to solve the problem, and (c) implement the solution, and (d) evaluate the degree to which the enacted solution was successful. It can be geared toward changing a problematic situation, the way in which one responds to the problematic situation, or both.

I encounter an interesting phenomenon when I supervise therapists-in-training, who say they are implementing problem solving with their clients. When I listen to recordings of their sessions, I often hear a dialogue that goes something like this:

Client:	I'm facing a really tough problem. I'm just so overwhelmed, and I don't know what to do.
Therapist:	Well, have you considered _______?
Client:	No, I haven't. That's a great idea.
Therapist:	Should you try that in between sessions?
Client:	Yes, I will.

[Client and therapist move on to discussing a new topic.]

Although the therapist in this dialogue means to be helpful, this is not a problem solving intervention. The reason for this is that the therapist has not asked Socratic questions that would allow the client to grapple with the issues and make strides toward drawing his or her own conclusion, nor has the therapist assessed whether the client has a deficit in problem solving skills, and if so, has helped the client to acquire any of these skills. Only in very rare instances do cognitive behavioral therapists supply solutions to clients for their problems, and even then, it is after much more systematic and careful discussion that is framed in a way for the client to have an important learning experience.

When I ask workshop participants and trainees whether they received systematic training in problem solving interventions in graduate school, most, if not all, indicate that they did not. Indeed, it seems that it is assumed that we, as therapists, are good problem solvers; therefore, it should be easy for us to transfer those skills to our clients. However, as can be seen from the above dialogue, in my supervisory and training experience, this is not always the case. In this section, I present a standard cognitive behavioral approach to problem solving, I illustrate its application to the two cases we have been following throughout the book, and I invite you to practice its application to one of your own clients.

Before proceeding, however, I encourage you to think about the way you approach problems in your own life. In the box below, think about a problem that you are currently facing or that you have recently faced, and outline the way in which you have approached problem solving.

BOX 5 A PROBLEM IN YOUR OWN LIFE

Think of a problem that you are currently facing. Describe the important components of the problem.

What aspects of the problem seem easy or relatively straightforward for you to face?

What aspects of the problem seem overwhelming or relatively difficult for you to face?

Are there any aspects of the problem that you do not have the ability to solve? If so, what types of other resources will you utilize?

Do you notice any ways of thinking about the problem that either interfered with problem solving, itself, or with your motivation to solve the problem? What were those ways of thinking? How could you apply cognitive restructuring to soften them?

Notice that I asked a question in the box about ways of thinking that either interfered with problem solving, itself, or with your motivation to solve the problem. This question reflects the important point that I made at the beginning of the chapter—that nearly all CBT interventions involve both cognitive and behavioral pieces, even if the primary activity that takes place during the intervention is one or the other. In the subsequent section on problem solving techniques, I mention some typical thinking styles to watch out for and ways to restructure them.

Techniques

When clients are overwhelmed and at a loss as to how to solve their problems, it is possible that they are characterized by a *problem solving deficit.* This means that the client lacks skill in one or more of the steps of problem solving and would benefit from coaching by the therapist. There are a number of problem solving templates available in various CBT protocols, many of which supply acronyms capturing the first letter of each step of problem solving to remember easily when implementing problem solving in session (e.g., ITCH [I = Identify the problem; T = Think of (brainstorm!) solutions; C = Choose a solution or solutions to implement; H = How did it work?]; Muñoz, Ippen, Rao, Le, & Dwyer, 2000). My "go to" sequence of problem solving steps is described in Nezu, Nezu, and D'Zurilla's 4th edition of a cognitive behaviorally-based approach to treatment called *problem solving therapy.* Like behavioral activation, problem solving therapy is a stand-alone treatment on its own, and its techniques can be integrated into a larger CBT package. According to Nezu et al. (2013), there are four steps in effective, *planful problem solving*:

1. Problem definition and formulation
2. Generation of alternatives
3. Decision making
4. Solution implementation and verification

Each of these steps is described in turn, below.

One can only solve a problem if the problem is clearly defined and its parameters clearly outlined. It was for this reason that, in Box 5 above, I asked you to describe the important components of the problem. Many clients report that they are experiencing multiple problems, some of which overlap or are entwined with each other, making it difficult for clients to know where to begin. This first step in problem solving provides the opportunity for clients to clearly define their problems and to identify one specific aspect of a problem that they could address in session and in the time between sessions. This step was demonstrated in my work with Marilyn, captured in Chapter 4 of this volume, in which I encouraged her to isolate one tangible issue for which there was some promise that headway could be made in session. During this phase of problem solving, clients set goals for problem solving and identify obstacles that might interfere with achieving goals.

The second step of problem solving is the *generation of alternatives.* Many clients refer to this step as *brainstorming.* The key to brainstorming is to encourage the client to generate all possible solutions without initially judging them or dismissing them. This can be quite the task for clients who struggle with depression, or who are otherwise pessimistic about their ability to solve problems. Thus, therapists often play the role of coaches that keep clients "on track" during this stage, catching the "yeah buts" that clients pair with many potential solutions that are generated but that would otherwise prevent them from considering the potential solution further.

Once clients have generated solutions to their problems, they turn to *decision making*. However, decision making is not as easy as it sounds. Cognitive behavioral therapists often find a need to coach their clients in finding a systematic way to evaluate each solution so that a sound decision can be made. A standard approach to arriving upon a solution is to facilitate an *advantages-disadvantages analysis*, such that clients weigh the pros and cons of each proposed solution. Because this task involves the processing of a great deal of information, it is often helpful to set up a grid in which clients can write out pros and cons for each proposed solution, side by side. They might also need assistance in developing a system for weighing the pros and cons, as some are likely to be more important than others. Clients often find that decision making is approached in this systematic manner, more than one solution has the potential to be successful, or a combination of solutions might be the most effective. Similar to what was described in the section on behavioral activation, they also can identify a sequence of solutions to try, such as having a "Plan B" if "Plan A" does not work.

A logical homework exercise for clients is to implement the solution that had been decided upon. Thus, the fourth step of problem solving is *solution implementation and verification*. Many cognitive behavioral therapists find it help to engage clients in *imaginal rehearsal*, or the use of vivid mental imagery to imagine walking through the steps of solution implementation, envisioning success, and conceptualizing obstacles that might be encountered. Verification refers to the fact that cognitive behavioral therapists invite their clients to discuss the implementation of their solution at the time of the next session, so that they can evaluate whether it was successful and what was learned from the exercise. The evaluation of solution implementation is crucial. Often, solutions do not work, or only partially work, and clients become discouraged. In fact, a failed solution provides an opportunity for clients to practice distress tolerance. Moreover, it provides important data about skills that the client may need to acquire in order to implement solutions more effectively in the future.

When cognitive behavioral therapists work with their clients to acquire and practice skills in planful problem solving, they combine the delivery of psychoeducation (i.e., teaching the client about key concepts associated with the intervention), modeling, and collaboration. They ask Socratic questions of their clients that help clients to evaluate the degree to which they are approaching problem solving in an effective manner. They record the fruits of their work on a sheet of paper or a white board so that clients have a visual demonstration of the work that was done in session. They encourage their clients to practice tangible behavioral skills that will increase the likelihood that their selected solution will be successful, such as practice in social skills if the solution involves asking something of another person. Moreover, they encourage their clients to think about ways to generalize their learning to solving problems that they might encounter in the future.

As mentioned previously, at times clients' difficulty with problem solving lies more in the cognitive realm than in the behavioral realm of enacting solutions to problems. Some clients are characterized by what is called a *negative problem orientation*, or a set of beliefs that a person holds about problems, which in turn provides the motivation (or lack thereof) to solve problems. People with a negative problem orientation view problems (a) as resulting from a personal defect, rather than as being a part of life; (b) as threats, rather than as challenges; (c) insolvable, rather than solvable; and (d) as issues that "should" be able to be resolved immediately, rather than those that will invariably require time, effort, and patience to resolve. They also resist the idea that they may experience negative emotions during the problem solving process and that these negative emotions are natural and transient (Nezu et al., 2013).

Many aspects of a negative problem orientation can be addressed using the cognitive restructuring techniques described in Chapter 5 of this volume. For example, clients can consider their past experiences with problem solving to objectively evaluate the evidence that supports and does not support an inability to solve problems. They can develop an adaptive plan for coping with the worst-case scenario of the solution being ineffective. They can treat solution implementation as a behavioral experiment, withholding judgment about the degree to which they expect a solution to be effective until they actually observe its effectiveness first-hand. Moreover, they can consider the effects of their negative problem solving, identifying specific ways in which it creates a self-fulfilling prophesy that decreases the likelihood that problem solving will be effective.

To get a sense of the "feel" of this framework, take a moment to apply this problem solving approach to the problem that you identified in Box 5. You have already defined the main components of the problem. What alternatives would you generate as possible solutions? How would you, systematically, evaluate those alternatives and decide upon a solution? Then, implement the solution to the problem, and evaluate the solution's effectiveness. In addition, consider whether any indications of a negative problem orientation emerged, and describe how you dealt with them.

BOX 6 APPLICATION OF PROBLEM-SOLVING SKILLS TO YOUR OWN PROBLEM

Brainstorm at least four alternative solutions to the problem. Write them down even if you find yourself dismissing them. Remember that the idea is to keep a fully open mind during the brainstorming process.

1.

2.

3.

4.

Evaluate the advantages and disadvantages of each potential solution.

SOLUTION #1

Pros:

Cons:

SOLUTION #2

Pros:

Cons:

SOLUTION #3

Pros:

Cons:

SOLUTION #4

Pros:

Cons:

Decide upon a solution and indicate here the specific way in which you will implement it.

(continued)

(continued)

[after implementing the solution] What about the solution was effective? What was ineffective? What did you learn from attempting to solve your problem?

Did any aspects of a negative problem orientation manifest? What were they? How did you restructure them?

Case Examples

Straightforward case. Recall Ashley, our relatively "straightforward" case, who was left in Chapter 5 of this volume with some trepidation about continued tension and even a potential confrontation with a dominant mother in her mothers' group, despite the fact that she had a very positive experience with her behavioral experiment. In cases like Ashley, who have a diagnosis of an anxiety disorder, it is important to differentiate between *actual* problems that clients are facing and *hypothetical* problems that are more reflective of excessive worry (Dugas & Robichaud, 2007). Although Ashley certainly had an unpleasant interaction with the dominant mother in her mothers' group on one occasion, the fear of a confrontation or "blow-up" was regarded as a hypothetical worry because there was no tangible evidence that another unpleasant exchange was on the horizon. Thus, we defined the problem as "feeling uncomfortable in the presence of the dominant mother in the mothers' group," and we began to brainstorm ways for Ashley to feel more comfortable and confident. In the dialogue in Chapter 5 of this volume, Ashley had already identified one potential solution—sticking close to a couple of the other mothers who had expressed similar viewpoints about the dominant mother. In the follow dialogue, Ashley continues to brainstorm ways to be more comfortable in spite of the presence of the dominant mother; she evaluates the advantages and disadvantages of her solutions, and she decides on a solution to enact.

Dr. Amy: So, one way to feel more comfortable that you had identified in the previous session is to align yourself with a couple of the other mothers who have expressed frustration about the one mother with whom you had problems and her children. You seemed to get along well with them when that mother was absent from the group. Might this be one solution that you continue to implement, even when this mother is in attendance?

Ashley: Yes, I still think that would be a good idea. We have another gathering in a couple of weeks, so I could try that.

Dr. Amy: That's terrific. Do you think it would be worthwhile to brainstorm additional ways for you to increase your comfort level with the group, in light of the fact that this woman will continue to attend gatherings?

Ashley: Oh definitely. Because one of the women I like—she only attends some of the gatherings. So, I'd be out of luck if she decides not to come one day.

Dr. Amy: Okay, let's brainstorm some other possibilities. Is it alright with you if we write them down on a sheet of paper, so that we can process all of them together?

Ashley: Absolutely.

Dr. Amy: I'm ready when you are. What are some other possibilities that would make it easier for you to be in this group in spite of that other mother's presence?

Ashley: Well. . . [trailing off] Gee, I don't know. I've always been such a shy person that I sort of have to muscle my way through social activities when I don't know a lot of people there.

Dr. Amy: [taking a different approach] What if you had a friend in a similar situation, and she asked you for advice? What advice would you give that friend?

Ashley: I'd definitely be able to empathize with her. I don't know, maybe volunteering to host an event so that it's on her "turf"?

Dr. Amy: Sounds like a good possibility to me. I'll write it down.

Ashley: [becoming sheepish] Oh gosh, I don't know if you should write that one down. I get so nervous about entertaining other people. What if I can't get the house clean enough? What if my daughter is not cooperating, and I have to spend the whole time tending to her? What if. . .?

Dr. Amy: [leaning forward and gently interrupting] I acknowledge your concerns, Ashley. At this stage, let's just brainstorm without judgment. The reason why I suggest this is that many people arrive upon some very good solutions to their problems, only to find that they would have dismissed the solution had they pre-judged it when they first thought of it. Can we add it to the list, and then when the list is complete, we can take a look at the pros and cons of each proposed solution?

Ashley: Oh gosh, I'm so sorry, I'm not doing this the right way.

Dr. Amy: [recognizing Ashley's tendency to be easily shamed, smiling in a warm, inviting manner, and normalizing her reaction] Honestly, there is very little "right" or "wrong" with this, Ashley. It's just my job to teach you a new skill, and believe me, all of us, including myself, can use some practice with brainstorming ideas in a way that is truly non-judgmental. Our anxiety can get the better of us when we are brainstorming.

Ashley: [relaxing] You can say that again.

Notice Ashley's immediate tendency to dismiss the idea of hosting the mothers' group at her home, identifying a barrage of hypothetical worries about bad things that might happen. When you implement the brainstorming stage of problem solving, you will almost invariably have to provide education about the purpose and benefits of brainstorming. Some clients, such as Ashley, have the tendency to berate themselves if they perceive that they are not compliant, so it is important to be alert for these reactions, normalize them, and ensure that they are not feeling shamed or punished. Another tactic I could have used would have been to assure Ashley that, if she were to have chosen that course of action, we could apply a combination of cognitive restructuring and problem solving to increase the likelihood that such an event would be successful.

Ashley ultimately identified five potential solutions—the two that were mentioned in the dialogue (i.e., staying close to the women who held similar viewpoints about the dominant mother, hosting an event on her own "turf"), and three additional solutions: (a) inviting the dominant mother and her children for a play date, so that she could get to know her better; (b) looking for additional mothers' groups to join, so that she would not be so dependent on the benefits this one group offered her; and (c) more actively and vocally expressing her viewpoint and defending her children if a similar situation were to occur. As might be expected, Ashley was most comfortable with sticking close to the mothers with similar viewpoints and least comfortable with being assertive with the dominant mother, although she recognized that she could benefit from practicing assertive communication skills. For her action plan, Ashley decided to stay close to the mothers whom she believed held similar viewpoints, and also search for additional mothers' groups and children's activities to expand her social circle. In addition, she agreed to consider hosting one of the mothers' groups events at her own house, albeit with careful problem solving and planning in future CBT sessions.

Ashley continues to represent as a relatively "straightforward" case here for many reasons. First, she demonstrated an openness to the problem solving intervention. Even though she began to dismiss some of the potential solutions generated (and began to make a self-deprecating statement about not doing the exercise "correctly"), she readily responded to psychoeducation, my attempt to normalize the tendency to dismiss potential solutions, and my effort to use aspects of the therapeutic relationship (e.g., warmth, genuineness) to reduce any shame she might be experiencing. Second, she demonstrated the capacity to develop a fairly sophisticated action plan that emerged from her problem solving work, committing to implementing two solutions and to use CBT to help prepare her to implement a third.

Now, take some time to reflect on my work with Ashley. What did you find effective? Was there anything that surprised you, or that you would have done differently? What other interventions might be useful here?

BOX 7 REFLECTIONS ON PROBLEM SOLVING WORK WITH ASHLEY

What did you find effective about the dialogue and the subsequent description of the course of problem solving?

What did you find surprising about my work with Ashley? What might you do differently?

If Ashley were to return to session having been successful with her problem solving homework, what might you do next with her?

If Ashley were to return to session having been *un*successful with her homework, why might that be? What might you do next with her?

Did you feel a pull to implement any other interventions at this point in the course of treatment? If so, what intervention did you see as indicated, and how would you implement it?

Difficult case. When Marilyn returned for her subsequent session after implementing activity scheduling, as described in the previous section, she reported that activity scheduling was about "75% effective." She followed through with pursuing one activity outside the home on both weekend days—a yoga class on Saturday and a service at the local Unitarian church on Sunday—although she noted that she continued to feel bored and lonely in the afternoons on both weekend days. To counteract these feelings of loneliness and boredom, she, indeed, read a book from the fiction series that she had identified in the previous session. However, she also had a few cocktails, admitting that she felt guilty about doing so and acknowledging the need to schedule activities during the late afternoons, specifically to maximize the benefits of behavioral activation. Marilyn also indicated that she read her fiction book on the two weekday evenings on which skating had not been scheduled and that she achieved a sense of eager anticipation and enjoyment from doing so.

In addition to this relatively favorable report, Marilyn also identified another activity from which she expected to achieve a great sense of accomplishment—taking classes toward a certificate in graphic design, which she expected would help her to pursue a career in this area and afford her the opportunity to leave her current position. However, she also encountered what she perceived to be a significant barrier—that one of the required core classes began at 4pm, and she worked until 5pm every day. Together, we applied the planful problem solving framework, and Marilyn recognized that the most logical solution to the program was to ask permission of her supervisor to begin work at 7:30am and leave at 3:30pm on the day of the class—an arrangement that was similar to ones made by some of her co-workers in the past. Unfortunately, Marilyn experienced a barrage of negative thoughts about the prospect of posing the question to her supervisor, as well as doubts about her ability to pose the request effectively. In the following dialogue, I demonstrate the way in which I handled her negative thought (i.e., "She's out to get me;" "She's find a bogus reason to deny my request"), as well the way in which I proposed working on social skills that would increase the likelihood that her request would be met with success and a plan for coping if her supervisor did not grant her request.

Marilyn: [becoming agitated] I know that the only way I can take this class is to ask my supervisor. But I also know that she's out to get me. I don't get to play by the same rules as everyone else. She'll find some bogus reason to deny my request, and I'll be stuck in this same God forsaken job for the rest of my life!

Dr. Amy: [demonstrating empathy] There is no question that your work environment is challenging, Marilyn. I do wonder, though—when you focus on those ideas of your supervisor being out to get you and the prediction that she will make up a bogus excuse to deny your request, does that increase or decrease the likelihood that you will ask for the accommodation?

Marilyn: [looking surprised] Well, it decreases it, I guess. There have been a couple of other times in the past when I needed to take off to go to appointments that could only be made during business hours. And I didn't even ask. I was just like, "Why bother?"

Dr. Amy: Oh, so in those instances, you decided not to try. What happened with the appointments?

Marilyn: [sighing] Nothing. I just didn't make them. I haven't seen my gynecologist in five years because of this.

Dr. Amy: Are you willing to forego the graphic design class for the same reason? That it's a foregone conclusion that she's got it out for you and will find a bogus excuse to deny your request?

Marilyn: [hesitating] Well . . . no . . . this is really important to me. I've got to do some things differently in my life. But it just seems so impossible! No matter what I do, I'm always met with a brick wall. Or with criticism. Or with people who talk behind my back.

Dr. Amy: I wonder if it would be useful for us, together, to put words to a somewhat different mindset that will help you overcome the mental part of the block in making a request of your supervisor? And then, perhaps we can craft and practice an effective way of posing the request?

Marilyn: [becoming tearful] I don't know if CBT will work here. My workplace defies all logic.

Dr. Amy: [speaking softly] I understand that there is no guarantee that your supervisor will accommodate your request. But the part that we can do, together, is to figure out how to put your best foot forward.

Marilyn: [looking skeptical] I'm worried that if this doesn't work, that this will make me even more depressed. And hopeless about my life.

Dr. Amy: Does that cost outweigh the benefit of being able to take the graphic design class if your request is granted?

Marilyn: I don't know. Maybe.

Dr. Amy: [demonstrating understanding] I can appreciate that you are vulnerable and that making this request seems very risky. If it works, though, what effect do you think it would have on your mood?

Marilyn: Oh, it would be a game changer. It would definitely achieve what you've been talking about. That activation stuff.

Dr. Amy: [smiling about Marilyn's retention of the psychoeducation about behavioral activation] That it would. I also think it would instill some hope that life could be different and also increase your confidence in your ability to solve some of the interpersonal problems that pop up at work.

Marilyn: Well, you're right, I guess. If I could make this happen, I would feel a lot better about a lot of things in my life.

Dr. Amy: How is this for a threefold plan? First, let's develop an adaptive response that you can carry with you in your mind as you go in to make the request of your supervisor. Then, let's consider the specific way in which you will make the request. Finally, we can develop a plan for coping and for what to do next if the worst-case scenario occurs, and she denies your request.

Marilyn: [sighing with more conviction] Okay, let's do it.

Notice that, at first, Marilyn was skeptical about implementing the proposed solution of asking her supervisor to adjust her work hours to allow her to take the class. I did not take the route of trying to convince Marilyn that the likelihood of a poor outcome would be low, as she had provided plenty of examples in the past suggesting that her supervisor managed her employees in a way that seemed, indeed, to be inconsistent. Instead, I focused on the effects of her negative mindset (i.e., that it prevents her from even trying to make requests), as well as the costs of not make the request and the benefits of, indeed, making the request. Marilyn introduced the understandable concern that it would be very discouraging for her if her supervisor denied her request. On the basis of this concern, I suggested that we add a component to our approach—developing a coping plan to deal with the worst-case scenario.

The remainder of the session was productive. We shifted her thinking from: "My supervisor is out to get me. She'll find some bogus reason to deny my request" to "My supervisor has approved these kinds of requests from other people, and this is my first time asking for an accommodation." We practiced making the request using effective communication skills, including (a) first asking the supervisor if there was a convenient time in which she could ask a question, (b) providing a rationale for the request, (c) demonstrating evidence that she could complete her work duties effectively, and (d) thanking the supervisor for considering her request. Finally, Marilyn's coping plan for the worst-case scenario included creative solutions to pursuing the graphic arts program if her supervisor denied her request (e.g., asking to take an independent study in place of the class) and applications of behavioral activation to be implemented after work (e.g., calling a friend, taking a bubble bath) to attain support and achieve a sense of self-soothing.

Now, take some time to reflect on my work with Marilyn. What did you find effective? Was there anything that surprised you, or that you would have done differently? What other interventions might be useful here?

BOX 8 REFLECTIONS ON PROBLEM SOLVING WORK WITH MARILYN

What did you find effective about the dialogue and the subsequent description of the course of problem solving?

What did you find surprising about my work with Marilyn? What might you do differently?

If Marilyn were to return to her next session indicating that her supervisor granted her request, what might you do next with her?

If Marilyn were to return to her next session indicating that her supervisor had not granted her request, what might you do next with her?

Did you feel a pull to implement any other interventions at this point in the course of treatment? If so, what intervention did you see as indicated, and how would you implement it?

Tips for Maximizing Effectiveness

My most significant tip for maximizing the effectiveness of problem solving interventions is a reiteration of a point that I made earlier—to spend a significant chunk of time in session carefully going through the steps of planful problem solving in a systematic manner, assessing the degree to which your client is acquiring new knowledge every step of the way. It is hoped that a problem solving intervention delivered in this manner is another way (such as the setting of an agenda) of organizing and addressing life's stressors and challenges in an adaptive manner that reduces the likelihood of emotional overwhelm.

Many therapists find that their clients identify sound solutions to their problems, but that they lack one or more skills to effectively implement the solution. This issue was illustrated in the dialogue with Marilyn, who had a history of negative interactions with her supervisor and lacked the confidence to make the request for a schedule adjustment in a way that would maximize the likelihood that her supervisor would agree. Thus, skills training is often paired with problem solving interventions to facilitate solution implementation. Like problem solving interventions, skills training interventions involve much more than making a simple suggestion to clients on how to develop a skill required for solution implementation. The following are steps that I outlined in one of my previous CBT texts for implementing training in one specific type of skill—communication skills (Wenzel, 2013).

1. Have the client model what he or she will say to the other person.
2. Ask the client to consider what it would be like to be on the receiving end of that communication, focusing on the communication's effectiveness and whether any aspect of it could be misinterpreted.
3. Decide on one specific skill to practice (e.g., making eye contact, providing validation to the other person, reducing the frequency of paraverbals).
4. Conduct a role-play in which you play the role of the client, and the client plays the role of the person on the receiving end of the communication in order to model the effective use of the skill for the client.
5. Reverse the role-play, such that the client plays him- or herself, and you play the person on the receiving end of the communication.
6. Continue to practice and hone the communication skill by evaluating the effectiveness of the client's use of the skill, making use of therapist modeling, and providing additional opportunities for the client to practice.
7. Consolidate the client's learning by asking him or her to articulate what was learned by this exercise.

Much of the time, solutions do not exactly work out the way that clients hope they will. Contrary to what you might expect, this is not at all negative—in fact, it provides useful information and a valuable learning experience. Regardless of whether a solution achieves its desired aim, clients can consider whether they learned from the experience. For example, they might learn that they need to further hone a skill that is necessary to implement the solution. They might realize that there is no one "right" solution and that many solutions will be adequate even if they are not perfect. Perhaps most importantly, they can learn that they can tolerate instances in which life does not turn out exactly as planned and that they can still achieve personal satisfaction and fulfillment. Thus, it is helpful to set up solution implementation as a "win-win proposition"—either clients solve an important problem that is causing emotional distress, or they learn that they can continue to live their lives in a meaningful, valued manner, even if particular stressors or challenges are not resolved in an optimal manner.

Application to a Client

Try your hand at implementing a problem solving intervention with one of your own clients. Think of a client on your caseload who is struggling with solving a problem in his or her life and could use some coaching in developing skills in one or more areas of problem solving. Use the following steps as a guide.

1. Problem definition and formulation: help your client to isolate a specific problem and defines its parameters.
2. Generation of alternatives: educate your client about the purpose of brainstorming and encourage your client to generate a pool of possible solutions, gently catching instances in which your client is judging or dismissing a potential solution.
3. Decision making: work with your client to lay out the possible solutions and evaluate their merits and drawbacks. Provide space for your client to decide upon either a single solution, a combination of solutions, or a sequence of solutions (e.g., first try "Plan A," then try "Plan B").
4. Solution implementation: ask the client to walk you though the specific steps he or she will follow to implement the solution. Consider using imaginal rehearsal to enhance the vividness of this practice.
5. Throughout this process, be alert for any manifestations of a negative problem orientation. Use cognitive restructuring skills (see Chapter 5 of this volume) to shape adaptive responses to these manifestations.
6. Assess for any skills deficits that could interfere with successful solution implementation. If you detect a skills deficit, follow the steps described earlier in this section to provide the client the opportunity to practice and enhance this skill.
7. Solution verification: at the time of the next session, ask permission to add discussion of solution verification to the agenda. In addition to allowing the client to describe the details of solution implementation, ask the client what he or she learned from the experience and the way in which he or she will apply the new learning to other problems in the future.
8. If the problem persists, use this framework to hone your client's problem solving ability and enhance your client's solution implementation skills.
9. In the box below, reflect on your problem solving work with your client.

BOX 9 **REFLECTION ON BEHAVIORAL ACTIVATION WORK WITH YOUR CLIENT**

What do you conclude from this experiential exercise? How effective was your problem solving intervention?

Was problem solving easier or more difficult to implement than you had expected? Why?

What, specifically, will you do differently in the future to implement problem solving?

How has your view about problem solving changed after participating in this experiential exercise?

Exposure

Whereas clients who are depressed avoid activities because of anhedonia, fatigue, and foggy-headedness, clients who are anxious avoid activities due to fear and dread. These clients believe that a dreaded, aversive outcome will occur if they have contact with a feared stimulus or situation, and they severely underestimate their resources to cope with adversity. *Exposure* is a standard and especially powerful strategy used in the treatment of anxiety, obsessive compulsive-and-related, and trauma- and stressor-related disorders (i.e., *anxiety-related disorders*) and involves the planned and systematic contact with feared stimuli and situations that clients have been avoiding (Abramowitz, Deacon, & Whiteside, 2011).

Exposure is a very versatile strategy that can take on many forms. *In vivo exposure* is actual, "real life" contact with a feared stimulus or situation. For example, a person with a fear of heights might engage in activities, such as going to the top of a skyscraper and looking down over the city; a person with a fear of contamination might touch trash cans or door knobs in public restrooms. *Imaginal exposure* makes use of vivid imagery to construct scenarios or reconstruct intrusive thoughts that are alarming to clients. It is especially indicated for clients with posttraumatic stress disorder (PTSD), for whom it would be difficult and unethical to recreate in vivo situations in which they face a past trauma. This is one instance in which CBT, indeed, focuses primarily on a past event and its implications for current functioning. Imaginal exposure is also indicated for clients with generalized anxiety disorder (GAD), who often catastrophize about worst-case scenarios that are unlikely to occur in the future. *Interoceptive exposure* involves the provocation of bodily sensations (e.g., racing heart, dizziness) that are often feared by clients with panic disorder and clients who have significant health anxiety concerns. An innovative approach to exposure that has been studied over the past 20 years is *virtual reality exposure*, which makes use of technology to simulate feared stimuli and situations that are difficult to replicate in "real life." Virtual reality exposure has been used for fears as diverse as the fear of flying, to combat experiences, and even to public speaking anxiety. Research shows that virtual reality exposure experiences are highly believable to clients and that it is just as efficacious as in vivo exposure (Morina, Ijntema, Meyerbröker, & Emmelkamp, 2015; Opriş et al., 2012). Table 6.1 summarizes efficacious approaches to exposure for various types of anxiety (and related) disorders.

Most people find that the concepts of anxiety, avoidance, and exposure have some relevance to an aspect of their lives. Think about whether anxiety (or fear or dread) and avoidance play any role in your own life. Are there stimuli or situations that you avoid, because you do not want to experience discomfort? Has there ever been a time when you found yourself faced with a situation that you would have rather avoided, and that by engaging in it (rather than avoiding it), you were able to work through your anxiety, fear, and/or dread? What did you find helpful in overcoming your fear?

Table 6.1 Exposure Exercises for Specific Anxiety and Related Disorders

DIAGNOSIS	*EXPOSURE EXERCISE*
Generalized Anxiety Disorder	• Primary imaginal exposure to predicted catastrophes • Primary imaginal exposure to uncertain outcomes of feared situations • In vivo exposure to uncertainty-inducing situations
Social Anxiety Disorder	• In vivo exposure to social and evaluative situations • In vivo exposure to social mishaps • Interoceptive exposure to feared anxiety symptoms, such as blushing • Secondary imaginal exposure to the consequences of a social mishap • (if necessary) Preliminary imaginal exposure to feared stimulus or situation
Panic Disorder	• Primary interoceptive exposure to feared physiological sensations • Secondary interoceptive exposure to situations that provoke feared physiological symptoms • In vivo exposure to other avoided situations • Secondary imaginal exposure to feared consequences of anxiety symptoms • (if necessary) Preliminary imaginal exposure to feared situation
Posttraumatic Stress Disorder	• Imaginal exposure to traumatic experience • In vivo exposure to situations that have been avoided after the trauma • (if necessary) Preliminary imaginal exposure to feared situations that have been avoided after the trauma
Obsessive Compulsive Disorder	• In vivo exposure to feared stimuli • Imaginal exposure to feared consequences of not engaging in ritualistic behavior • (if necessary) Preliminary imaginal exposure to feared stimulus or situation
Specific Phobia	• In vivo exposure to feared stimulus or situation • (if necessary) Preliminary imaginal exposure to feared stimulus or situation

Note: Table adapted with permission from Wenzel, A. (2013, p. 173). *Strategic decision making in cognitive behavioral therapy.* Washington, DC: American Psychological Association.

BOX 10 REFLECTIONS ON ANXIETY, AVOIDANCE, AND EXPOSURE

Describe one or more stimuli or situations in which you experience anxiety, fear, and/or dread. To what extent do you go out of your way to avoid it or them?

Do you notice that your anxiety, fear, and/or dread get worse or become more entrenched when you avoid? Why do you think that is?

Have you been in a position in which you have had the opportunity to face the stimulus or situation associated with anxiety, fear, and/or dread? What happened?

What else was helpful as you attempted to overcome your anxiety, fear, and/or dread of the stimulus or situation?

The field is undergoing quite an evolution regarding its understanding of the way in which exposure works. Edna Foa and Michael Kozak published a seminal article in 1986 describing the way in which fear is represented internally, which has implications for the mechanism by which exposure works. Specifically, they indicated that people with anxiety and related disorders are characterized by *fear structures*, which are representations of cognitive, affective, and behavioral reactions to feared stimuli and situations. To successfully treat an anxiety-related disorder, they indicated that the fear structure must be activated, and the client should demonstrate *habituation*, or the lessening of the fear response with prolonged and repeated contact with the feared stimulus or situation in the absence of the aversive outcome. Habituation is much like what happens when we enter into a cold swimming pool. At first the water is cold, but if we stay in long enough, eventually the water does not feel so cold. The temperature of the water has not changed; instead, our bodies have adapted to it (cf. Abramowitz et al., 2011). Habituation is demonstrated when, within a single exposure trial, a client's self-reported anxiety decreases substantially (i.e., *within-session habituation*), and across exposure trials, when a client's beginning-, peak-, and ending-anxiety levels are lower on later trials than on earlier trials (i.e., *between-session habituation*).

Although the habituation model makes intuitive sense and is straightforward to implement with clients, one reality of it is that sessions usually needed to be longer than the typical 45 to 50 minutes in order for clients to achieve within-session habituation. Many therapists in private practice settings found these lengthy sessions difficult to implement not only from a scheduling perspective, but also because insurance usually would not reimburse for lengthy sessions (particularly those that took place outside of the office). From an empirical perspective, the eminent psychologist Michelle Craske and her research team did a critical review of the literature and concluded that there was weak evidence, at best, that habituation is associated with successful outcome with exposure (Craske et al., 2008). They proposed an alternative framework called the *inhibitory learning* model to account for the way in which exposure works. This model has its basis in classical conditioning theory. An *excitatory* learning experience is one in which an aversive consequence follows the presentation of a conditioned stimulus (e.g., the person is in the presence of a dog, and the dog bites the person). In contrast, an *inhibitory* learning experience is one in which an aversive response does not follow the presentation of a conditioned stimulus (e.g., the person is in the presence of a dog, and the dog does not bite the person). Successful exposure occurs when the client has formed a new pathway of learning through repeated inhibitory learning experiences. New learning is the goal of exposure in both paradigms, but in the inhibitory learning paradigm, even if the client does not achieve habituation in the form of a substantial reduction in self-reported anxiety, exposure is still regarded as successful because of the new learning that has occurred. The goals of exposure associated with the inhibitory learning paradigm are (a) new learning of nonthreat associations between feared stimuli and situations and outcome; (b) the ability to access this new learning in different contexts; and (c) fear tolerance rather than fear reduction per se.

Like behavioral activation, there is strong empirical evidence suggesting that exposure is just as efficacious as a full package of CBT (including both exposure and cognitive restructuring) (e.g., Siev & Chambless, 2007). As a practitioner-scientist, I am strongly influenced by the data, and from the data I conclude that exposure is essential in the treatment of anxiety, obsessive compulsive and related disorders, and trauma- and stressor-related disorders. In fact, I have worked with many clients with anxiety-related disorders who can beautifully restructure inaccurate and unhelpful thoughts about feared stimuli and situations, but if they are still engaging in avoidance behavior, then it is my belief that CBT is far from successful. This being said, many therapists-in-training find exposure to be a bit daunting and even report being quite squeamish about implementing it. In fact, in their review of the usage of exposure for anxiety-related disorders, Olatunji, Deacon, and Abramowitz (2009) observed that only a minority of therapists implement exposure despite knowledge of its efficacy and having received systematic training.

What accounts for the discrepancy between the impressive efficacy data and the low percentage of well-trained therapists who regularly implement exposure to indicated clients? The three most common reasons that I have encountered in my training and supervision experiences are as follows (cf. Feeny, Hembree, & Zoellner, 2003; Olatunji et al., 2009):

1. Exposure is aversity enough that clinicians sometimes perceive that clients will refuse to participate or drop out at a much higher rate than is typical for mental health treatment.
2. Exposure is thought by some clinicians to "re-traumatize" the client.
3. Exposure is simply too uncomfortable for the clinician to tolerate.

Allow me to address each of these concerns in turn.

Under tightly controlled conditions, such as the "gold standard" randomized controlled trials (RCTs) that are typically conducted in the walls of academia, data show that there is no difference in rates of drop-out from treatment between clients who participate in exposure-based therapies and clients who participate in other types of psychotherapy (e.g., Hembree et al., 2003). However, expert therapist Lisa Najavits (2015) has critically reviewed the literature and concluded that exposure is, indeed, associated with higher-than-average drop-out rates in the treatment of clients with post-traumatic stress disorder (PTSD) in "real-world" settings. One reason for this is that therapists—even those who are trained in the delivery of exposure-based therapies—often bring a negative mindset to treatment, assuming that clients will have an aversive response to exposure-based therapies (Zayfert et al., 2005), thereby creating a self-fulfilling prophesy. Thus, it is possible that data that do, indeed, reflect higher drop-out rates from exposure-based therapies could be confounded by therapist attitude or comfort level with the treatment, a point about which I speak more below.

Second, there is no evidence that exposure "re-traumatizes" the client (Olatunji et al., 2009). In fact, many therapists-in-training express the concern that they expect their clients to have full-fledged panic attacks during exposure, and they worry that they will not know what to do if that happens. In reality, research shows that most clients report only a moderate level of anxiety during exposures (e.g., Grayson, Foa, & Steketee, 1982), which is consistent with the anxiety associated with their anxiety-related disorder that they experience in their daily lives. In other words, the anxiety experienced during exposure is no different than the anxiety that they would be experiencing anyway (Abramowitz et al., 2011). There is, indeed, a small set of anxious clients who report an exacerbation of anxiety following exposure, but it is far from "re-traumatization," it is able to be managed, and it does not predict poor outcome in treatment (Foa, Zoellner, Feeny, Hembree, & Alvarez-Conrad, 2002). In fact, in many ways it can be considered beneficial when clients experience a relatively high level of anxiety during exposure, as it provides much room for them to observe habituation from a habituation framework, and it also allows them to learn that they can tolerate anxiety from an inhibitory learning perspective.

The third concern—that exposure is simply uncomfortable for the therapist—is one on which there is a paucity of data, but one that I encounter frequently in my training and supervision experiences. Some reasons for the discomfort involve concerns about client well-being, as captured above. If you are a person that has the belief that exposure can be harmful to the client, I am hopeful that the discussion to this point has helped to modify that concern. However, perhaps even more common is a concern that is expressed something like, "I just don't think I can do it," usually accompanied by a facial expression suggestive of disgust or a "deer in headlights." In the spirit of not asking our clients to do things that we ourselves would not do, it is important for us, as therapists, to model confidence and tolerance of discomfort during exposure exercises. This very well might mean that we need to reframe our own unhelpful automatic thoughts about exposure exercises and, if necessary, practice ahead of time in order to achieve a sense of confidence and tolerance of discomfort that can be modeled to clients. I often encourage therapists-in-training to approach the implementation of exposure as a behavioral experiment, carefully observing the way in which exposure becomes more natural to implement with clients with repeated practice. Moreover, if you are struggling with a particular anxiety-related disorder yourself, then I encourage you to refrain from taking on clients with that diagnosis until it is successfully treated.

Implementing Exposure

The first step in conducting exposure with clients is to provide a sound rationale for the strategy and ensure that the client is on board. After all, in many instances, clients are facing their worst fears that they have avoided for most of their lives, and the prospect of staying present with that stimulus or in that situation can be daunting. Thus, although the suggestion to provide a sound rationale and ensure that the client is on board is a sound suggestion for the implementation of all cognitive behavioral strategies, I believe that it is especially crucial in maximizing the likelihood of success with exposure. With the sound rationale, clients learn to "invest anxiety now for a calmer future" (Abramowitz et al., 2011).

After clients have agreed to pursue a course of exposure, they work with their therapist to develop a fear hierarchy that will guide the particular exercises in which the client will engage. A *fear hierarchy* is an ordered sequence of feared stimuli and situations, beginning with stimuli and situations that are associated with mild to moderate levels of fear, and moving toward those that are associated with high levels of fear. Clients assign fear ratings (either ranging from 0 to 10, or 0 to 100, with 10 or 100 being the highest level of fear that they can imagine) to each of the items that they identify, and they use those numbers to guide the arrangement of the hierarchy. If you read other CBT texts on exposure, you might see these ratings called SUDs ratings (i.e., *Subjective Units of Discomfort ratings*), a term coined by the late Joseph Wolpe, a behavior therapist whose scholarly and clinical work significantly advanced the practice of exposure in the middle of the twentieth century (Wolpe, 1959). It has been convention for many decades to begin practicing exposure with the lowest rated item on the hierarchy and work toward the highest rated item; indeed, my clinical experience suggests that this approach helps ease clients into exposure and allows them to have success early on, which provides motivation to keep moving forward. However, flexibility is key, as it does not always work that way because clients typically encounter random opportunities to face items that were placed higher on the hierarchy than the items that they are currently practicing. Fortunately, results from at least one study demonstrate that outcome in exposure is *better* when a random order on the hierarchy is followed, rather than when the hierarchy is followed exactly sequentially (Lang & Craske, 2000).

A model of conducting exposure for which I have advocated in the past (Wenzel, 2013) is to conduct and exposure in session, and then encourage the client to implement the same exposure (or something similar to it) every day for homework between sessions. This suggestion comes from the observation that it is easy to fall into the trap of *talking about* doing exposure in session, but not *actually doing* it, which could inadvertently reinforce avoidance behavior in the client. This is true for any CBT intervention, but I view it as being a particularly astute observation for exposure. In addition, many CBT experts recommend an *expanding spaced* schedule of practice to capitalize on the benefits of both massed practice and the partial forgetting and subsequent retrieval that occurs during spaced practice (cf. Bjork & Bjork, 1992; Craske et al., 2008). For example, sessions might begin at a twice weekly rate, then drop back to once weekly, then drop back to once every other week, and then drop back to even less frequent sessions (Abramowitz & Arch, 2014; Abramowitz et al., 2011).

In addition, the inhibitory learning model of exposure that has been advanced in the past decade carries with it several implications for practice (Abramowitz & Arch, 2014; Craske et al., 2008; Craske, Treanor, Conway, & Zbozinek, 2014). Because the empirical literature has not fully supported the notion that clients must remain in the exposure trial until habituation has occurred (that is, until their anxiety ratings have decreased to only a mild level), less emphasis is now placed on tracking anxiety ratings throughout exposure trials, and more emphasis is placed on making "crystal clear" when new learning occurs. Perhaps the most straightforward way for new learning to occur is for clients to violate their previous expectancies during an exposure trial. As is demonstrated in the case example later in the chapter, clients can make estimates of the length of time they believe they can remain in the exposure before something catastrophic happens, and they can then practice the exposure for a time that is longer than their estimate to have a corrective learning experience. In addition, research shows that learning is enhanced when multiple cues are presented in a single learning trial (cf. Craske et al., 2008), such that clients can be presented with two feared stimuli or situations at once (e.g., touching door knobs in a public restroom and simultaneously imagining the contamination of family members). Moreover, research shows that variation in exposure trials is key to achieve a generalization of learning to related contexts (Rowe & Craske, 1998). For example, if you are working with a client with blood/injury/injection phobia who avoids hospitals at all cost, you would have her walk into many different hospitals and clinics, rather than just one, to enhance learning.

Experiential Exercise

Earlier in the chapter, I provided space for you to reflect upon something that you fear or dread and subsequently avoid. At this point in the chapter, I encourage you to apply the principles of exposure to facing that stimulus or situation and overcoming your tendency to avoid. In Table 6.2,

Table 6.2 Your Own Exposure Practice

EXPOSURE EXERCISE	*ANXIETY LEVEL (0 = NO ANXIETY; 10 = THE MOST ANXIETY YOU CAN IMAGINE EXPERIENCING)*

EXPOSURE PRACTICE				
EXPOSURE	*DATE*	*BEGINNING ANXIETY LEVEL*	*PEAK ANXIETY LEVEL*	*ENDING ANXIETY LEVEL*
#1				
#1				
#2				
#2				
#3				
#3				

please write down three manifestations of the feared stimulus or situation that you can practice for exposure. For example, if you identified a fear of making phone calls due to social anxiety, you might include in the table making a phone call that you view as relatively easy (e.g., to a close friend), a phone call that you view as being of moderate level of difficulty (e.g., to a person who you do not know personally, perhaps someone who provides a professional service), and a phone call that you view as being especially difficult (e.g., to a person who might give you some negative feedback). Arrange them in a hierarchical format, from least anxiety-provoking to most anxiety-provoking. Then, across the course of the next several days, practice exposure to these three items on the list. Although there is no "magic number" of times to practice exposure to any one individual stimulus or scenario, for the purpose of this exercise, I ask that you practice exposure at least twice to each item so that you can observe the way in which your anxiety decreases. You will see in the table that there is space for you to record the amount of anxiety that you are experiencing at the beginning of each exposure, the peak anxiety that you experienced during the exposure, and the amount of anxiety that you experienced at the end of the exposure. After completing the exercises, reflect on your experience in the box below.

BOX 11 **REFLECTION ON EXPOSURE PRACTICE**

Describe what you learned from these exposure exercises. To what degree do you believe that you will be able to carry forward the momentum that accumulated from participating in these exposures?

Describe the obstacles that you encountered as you implemented the exposure exercises (e.g., lack of motivation, lack of time). How did you overcome those obstacles?

What did you learn from these exercises that you will apply to your work with your clients?

Case Example

Exposure was not indicated for Marilyn, who was diagnosed with major depressive disorder, recurrent, and who exhibited features of borderline personality disorder. Ashley, however, carried a diagnosis of GAD, and as was seen across these two chapters, she also exhibited social anxiety. Ashley addressed the social anxiety component of her clinical presentation effectively with cognitive restructuring and problem solving, and at the time of her tenth CBT session, she reported decreased anxiety about a "confrontation" happening during her mothers' group, or feeling the need to leave her mothers' group because she did not belong. However, consistent with a GAD clinical presentation, as her social anxiety abated, a new concern arose—a fear of her anxiety, itself. Specifically, Ashley began to attach a great deal of significance to her anxiety, worrying that it meant (a) that she was seriously mentally ill; (b) that it was just going to worsen, to the point that she would be hospitalized long-term as an inpatient; and (c) that her anxiety would become impairing enough that, if she and her husband divorced, he would get full custody of the kids.

This is an example in which cognitive restructuring *can* be indicated, but it is often ineffective because anxious clients have a tendency to become what I call "yeah, but-ers," such that they find tiny loopholes in the logic that is arrived upon when they work with their therapists to reframe their unhelpful thoughts. Recall in Chapter 5 of this volume that I cautioned against "digging heels" in with your client, such that the two of you become entrenched in divergent views of a situation and are trying to convince one another of different conclusions. Typically, a far more effective strategy is for the client to experience, first-hand, evidence that is inconsistent with the negative predictions that he or she is making—this is the behavioral experiment. Fortunately, exposures can be set up as behavioral experiments so that clients can achieve the full benefit of exposure and use that benefit to shift their view of the feared stimulus or situation.

I worked with Ashley to develop a hierarchy of stimuli and situations for exposure, which reflected an interesting combination of in vivo exposure, imaginal exposure, and interoceptive exposure. Table 6.3 summarizes her hierarchy, containing the specific exposure to pursue,

Table 6.3 Ashley's Hierarchy for Exposure

EXPOSURE IDEA	*ANXIETY RATING (0–10)*
Driving past a psychiatric ward	2
Telling myself I'm not sure if and when the anxiety will abate	4
Walking into a hospital	4.25
Reading a story about someone who had to be hospitalized for psychosis	5
Talking to a friend who is struggling about her problems	5.25
Being home overnight with the kids while husband is traveling	5.5
Taking care of the kids after not getting enough sleep	5.75
Driving the kids after not getting enough sleep	6
Putting my head between my legs for 30 seconds and lifting up quickly	6.5
Spinning in a chair for 60 seconds	8
Imagining being in a psychiatric hospital and not knowing when I will get out	8.25
Staring into my own eyes in a mirror for 60 seconds	8.5
Reading a story about someone who had to be hospitalized for anxiety	8.75
Staring into my own eyes in a mirror for 120 seconds	9
Staring into my own eyes in a mirror for 120 seconds and then putting my head in my lap for 30 seconds and lifting quickly	9.5
Reciting a scenario in which my husband says he is seeking custody, and it is unclear what will happen	9.75
Having a panic attack	10

along with the corresponding anxiety rating on a scale of 0 (none) to 10 (most that she could imagine experiencing).

Some items on the hierarchy capture in vivo exercises, such as riding past a psychiatric ward and walking into a hospital. Others reflected imaginal or internal work, such as telling herself that she is unsure if and when the anxiety will abate. Many of the higher items on the hierarchy took on an interoceptive flavor, such that we intentionally brought on symptoms of anxiety to test the idea that she could not take them or would go crazy and need to be taken to the hospital. In the following dialogue, I prepare Ashley to stare into her own eyes in a mirror for 60 seconds, and after she conducts the exercise, I spend some time debriefing with her.

Dr. Amy: What do you predict will happen in this exercise?
Ashley: [appearing hesitant] I don't know. I think I could really lose it.
Dr. Amy: [being mindful of the inhibitory learning framework] How long do you think you can stare at your eyes in the mirror before really losing it?
Ashley: Hmmm, maybe 20 seconds?
Dr. Amy: So, if we do this exercise for 60 seconds, what might you learn?
Ashley: I guess I can learn that I can wishstand more than I think I can.
Dr. Amy: Is it okay to proceed with the exposure exercise?
Ashley: Yes, I guess that is the next step, isn't it?
Dr. Amy: It sure is. On our scale of 0 to 10, where would you place your anxiety right now?
Ashley: Um, I guess at a 7.
[Ashley stood in front of a mirror in my office for 60 seconds, looking at her eyes in the mirror, and taking care not to engage in safety behaviors, such as mental distraction or focusing on a different part of her body.]
Dr. Amy: Sixty seconds is up, Ashley. [Ashley looks away from the mirror and toward me.] How do you feel? Are you losing control?
Ashley: No, it's okay.
Dr. Amy: On or 0 to 10 scale, where is your anxiety now?
Ashley: It's pretty low. Like a 4.
Dr. Amy: What was the highest level that it reached during the exposure? [I refrained from asking Ashley to give me anxiety ratings during the 60-second exposure, so that I would not interrupt her concentration and distract her.]
Ashley: [providing a response that I find to be typical in my clinical practice] I don't think it got any higher than my first rating. The 7.
Dr. Amy: Ah, no higher than a 7. What rating would you typically associate with "losing it"?
Ashley: Oh, a 9 or a 10, definitely. Probably more like a 10. A panic attack.
Dr. Amy: Did you have a panic attack during the exposure?
Ashley: Nope.
Dr. Amy: What do you conclude from this exercise?
Ashley: That it's not so bad. That the anticipation is way worse than the actual experience.
Dr. Amy: I conclude the same thing, Ashley. How does this conclusion apply to the rest of your life?
Ashley: [furrowing her brow] Well, I go way out of my way to avoid uncomfortable physical sensations, because I think they will send me into a tailspin. But maybe that is unnecessary.

Dr. Amy: You could very well be right, Ashley. I have an idea. Would you be willing to practice this very same exposure daily between our sessions to gather information that will show you the applicability of your conclusion in your everyday life?

Ashley: Yes, I can do that. It helps that I had practice here. It gives me confidence that I can do it on my own.

In this example, Ashley demonstrated to herself that she could remain in the exposure much longer than she had predicted without "losing it." On the basis of this success, she was willing to replicate the exposure on her own each day between sessions for homework. However, did you catch something interesting at the end of the dialogue? Ashley mentioned: "It helps that I had practice here. It gives me confidence that I can do it on my own." On the one hand, this dialogue models the principle that I mentioned previously—that it is ideal to conduct exposure in session, and for the client to commit to implement exposure homework between sessions. In this case, I got the sense that Ashley might have been using the in-session practice, itself, as a safety signal, such that if she did not "lose it" in the office with me, it meant that she would not "lose it" when she practiced on her own. I filed away this hypothesis and, at the time of the next session, raised the possibility of doing some exposures on her own *without* the benefit of having done them in my office. Ashley understood the rationale for this suggestion and was, indeed, willing to try this.

In the box below, take this opportunity to reflect upon my work with Ashley. What did you find effective about this work? What surprised you? What might you do differently?

BOX 12 **REFLECTIONS ON EXPOSURE WORK WITH ASHLEY**

What did you find effective about the dialogue describing my exposure work with Ashley?

What did you find surprising about my work with Ashley? What might you do differently?

If Ashley were to return to her next session indicating that she completed her exposure exercises, what might you do next with her?

(continued)

(continued)

If Ashley were to return to her next session indicating that she did not complete her exposure exercises, what might you do next with her?

Did you feel a pull to implement any other interventions at this point in the course of treatment? If so, what intervention did you see as indicated, and how would you implement it?

Tips for Maximizing Effectiveness

Although exposure is a highly efficacious CBT strategy for the treatment of anxiety-related disorders, it is understandable that clients would demonstrate some degree of ambivalence about it, as it involves the prospect of facing their worst fears. I have encountered many instances in which clients, intellectually, believe that exposure is a necessary and even central component of treatment for them, but that, emotionally, they have difficulty mobilizing themselves to engage in it. For clients who express or demonstrate ambivalence about participating in exposure, motivational interviewing can be a useful intervention. *Motivational interviewing* is a style of counseling that allows space for clients to "dig deep" and acknowledge their own reasons for change, rather than complying with treatment simply because they are being told to do so. Therapist who deliver motivational interviewing reinforce clients' language that indicates reasons for change, allowing clients to elaborate on those reasons and decide, for themselves, that those reasons are worth a commitment to the treatment process. Although a full discussion of the principles and techniques of motivational interviewing is beyond the scope of this chapter, interested readers are encouraged to consult motivational interviewing resources (e.g., Miller & Rollnick, 2013) and think critically about how to incorporate them into their cognitive behavioral practice to reduce ambivalence about treatment and enhance a commitment to treatment. Increasingly, clinical trials examining the addition of motivational interviewing with CBT for anxiety-related disorders have demonstrated that it enhances outcome (e.g., Westra, Arkowitz, & Dozois, 2009; cf. Westra, Aviram, & Doell, 2011). I have written previously about this topic as well, suggesting that a motivational interviewing style of therapy is not at all incompatible with CBT and can, in fact, contribute to a strong therapeutic alliance and increase therapist-client collaboration (Wenzel, 2017).

Many therapists wonder whether some exposure exercises are "too much" for clients. According to Abramowitz et al. (2011), the "rule-of-thumb" is that exposure exercises should reflect no more than an everyday level of risk. This being said, it is important that the therapist have an accurate definition of what is meant by an everyday level of risk. For example, in the United States, it is customary for people to wash their hands after using the restroom, and many Americans (therapists include) exhibit a visceral reaction if it is suggested that they not wash their hands after using the restroom. However, in some cultures, this same habit is not customary, and people do not regularly wash their hands after using the restroom. Moreover, there are times when circumstances prevent us from washing our hands after using the restroom. Thus, a sound definition of an "everyday level of risk" is that it is a situation in which people occasionally might inadvertently find themselves.

I also encourage you to be as specific as possible when you are developing exposure exercises with your client. Consider, for example, a client with a driving phobia. If she simply writes "drive" on her hierarchy, it will be unclear how to replicate the exposure on her own. Should she drive during the day or at night? During rush hour or quieter times? During good or bad weather? On a highway or a local road? For one mile or for ten miles? Clients usually find that there are many permutations of a single type of stimulus or situation that is associated with anxiety and avoidance. What might begin as one general exposure, then, can quickly morph into many, many specific exposures (e.g., drive two exits on Interstate 76 at 8am on a weekday; drive two exists on Interstate 76 at 10am on a Sunday, etc). As clients begin to embark on exposure, they see that there are many specific contextual factors that affect their emotional distress. These contextual factors should be factored into the descriptions of exposures so that they can be accounted for and also replicated whenever the client is doing exposure on his or her own.

In addition, a creative use of resources can also help to generalize exposure opportunities toward specific stimuli and situations. YouTube, in particular, is a terrific repository of videos that activate anxiety reactions in clients with anxiety-related disorders. I have used YouTube videos that depicted extreme turbulence on international flights, the climbing of great heights under dangerous circumstances (e.g., portions of pyramids in Central America that were off-limits due to an unstable structure), and injections. Furthermore, the creative use of exposures that involve various sensory experiences can heighten the experience of anxiety in many clients (and, thereby, provide an opportunity that is ripe to show themselves that they can tolerate it). For example, patients with vomit phobia can view images of vomit and people retching; they can create concoctions that smell like vomit; they can listen to sounds of people retching; and they can touch squishy substances that feel like vomit. In one instance, I had "Bertie's Botts Every Flavor Beans" left over from my daughter's Harry Potter-themed birthday party, and a vomit-phobic client ate the vomit-flavored jelly bean.

Finally, it is of critical importance to pay attention to clients' use of safety behaviors. *Safety behaviors* are behaviors, often ritualistic in nature, in which clients engage to reduce their anxiety when they are faced with a feared situation or stimulus. When clients engage in safety behaviors, they attribute the success of the exposure to the fact that they enacted the safety behavior, and they deprive themselves of the opportunity to learn that the aversive outcome is very unlikely to occur, and even more importantly, that they can tolerate their emotional distress. A "classic" example of a safety behavior is when a client with obsessive compulsive disorder (OCD) washes his hands after touching something he views as contaminated with germs. Many mental health professionals automatically diagnose clients with OCD when they observe the presence of safety behaviors. However, clients with many anxiety-related disorders engage in safety behaviors, so it is not limited to those with OCD. Moreover, safety behaviors can take the form of mental rituals, such asrepeating a certain word over and over again, counting, praying, and minimizing. Thus, astute cognitive behavioral therapists are on the lookout for subtle safety behaviors that are maintaining clients' anxiety, and they encourage their clients to participate in exposure exercises without engaging in safety behaviors so that they can have a full corrective learning experience.

Application to a Client

Now you can take the opportunity to implement exposure with one of your own clients. I suggest that you start with a client with a relatively straightforward anxiety disorder, such as a phobia, rather than an anxious client with a complicated clinical presentation, such as multiple anxiety disorders, OCD, or posttraumatic stress disorder (PTSD). Orient your client to exposure, and work with him or her to develop and implement a hierarchy of exposure exercises. Use the following steps as a guide.

1. Explain the rationale for exposure and secure your client's commitment to embark on a course of exposure.
2. (if necessary) Address the client's ambivalence and allow space for the client to contemplate the reasons for participating in exposure.
3. Work with your client to develop a fear hierarchy.
4. Begin with the lowest rated item on the hierarchy, practice in session if you can, obtain pre-, peak-, and post-exposure ratings, and secure the client's commitment to continue practicing the exposure exercise (or variations of it) for homework.
5. When the client returns for the next session, review his or her exposure homework. If he or she did not complete it, discuss obstacles that interfered with homework completion and ways to overcome those obstacles. If the client agrees, repeat the same exposure exercise in session and for homework. If he or she completed the homework, move onto the next item on the hierarchy.
6. Continue in this manner for the next several sessions until the client has completed the items on the hierarchy. Approach this plan in a flexible manner, knowing that new exposure ideas will arise, that opportunities will present themselves for exposure exercises to be completed "out of order," and that clients will have varying levels of success depending on the specific item.
7. In the box below, reflect on your exposure work with your client.

BOX 13 REFLECTIONS ON EXPOSURE WORK WITH YOUR CLIENT

What do you conclude from this experiential exercise? How effective was your exposure intervention?

Was exposure easier or more difficult to implement than you had expected? Why?

Did you notice any of your own hesitations or fears that arose as you were implementing exposure? What were they, and how did you address them?

What, specifically, will you do differently in the future to implement exposure?

How has your view about exposure changed after participating in this experiential exercise?

CHAPTER 7 MINDFULNESS AND ACCEPTANCE

Mindfulness and Acceptance CHAPTER 7

One reason why CBT received so much positive attention as it gained momentum was that clients seemed to achieve a great deal of change in a much shorter time frame than had been typical in psychotherapy. Indeed, cognitive and behavioral change, as well as resulting emotional change, are laudable goals of any psychotherapeutic approach. That being said, the agenda of "change" can sometimes be pushed too hard and too far. Many clients find themselves in difficult circumstances beyond their control, and they would be "beating their head against a wall" if they focused their efforts exclusively on trying to change the situation. Furthermore, an exclusive focus on change can inadvertently communicate to the clients that their emotional distress is intolerable and that they cannot lead the life they want to live if it is present. For these reasons, for more than two decades, many cognitive behavioral researchers and therapists have moved toward the integration of acceptance in CBT, such that a balance is achieved between an emphasis on change and an emphasis on acceptance (e.g., Linehan, 1993). When I first describe CBT to my new clients, I often describe it as a three-legged bar stool, with cognitive change strategies representing one leg of the stool, behavioral change strategies representing a second leg of the bar stool, and acceptance-based strategies representing a third leg of the bar stool (and I even joke that we should rename the treatment approach to CBAT—cognitive-behavioral-acceptance therapy!).

Acceptance is not resignation. It is an empowered response that allows a person to let go of unnecessary struggle and stay present even with aversive physical, emotional, and cognitive experiences. It is the decision not to spend one's energy and resources fighting to change something that is what it is, or to wish it away, and instead living a valued life in spite of sub-optimal circumstances. The ability to accept reflects maturity, wisdom, and far-sightedness.

It is part of human nature for all of us to encounter times in which we feel a tension between change and acceptance. Think of a circumstance in your own life that you find aversive but cannot change. What are the effects of fighting against it or wishing that the situation is different? What could be the effects of acceptance and letting go of the struggle against it?

BOX 1 **REFLECTION ON ACCEPTANCE IN YOUR OWN LIFE**

Think of a circumstance in your own life that you find aversive but cannot change. What are the effects of fighting against it or wishing that the situation is different?

What could be the effects of acceptance and letting go of the struggle against it?

What are some steps that you could take to move toward acceptance?

Have you noticed anyone else in your life who seems especially adept at achieving acceptance? What kinds of aversive experiences has he or she accepted? What effects have you noticed? What can you learn from this person?

Acceptance-Based Constructs and Techniques

Although most of my clients are intrigued by the idea of acceptance, they quickly draw the conclusion that it is "easier said than done." Acceptance is a construct that defies a step-by-step procedure in the same way as we saw with cognitive restructuring, behavioral activation, problem solving, and exposure. Nevertheless, in this section, I present some constructs that are associated with some interventions with which I have had success in facilitating a sense of acceptance in my clients.

Radical Acceptance

Radical acceptance is one of many distress tolerance techniques incorporated into Marsha Linehan's Dialectical Behavior Therapy (DBT; Linehan, 1993, 2015). It is defined as acceptance with one's entire heart, mind, and body. The purpose of the inclusion of the word "radical" is that many of our clients are facing awful life circumstances and are living lives that they would never have wished upon themselves, so (for lack of better words) *it is a big deal* for them to come to a state of acceptance. However, as I alluded to in my introduction to this chapter, it is quite empowering because clients are making an informed choice to let go of the struggle against reality and to learn to be as effective as possible within the parameters of their reality.

Although there is no "formula" for radical acceptance, I encourage my clients to apply the construct in the following manner.

1. Recognize why they are struggling against reality and exerting a great deal of energy (unsuccessfully) to make it something that it is not).
2. Remind themselves of the concept of radical acceptance and think about the way in which it applies to their current situation.
3. Observe the cognitive, emotional, and physiological benefits of radical acceptance. For example, does the client feel "lighter?" "Freer?" less burdened?
4. Invariably, clients will begin to struggle against reality again. Remind them to, once again, take the path of radical acceptance. Linehan (2015) has referred to this technique as *turning the mind*, or choosing radical acceptance over and over, as much as is needed in the situation.

Many of my clients report that the term "radical acceptance" resonates in their mind when they are facing circumstances (external or internal) that they find especially aversive. I tell my clients that they are cultivating an essential life skill when they learn to achieve radical acceptance and let go of the way they wish reality would be different, and they have often told me that they remember that they are doing important work when they choose the path of radical acceptance. In a humorous anecdote, I once had a client miss a session without giving me 24 hours' notice of a cancellation, necessitating that he would have to pay me my full session fee. He left me a message apologizing for the missed session, rescheduling for the following week, and indicating that he was "radically accepting" that he was going to owe me double my price at the time of the next session.

In my clinical experience, I have found that radical acceptance is a sound match for clients like Finn, described earlier in this volume. Recall that Finn was a client in his 50s who had overcome much adversity in his life and thrived on being active and athletic, only to be stymied by an accident that robbed him of the ability to use his legs. At the time at which I saw him in CBT, there was some hope that we would regain limited mobility, but the prognosis was such that he expected not to be able to resume participation in extreme sporting activities, which were his passion. Thus, we applied the concept of radical acceptance to achieve a sense of acceptance about the fact that the accident occurred, as well as its sequelae. Then we applied some advanced cognitive restructuring techniques to redefine his adaptive core beliefs (e.g., shifting from the identify of being a physically strong individual to an individual who is mentally strong and who appreciates nature), as well as behavioral activation and problem solving techniques to cultivate new passions (e.g., drawing and painting, nature photography). At the close of our work together, although he continued to struggle with radical acceptance at times, Finn continued to adopt his mentality of making the most out of life and was actively pursuing artistic endeavors.

Cognitive Defusion

Researchers and practitioners of *acceptance and commitment therapy* (ACT), a psychotherapy that has its roots in CBT and is considered to be in the broad family of CBTs, have advanced an alternative to cognitive restructuring (e.g., Hayes, Strosahl, & Wilson, 2012). Specifically, they have proposed that when we buy into our negative thoughts and take them as fact, we are "fused" with them. However, language is an imperfect representation of reality, and we can "defuse" our thoughts if we recognize that they are simply composed of meaningless words that have no literal value. *Cognitive defusion* is a strategy in which we employ one or more techniques to deliteralize the language that we use to represent our thoughts in order to get distance from them and attach less significance to them. The idea is that there is no need to "fight" with our thoughts to "prove" that they are not true; instead, we can simply recognize that they are "mental noise" of our own social construction and that we can go about living our lives in a valued manner even in their presence.

There are many cognitive defusion techniques; the underlying theme associated with all of them is that they are meant to be delivered in an experimental manner so that people see the arbitrariness (and even the silliness) of language itself. Table 7.1 displays a list of some standard cognitive defusion techniques.

In addition to the relatively straightforward techniques summarized in 7.1, researchers and practitioners of ACT have developed rich metaphors that demonstrate the power that thoughts can hold over us and our ability to carry on in spite of them (Blackledge, 2015; Hayes et al., 2012). For example, in the *passengers on the bus metaphor*, clients are encouraged to imagine that they are a bus driver and that various thoughts are passengers on a bus that get on and off at random times. In the metaphor, the client is encouraged to imagine that some of the passengers become unruly (as do negative thoughts) by shouting insults or throwing garbage at the bus driver. Does the bus driver stop doing his or her job? No, the bus driver will continue driving the route, even if it is unpleasant. Again, the message from this metaphor is that we can all continue to "do our jobs" (i.e., live our lives), even if we are experiencing a barrage of unruly passengers. I recently developed a similar metaphor for my sports fans, likening negative thoughts to a crowd of hostile baseball fans in their home stadium when their team is losing the game. These hostile fans are heckling the visiting closing pitcher, who must strike out batters in order for his team to win the game on the road.

Table 7.1 Cognitive Defusion Techniques

- Insert the phrase, "I'm having the thought that," before stating the thought to recognize that it is only thinking, and not necessarily fact.
- Recognize what life looks like when one is wearing goggles or colored glasses, and acknowledge that language works in the same way to distort reality.
- Repeat the key word in the thought over and over until it sounds strange and carries little, if any, meaning.
- Repeat a thought using very slow speech so that the meaning is lost.
- Repeat a thought using a silly voice so that the meaning is lost.
- Rearrange the words of thoughts (as in a game of Scrabble) so that the meaning is lost.
- Sing a thought, rather than stating the words outright so that the meaning is lost.
- Imagining thoughts as leaves on a stream that gently float away.

Source: Blackledge, J. T. (2015). *Cognitive defusion in practice*. Oakland, CA: New Harbinger Press.

Many therapists-in-training wonder how cognitive defusion is reconciled with cognitive restructuring—after all, isn't cognitive defusion essentially about accepting the presence of our thoughts, whereas cognitive restructuring is essentially about changing our thoughts? I believe this distinction is a bit simplistic, but there is some truth to it. I just encourage you, as you move from being a beginning cognitive behavioral therapist to a cognitive behavioral therapist who has an increasingly sophisticated grasp on the research and practice associated with CBT, to recognize that there is more overlap between the two than there might seem to be at first glance. For example, I believe that the empowered choice to accept a thought is, in itself, a form of an adaptive response that we can arrive upon in cognitive restructuring. Moreover, it is also important to remember that the application of cognitive restructuring does not *necessitate* that a thought be changed into an adaptive response. Rather, it provides a process for evaluating the accuracy and usefulness of thoughts, with one outcome being that after the evaluation, the thought is changed into something more balanced and adaptive.

Figure 7.1 displays a heuristic that I have developed in my clinical practice to guide my application of cognitive restructuring versus cognitive defusion. When a client is expressing a thought for which there is clear evidence against its accuracy, I typically employ cognitive restructuring. For example, at the moment I am working with a young woman with depression who tends to isolate herself from her close friends and family. When she planned to go on the occasional social outing with friends, she reported the automatic thought: "They don't even want me there. My friends hate me." This client had an abundance of evidence to the contrary, such as heartfelt text messages from friends who implored her to join them for social gatherings and expressed how much they enjoyed seeing her. This client was able to examine the evidence, using those text messages as hard "data," and recognize that it was her depression talking,

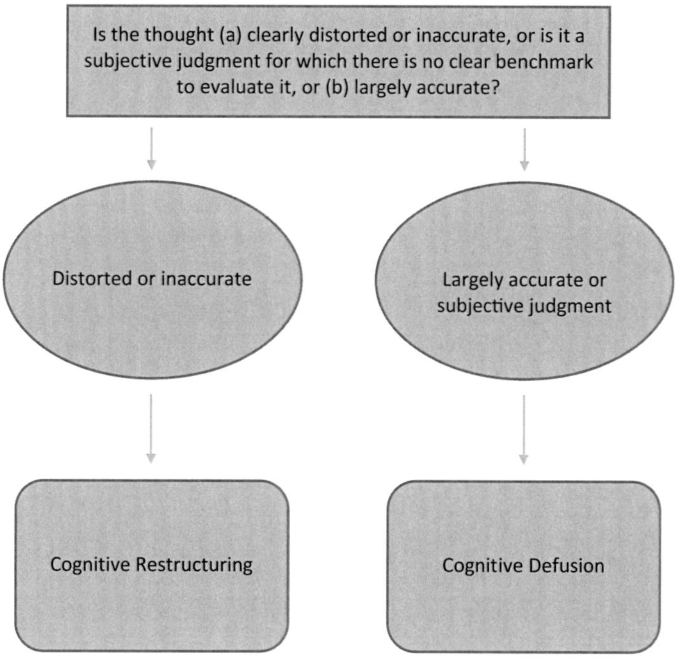

Figure 7.1 Integrating Cognitive Restructuring and Cognitive Defusion

rather than any semblance of truth. When the "data" are readily available to refute a clearly inaccurate thought, cognitive restructuring is a terrific strategy. This is a "real life" example from my clinical practice that, in fact, served as the impetus for the first example included in Table 5.2 of this volume and the discussion in Chapter 5 of this volume about rating the emotional intensity of adaptive responses.

In contrast, other thoughts cannot be so easily evaluated. Many clients present with thoughts tinged with judgment, such as "I'm a failure" or "I'm worthless." Although, obviously, these thoughts are a bit extreme and "all-or-nothing" in nature, there is not really a universal metric by which we can evaluate the degree to which a person is a success or has worth (and, it can be argued from a humanistic perspective, that doing so is riddled with problems from the outset because all human beings inherently have worth). Even in instances in which a person can acknowledge tangible accomplishments and achievements (e.g., graduating from medical school, making a certain amount of money), it is easy to counteract those facts with "yeah buts" (e.g., "Yeah, but I've had three failed marriages") and comparisons with others (e.g., "Yeah, but others in my field make more money than I do"). Other clients present with thoughts that, though negative, are largely factual or do, indeed, characterize reality (e.g., "My next several months will be devoted to supporting my son as he goes through rehab and transitions to a halfway house"). In these cases, I find that cognitive defusion facilitates them in recognizing their thinking, proactively deciding to continue to live their lives according to their values and having enriching experiences even with upsetting thinking still in the background.

Mindfulness Meditation

Mindfulness is defined as "paying attention in a particular way; on purpose, in the present moment, and non-judgmentally" (Kabat-Zinn, 1994; p. 4; see also Kabat-Zinn, 2003). Mindfulness meditation has been practiced by practitioners of Zen Buddhism for over 2,000 years; however, over the past few decades, it has been infused into many aspects of modern medicine for the purpose of stress reduction and to enhance well-being. It is common for mental health providers to incorporate mindfulness meditation into their psychotherapeutic work for these same purposes. In fact, mindfulness meditation is an integral component of many specific approaches within the family of CBTs, including dialectical behavior therapy (DBT) (Linehan, 1993, 2015), ACT (Hayes et al., 2012), emotion regulation therapy for generalized anxiety disorder (Fresco, Mennin, Heimberg, & Ritter, 2013), and mindfulness-based cognitive therapy (MBCT) (Segal, Williams, & Teasdale, 2013). Many contemporary cognitive behavioral therapists readily incorporate mindfulness meditation into their clinical practice.

There is an abundance of scholarly, clinical, and self-help literature on the practice of mindfulness meditation, and interested readers are encouraged to pursue additional reading from this literature to develop a sophisticated understanding of the way in which mindfulness meditation works and specific mindfulness meditation exercises (e.g., Brown, Creswell, & Ryan, 2015). For the purpose of this discussion, I make some general observations about mindfulness. First, I believe that mindfulness meditation exercises provide invaluable practice with acceptance, as the idea is for people who practice mindfulness to stay present with whatever their experience is in the moment, whether it is good or bad. Thus, if clients are practicing mindfulness and are experiencing unhelpful thoughts or aversive emotions, they can learn to experience those thoughts and emotions as they are, refraining from pushing them away or wishing that their experience is different. This practice allows clients to form a different relationship with their unhelpful thoughts and aversive emotions so that they no longer view these unpleasant internal experiences as their adversaries.

Second, mindfulness meditation increases awareness of subtle internal changes that signal a recurrence of a mental health problem (cf. Segal et al., 2013). The more people practice mindfulness, the more they are able to live in a state of awareness, rather than in a state in which they are operating as if they are in "automatic pilot" mode. Not only does living with awareness increase the richness of our experiences, it allows us to detect signs of stress, tension, or distress and to do something effective to deal with them before they overtake us.

Finally, many mindfulness meditations involve a simple focus on the breath. The reason for this is that the breath is always with us, so even in times of chaos and upheaval, we can still rely on our breath to anchor us and focus our attention. This being said, there is no rule that says that a person absolutely must focus on the breath during mindfulness. We can practice mindfulness while engaging in any activity—eating, walking, and even mundane activities, such as brushing our teeth or washing our hair. The idea is to bring an intentional,

Table 7.2 Sample Mindfulness Exercises

NAME OF PRACTICE	*DESCRIPTION*
Raisin exercise	Therapist helps clients to examine various aspects of a raisin (e.g., the way it feels, the way it smells), as if they have never seen a raisin before, in order to demonstrate the extent to which we live our lives in "automatic pilot."
Body scan meditation	Clients lie down and bring gentle awareness to each area of their bodies in turn in order to bring awareness to places in the body where tension is resting.
Mindfulness of the breath	Clients sit for 10 minutes, focusing on their breathing.
Seeing exercise	Clients focus on the elements of the scene (e.g., colors, shapes), rather than thinking about what they are seeing, in order to move toward the "being" mode rather than the "doing" mode.
Three-minute breathing space	Within a three-minute time frame, clients move from bringing awareness of their current experiences (i.e., awareness) to focusing attention on the breath (i.e., gathering) to allowing awareness to expand to the body as a whole (i.e., expanding). This exercise can be paired with an "action step," such that following the three-minute breathing space, they do something pleasurable, that gives them a sense of accomplishment, or in a mindful way.
Mindful stretching	Clients engage in various stretches (e.g., stretch their arms in the air), noticing sensations in the body and their breathing.
Mindfulness of sounds and thoughts	Clients focus attention first on sounds, then on thoughts, allowing themselves to be in the moment completely whatever their experience.
Mindful walking	Clients notice the sensations associated with walking, such as the ways in which their feet touch the ground, the weight of their body in each of their legs, and the emptiness they feel when they lift each leg.

Source: Adapted from Wenzel, A. (2017, p. 146–7). *Innovations in cognitive behavioral therapy: Creative interventions for strategic practice.* New York: Routledge.

present-focused, non-judgmental awareness to whatever we are doing in the moment. Table 7.2 lists some common mindfulness meditation exercises that are incorporated into MBCT, as well as many other mindfulness protocols.

Compassion

According to Neff (2011), *compassion* involves (a) the acknowledgment of suffering; (b) kindness for people who are suffering; (c) a desire to lessen suffering that emerges from that kindness; and (d) the recognition that we all share the human condition, "warts and all." Practitioners who advance acceptance-based approaches encourage their clients to apply these strategies from a compassionate stance, such that clients view their internal experiences in a gentle, curious way and recognize that they are human and therefore imperfect. The compassionate stance certainly suggests that withholding judgment and malice toward others is associated with emotional well-being and adjustment. However, many clients present with an extraordinarily self-deprecating way of chastising themselves (one of my clients calls it "self-flagellating"). These clients can benefit from adopting a stance of self-compassion.

The compassionate stance can serve as a filter through which many of the other acceptance-based techniques in this chapter can be viewed. In fact, many mindfulness meditations incorporate a focus on compassion, my favorite being the befriending meditation that encourages mindfulness practitioners to take a compassionate stance toward family members and friends, people with whom they are struggling, and themselves (https://soundcloud.com/hachetteaudiouk; Retrieved 11 July 2018). A related set of constructs that I use in my clinical practice to foster self-compassion is to encourage clients to face adversity with grace and dignity, carrying themselves with acceptance, self-compassion, and fortitude. I have found that this mindset is particularly helpful for clients who are going through significant health challenges, have been victims of crime, or, more generally, who find themselves in devastating circumstances at no fault of their own.

Experiential Exercise

Before considering the way in which you would apply acceptance-based strategies with your clients, take a moment to first apply these constructs and techniques in your own life. I encourage you to complete two different exercises before proceeding with the remainder of the chapter. First, think of an issue in your own life that presents an ongoing struggle for you—one that evokes a great deal of cognitive and emotional angst; one for which there is no easy solution. It could be the issue that you referenced in Box 1, or it could be a different issue. Over the course of the next week, when you catch yourself struggling with it, practice applying the constructs of (a) radical acceptance, (b) cognitive defusion, and (c) compassion (especially self-compassion). Second, choose one mindfulness exercise, and practice it daily for the next seven days. It can be a mindfulness exercise that you already know, one that you find on your own, or one of the ones described in Table 7.2. If you choose one of the exercises listed in Table 7.2 and think you need more specific instruction, insert the name of the mindfulness meditation in a Google search, and you will see many audio tracks and written instructions that you can follow. In the box below, reflect on your experiences with both exercises.

BOX 2 REFLECTIONS ON ACCEPTANCE AND MINDFULNESS PRACTICE

Describe what you learned from radical acceptance. How easy or difficult was it to apply? How will you carry forward what you learned from it?

Describe what you learned from cognitive defusion. Which specific cognitive defusion technique did you try? How easy or difficult was it to apply? How will you carry forward what you learned from it?

Describe what you learned from compassion. How easy or difficult was it to apply? How will you carry forward what you learned from it?

Describe what you learned from practicing your mindfulness exercise. Which specific mindfulness exercise did you try? How easy or difficult was it to apply and practice across the course of the week? How will you carry forward what you learned from it?

In general, reflect for a moment on the application of acceptance-based strategies in your life, in comparison with the application of change-based strategies in your life. How can you achieve a balance between acceptance and change moving forward? Where does your natural inclination lie?

Case Examples

I incorporated a focus on acceptance into my work with both Ashley and Marilyn, the cases that we have been following in this volume to this point, albeit for different reasons. Consider the application of acceptance and mindfulness strategies in the following dialogues.

Straightforward Case

As might be expected, Ashley was quite successful with the interventions that had been delivered, including cognitive restructuring, exposure, and social problem solving combined with communication skills practice. At the time of her fourteenth session, the anxiety rating that she supplied during the brief mood check had been in the "none to mild" range (i.e., between a "0" and a "3") for three consecutive sessions. She readily incorporated cognitive restructuring into her life on a daily basis; she had practiced most of the items on her fear hierarchy, and she had successfully navigated relationships with mothers in her mothers' group. Regarding the latter point, she began to socialize outside of the group with the two other mothers with whom she felt most aligned, and that confidence allowed her to form connections with other women who had young children outside of the group. Ashley even perceived that her relationship with her husband had improved, despite the fact that it usually was not a topic of discussion during session. She attributed to the fact that she was coping more effectively with her anxiety, thereby needing less reassurance from him, which tended to annoy him. Because Ashley had achieved such significant and sustained gains in CBT, we decided to decrease the frequency of sessions and move toward a focus on relapse prevention (see more about relapse prevention in Chapter 8 of this volume). Using MBCT as a guide, I implemented a focus on mindfulness over the final three sessions. Below is a dialogue that captures our mindfulness work in Ashley's fifteenth session, after she had practiced a mindfulness of the breath exercise for homework.

Ashley: Oh boy, that was harder than I thought it would be. I had really been looking forward to mindfulness because I had heard such great things about it. But I won't lie to you, I started to dread it, because I know I wasn't doing that right.

Dr. Amy: [recognizing an unhelpful thought that was affecting Ashley's view of mindfulness] When you have that idea that you're not doing it right, what happens to your motivation to practice?

Ashley: [laughing] Oh, I know that's an automatic thought. I was able to recognize that this is where my mind goes—always thinking that the problem is me—so I gave myself a break and told myself that I'm still new to this. And I read online that lots of people struggle with mindfulness when they first start.

Dr. Amy: Great reframe, Ashley. So, you were able to practice regularly in between our sessions?

Ashley: Yes, every day except one, when we went on a family day trip out of town.

Dr. Amy: I have an idea. Let's practice Mindfulness of the Breath here, together, and then we can talk about your experience in the context of your practice this past week.

Ashley: Sounds good.

[We listened to a mindfulness of the breath track that I regularly use in my practice: https://mindfulwaythroughanxiety.com/wp-content/uploads/2012/08/Mindfulness-of-Breath.m4a]

Dr. Amy: [allowing Ashley some time to open her eyes and reorient herself to our conversation] Tell me about your experience.

Ashley: My mind always wanders during the exercise. It's so frustrating. I wonder if my mind is just not geared toward mindfulness, because of my generalized anxiety.

Dr. Amy: You mentioned that you read online the other people experienced similar challenges.

Ashley: Well, yes. Mind wandering seemed to be a pretty common experience.

Dr. Amy: What might that tell you?

Ashley: [sighing] I guess that it's normal?

Dr. Amy: Yes, exactly. Is it okay if I share my perspective on this?

Ashley: Definitely!

Dr. Amy: Minds wander. It's what they do. Even people who have practiced mindfulness meditation for years and years notice that their minds wander during practice. There is no need to stop your mind from wandering; in fact, it would probably be fruitless, because everyone's mind wanders. Rather, the trick is to remember to stay present, notice where it goes in a compassionate, non-judgmental way, saying "Oh, there you are mind. Look at where you've gone now." And then gently bringing it back to the focus on the breath. In this way, I look at mindfulness much more as a process, kind of mimicking an orbit going around Planet Breath, as opposed to a laser-sharp focus on the breath that leaves no room for mind wandering.

Ashley: [looking thoughtful] Hmmm. So, you're saying that I'm doing mindfulness even if my mind wanders? Like if I stick with it and refocus, I'm doing mindfulness?

Dr. Amy: [smiling] Yes, you are, Ashley. In fact, I would go so far as to say that you are engaging in important practice even if you don't immediately refocus your mind. The intentional, non-judgment mental *process* of mindfulness is what is central here, rather than the *outcome* of a sole focus on the breath.

This dialogue illustrates a common phenomenon often seen in clinical practice—that mindfulness meditation is experienced as more difficult than was expected, and clients conclude that they have failed. I applied cognitive restructuring the first time that Ashley mentioned this in order to reinforce the skill that she had already acquired. However, I mainly focused on acceptance of the fact that her mind wandered, a non-judgmental stance about her mind wandering, and shifting her focus from one on outcome to one on process. In addition, notice in the dialogue that we took the time to experience the mindfulness meditation together in session. This example reinforces a point I made earlier in the volume—that it is important to conduct experiential exercises in session, rather than just talking "about" doing the exercises and asking clients to do them for homework. This strategy allowed Ashley to experience her mind wandering right there with me and reflect on this experience in a way that was fresh and present-focused, rather than retrospectively in nature.

In the box below, take this opportunity to reflect upon my mindfulness work with Ashley. What did you find effective about this work? What surprised you? What might you do differently?

BOX 3 REFLECTIONS ON MINDFULNESS WORK WITH ASHLEY

What did you find effective about the dialogue describing my mindfulness work with Ashley?

What did you find surprising about my work with Ashley? What might you do differently?

What other acceptance-based strategies do you see as relevant to incorporate with Ashley? Why?

Think about the balance between cognitive restructuring and acceptance-based work in this dialogue. Did you think that balance was effective? What might you do differently?

What intervention might you implement next with Ashley?

Difficult Case

By the sixteenth session of CBT, there were many ways in which Marilyn had made substantial progress. I viewed it as a victory that she did not drop out of therapy and that she attended sessions on a regular basis (although at one point, she left me a message saying that she did not think CBT was "right" for her, only to call me back four days later to indicate that she was having a bad day and wanted to keep her next session). After a period of time in which she was a bit guarded against my optimism and genuine positive affinity toward her, she "softened" and began to acknowledge that she knew I was "on her side." Thus, I viewed our therapeutic relationship favorably and recognized that it was likely a central reason why her course of treatment was going fairly well. In addition, Marilyn was able to implement some of the techniques that she practiced in session, such as rudimentary cognitive restructuring, effective communication skills, and longer-term problem solving to go back to school for graphic design.

Despite these gains, Marilyn's first reaction was continued to be one such that she rejected psychoeducation and the introduction of various CBT strategies when they were first presented to her, claiming that a previous therapist had tried them with her in the past and that they did not work, or that my suggestion implied that she was living her life "wrong" and that everything she does is wrong. She also continued to be very hard on herself and made many self-deprecating statements about not being good enough or as failing. Thus, I implemented the principles of cognitive defusion with her, as illustrated in the following dialogue.

Marilyn: [demonstrating some insight] I know that I probably sound bad, like I'm just rejecting what you are saying outright. But I can't help it! It's just how I feel!

Dr. Amy: Then it's my job to take what you are giving me, Marilyn, and to work together with you to dig deep and be creative, so that we can help you form a different relationship with these thoughts.

Marilyn: [rolling her eyes] A different relationship? What do you mean?

Dr. Amy: Well, I've taught you some skills for evaluating and responding to your thinking, and I think it has been helpful in some instances, and in other instances it just didn't ring true, yes?

Marilyn: Yes, you're right there.

Dr. Amy: What if, instead, we shifted focus away from trying to soften—essentially change—your thinking, and instead you were able to recognize that your thoughts are just thoughts, just background noise, and that you can still live your life the way you want to live even if they are present?

Marilyn: How in the world can I do that? I'm over 50 years old. I'd think that if I had the ability to do that, I'd have already figured it out.

Dr. Amy: I might beg to differ, Marilyn. You see, it's human nature to be tied to language. After all, the use of language is what makes us uniquely human. But something funny has happened with language. We take it so *literally*. But, really, it is not literal at all. It's an approximately, maybe even a social construction, rather than reality.

Marilyn: [looking confused] Huh? You lost me.

Dr. Amy: [smiling] Let me give you an example. For us here in the Philadelphia area, snow is snow is snow, right?

Marilyn: [hesitating] Well . . . yeah.

Dr. Amy: But Eskimos, who obviously live much more of their lives in the snow, have over 50 words for the word snow. One word for snow actually means "slightly falling snow," and another word for snow actually means "snow that is good for sledding." So, if we were to simply call snow "snow" to an Eskimo, that person wouldn't understand what, exactly, we were referring to.

Marilyn: That's actually kind of interesting. Because I bet the Eskimo would react differently depending on the type of show that was being referred to.

Dr. Amy: Exactly. And another thing that I find interesting is that Eskimos are used to, and probably even live their lives around these nuances, but we couldn't care less, because we have not lived our lives around them. So, what does this tell you about some of the language that you use to describe yourself?

Marilyn: Okay, I see where you are going. That the language I use depends on my culture, and it's kind of subjective.

Dr. Amy: Yes! Exactly! So, what if we recognized that those thoughts are a product of imperfect language, that they do not necessarily reflect fact? Kind of in the same way that the word "snow" would be meaningless to an Eskimo living up north?

Marilyn: It's an interesting concept. I don't want to just reject everything you say. I truly don't. But I don't know . . .

Dr. Amy: Would you be willing to try an experiment, Marilyn?

Marilyn: Okay, I guess.

Dr. Amy: I'd like you to say the word "milk" over and over again until I tell you to stop. I know it might sound odd, but just go with it. And after I say stop, we'll talk about what you experienced. [Marilyn says "milk" over and over the 30 seconds.]

Dr. Amy: Tell me what you got from that exercise.

Marilyn: After awhile, it didn't even seem like I was saying a word. It seemed like it was just a bunch of garbled sounds!

Dr. Amy: Exactly. Some of my clients tell me that at first they can picture a glass of milk or something like that, but then the word loses all of its meaning.

Marilyn: Yes! It did that for me too!

Dr. Amy: Can we try now with a different word? [Marilyn nods] How about the word failure?

Marilyn: Oooo, okay, that will be more challenging, to say the least. [Marilyn says "failure" over and over for 30 seconds.]

Dr. Amy: What happened this time?

Marilyn: The same thing happened. It was a bunch of sounds. Or like two types of intonation—more emphasis on the first syllable, and less emphasis on the second syllable.

Dr. Amy: How can the results of these experiments apply to your life, more generally?

Marilyn: [looking thoughtful] I think that trying to change the belief of being a failure doesn't work for me. It's engrained, and it probably always will be. But if I can sort of detach myself from it . . . I don't know, maybe it won't torment me so much.

Dr. Amy: If you weren't tormented so much by that failure belief, what would you be doing differently?

Marilyn: Probably lots of things. Standing up for myself at work without doubting myself and thinking that I'm in the wrong. Going after that graphic arts certificate. Maybe even putting me out there with my friends, suggesting that we go to new restaurants. Travel. Things like that.

Dr. Amy: You mean doing the things that are important to you? That you value?

Marilyn: [appearing as if she has had an epiphany] Yeah, exactly.

Here is another example of my suggestion to conduct the exercise in session in an experiential manner so that the client can have a powerful experience and reflect upon the way that experience can apply to his or her life. Marilyn was not fully "buying into" cognitive restructuring with regard to her self-deprecating thoughts and beliefs, but the cognitive defusion psychoeducation and experiential exercises seemed to "loosen up" the hold those beliefs had on her. Moreover, notice my reference to values at the end of the dialogue. Many cognitive behavioral therapeutic approaches, such as ACT and behavioral activation, place a special emphasis on clarifying and acting according to our values. The goal is to teach clients that they can live out their values, being true to themselves, in spite of the mental noise that can come along with mental health disorders.

In the box below, take this opportunity to reflect upon my cognitive defusion work with Marilyn. What did you find effective about this work? What surprised you? What might you do differently?

BOX 4 **REFLECTIONS ON COGNITIVE DEFUSION WORK WITH MARILYN**

What did you find effective about the dialogue describing my mindfulness work with Marilyn?

What did you find surprising about my work with Marilyn? What might you do differently?

What other acceptance-based strategies do you see as relevant to incorporate with Marilyn? Why?

The difficulty with which Marilyn poses in session seems to have decreased to some degree in these later sessions of CBT. Why do you think this is? Did you expect this?

What intervention might you implement next with Marilyn?

Tips for Maximizing Effectiveness

On a personal note, I have found that acceptance-based strategies have significantly enhanced my cognitive behavioral practice. The balance between acceptance and change is one that forms the basis of one highly-researched type of CBT (i.e., DBT; Linehan, 1993), and my clinical experience is that it is one to which clients readily respond when (a) the rationale for both approaches are described; (b) a compelling example of the application of both approaches is given; and (c) the therapist demonstrates the way in which both approaches can be used synergistically and in a way in which they support one another, rather than in a way in which they work in opposition or confuse the client. Clients tend to take a holistic view of their internal experiences when they learn both approaches, realizing that the backdrop of acceptance is often a foundation, and that the techniques of change can facilitate immense relief when they are applied in relevant situations. In this section, I include three important tips to maximize the effectiveness of acceptance-based strategies.

First, some clients apply acceptance-based strategies, particularly various mindfulness meditation exercises, as a way to "feel better" or to "relax." Although many people do, indeed, feel better or more relaxed when they practice mindfulness or other acceptance-based strategies, implementing the exercise in pursuit of that goal is inconsistent with the basic premise of these strategies because they are trying to change their internal state. In contrast, clients who apply these strategies are taught that they might feel better or more relaxed, or they might not, and it is okay either way. The point is that they are being present and accepting of their experience, whatever their experience is—feeling good, or not feeling good. I point out to my clients that the quest to feel better can ultimately present a paradox—the more we focus on it, and the more we enact various strategies to achieve this goal, the more it can elude us. For this reason, I encourage my clients to take a "process" orientation to mindfulness rather than an "outcome" orientation, such that they ultimately savor the fact that they are practicing a present-focused, mindful lifestyle, rather than achieving any sort of outcome. Indeed, this was the insight achieved by my client, "Matthew," whom I described as a CBT success in Chapter 1 of this volume.

Second, I encourage therapists to refrain from simply "throwing in" a mindfulness or acceptance-based strategy at whim because it seems right in the moment. Acceptance and mindfulness are lifestyle choices, and as such, the application of acceptance-based strategies should be done in a thoughtful, systematic manner. In MBCT, for example, clients are encouraged to engage in oftentimes an hour of systematic practice, look for opportunities to practice mindfulness during everyday activities in their lives, and, at the end of the course of treatment, commit to living a mindful lifestyle. Thus, I encourage therapists-in-training not to view mindfulness as a technique that clients choose to reduce anxiety or stress, but rather, as a lifestyle choice that facilitates acceptance and the thoughtful, effective application of other cognitive behavioral strategies that they have learned.

Finally, many clients believe that they must have optimal conditions to practice mindfulness, such as a quiet environment. I encourage my clients to practice mindfulness in *any* environment, and that it can be *particularly* enlightening to practice it in non-optimal circumstances, such as those in which there is a lot of noise or interruption. I think back to a story I heard about an avid practitioner of meditation who was very much looking forward to a weekend meditation retreat. Unfortunately, weekend construction was occurring at the next-door building, making for a noisy environment that he saw as being distracting and as taking away from his meditation experience. Throughout the weekend, he learned to accept the noise from the construction, and eventually, he became grateful for it. By the end of the weekend, he concluded that he had gotten more out of this retreat than out of any other one because he learned an important lesson—that mindfulness and acceptance applied to *any* circumstances, not just those that we view as "conducive" to facilitating them, and that mindfulness meditation, itself, helped him to achieve acceptance of his disappointment and anger that construction was going on next door to his retreat.

Application to a Client

It is time, now, for you to implement an acceptance-based strategy with one of your clients. Think of a client who struggles with many upsetting internal experiences despite the seemingly effective application of traditional cognitive behavioral strategies, such as cognitive restructuring, behavioral application, problem solving, or exposure. Observe the "feel" of the intervention, relative to the ones presented in the volume thus far that are more change-based. Use the following steps as a guide.

1. Select one or more acceptance-based strategies that would address key aspects of your client's case formulation.
2. Describe the rationale for the intervention with your client.
3. Practice the intervention, experientially, in session.
4. Work with your client to devise a way for him or her to continue to implement the strategy(ies) for homework between sessions.
5. When the client returns for the next session, discuss the way in which he or she applied the strategy(ies) in his or her life and the important conclusions or insights that were drawn.
6. Discuss with you client the way in which the strategy(ies) can be generalized to his or her life.
7. In the box below, reflect on your acceptance-based work with your client.

BOX 5 **REFLECTIONS ON ACCEPTANCE-BASED WORK WITH YOUR CLIENT**

What do you conclude from this experiential exercise? How effective was your acceptance-based intervention?

Was the acceptance-based intervention easier or more difficult to implement than you had expected? Why?

What, specifically, will you do differently in the future to implement acceptance-based interventions?

How has your view about exposure changed after participating in this experiential exercise?

CHAPTER 8 RELAPSE PREVENTION AND THE COMPLETION OF TREATMENT

Relapse Prevention and the Completion of Treatment

CHAPTER 8

CBT is a psychotherapy for which there is meant to be a definite end. The goal is for clients to become their own cognitive behavioral therapists; in fact, I often say jokingly that cognitive behavioral therapists want to put themselves out of business, because they want clients to learn the principles, strategies, and tools of CBT and no longer need the regular help of a therapist to guide them! Cognitive behavioral therapists observe that some of the greatest change occurs *after* clients have completed treatment, demonstrating the power of allowing clients space to consolidate and apply their new learning in their own way in their own lives. Empirical research confirms that CBT has enduring effects, much more so than an alternative treatment approach, such as pharmacotherapy (e.g., Hollon et al., 2005).

Remember what I said in Chapter 1 of this volume—you need not be tied to a specific number of sessions unless you are following a very specific treatment protocol, or if there are outside forces (such as an insurance or a company policy) that specifies a maximum number of sessions with clients. How, then, do you know when clients are ready to move toward the completion of treatment? Table 8.1 includes some guidelines to inform your clinical judgment.

There is no hard-and-fast rule that specifies exactly when you move toward the completion of treatment. For this reason, I give the suggestion in the first row of Table 8.1 that the client scores in no more than the mild range in symptoms for three consecutive sessions. However,

Table 8.1 Indicators that Clients Can Move Toward the Completion of Treatment

- Client is scoring in no more than the mild range of emotional distress or other symptoms on brief mood check ratings or scores on self-report inventories for a number of consecutive sessions (e.g., 3 sessions).
- Client has met the goals set in the early phase of treatment.
- Client has regularly completed homework and has successfully implemented cognitive and behavioral tools in his or her life.
- Sessions have a "feel" of being less focused or more chatty.
- Client expresses a desire to taper or discontinue sessions.

it very well could be the case that you are working hard toward achieving a treatment goal and that there might be more than three consecutive sessions in which the client is scoring low on mood ratings; in this case, it is still indicated for the client to continue with regular sessions. You might simply have a subjective sense that sessions have become "looser"—less focused, more "chatty," and less driven by the case formulation and clinical strategy. If you notice this happening in session, you can make the observation and ask the client if it is okay to put discussion of treatment progress on the agenda, at which time you very well might determine that the goals of CBT have largely been met and that you can move toward the completion of treatment. Regardless of the metric that you use to determine the timing of treatment completion, the most important principles to keep in mind are that (a) the client knows from the beginning of the course of treatment that there will eventually be an end; and (b) the decision of when to end treatment is a collaborative one between you and the client, rather than one that is sprung on the client unexpectedly.

In this short final chapter of the volume, I provide some guidelines for the major activity that occurs in the late phase of CBT—relapse prevention—as well as approaches to tapering sessions and ending treatment. In addition, I summarize the ultimate outcome in treatment and the way in which treatment ended for the main cases that we have followed throughout the volume—Ashley and Marilyn. I end the chapter with space for you to reflect on your own learning and decide upon the next steps you will take to refine your skills as a cognitive behavioral therapist.

Relapse Prevention

Relapse prevention is a strategy in which clients think ahead to signs that they are experiencing another episode of their mental health disorder and ways to, proactively, apply the CBT principles and strategies that they have learned. Worksheet 8.1 is an example of a Relapse Prevention Plan that I use with my clients. Notice the question in the first row—how do I know that I am at risk for a relapse or a recurrence? Although it is not essentially for clients to grasp the finer points of this difference, I define these terms here because you will encounter them in the empirical literature. A *relapse* occurs when a client experiences an exacerbation of symptoms of the current episode of his or her mental health disorder, whereas a *recurrence* occurs when the initial episode of the mental health disorder has remitted, and there is an onset of a new episode. The principles of relapse prevention apply to both a relapse and a recurrence of symptoms.

Worksheet 8.1

Relapse Prevention Plan

MY RELAPSE PREVENTION PLAN
How do I know that I am at risk for a relapse or a recurrence?
How can I cope with these risks?
Who can I reach out to for help?
When should I contact a professional?
Professional contacts:

The other parts of the Relapse Prevention Plan allow clients to consolidate their resources. What were the most effective CBT tools they learned that can help when they are at risk of a relapse or a recurrence? Sometimes, my clients will create a "Top 5" or a "Top 10" list in this space. Who can they turn to for help or support? In this section, they can list people they feel comfortable sharing with that they are struggling, as well as people with whom they might not share such intimate details about themselves, but who, nevertheless, serve as a source of social support and comfort. When is additional professional help warranted? It is helpful for therapists and their clients to have a discussion in which clients define the threshold at which they would resume sessions. I also strongly encourage clients to write down not only the names of professionals who can be of help, but also those professionals' contact information, so that such contact information is readily available. After clients have completed the Relapse Prevention Plan, I also talk with them about where they will keep the worksheet and how they will remember to use it as needed.

Ending Treatment

Treatment does not usually end abruptly; more typically, clients taper from attending more frequent sessions (e.g., once a week) to less frequent sessions (e.g., scheduling a session or two with two weeks in-between, then scheduling a session for one month later). After treatment has ended, it is common to have a "booster session" a few months later, with the idea that clients will return for a "check-in" to describe the way in which they generalized CBT principles and strategies to their lives without the aid of a therapist. Many clients look forward to booster sessions as a way to revel in their progress and share their success stories with their therapist, with whom they have developed a close, supportive relationship. There is no standard "rule-of-thumb" for the schedule of tapering sessions, or for the specific amount of time that will have passed before scheduling a booster session. The decision is made collaboratively between the therapist and client on the basis of the client's needs and preferences and the therapist's clinical judgment.

In addition to the focus on relapse prevention, in the last sessions before the completion of treatment, cognitive behavioral therapists typically discuss clients' reflections on the course of treatment and their reactions to the end of treatment. Any unhelpful automatic thoughts about the ending of treatment can be addressed using the same strategies that have been practiced throughout the course of treatment (e.g., cognitive restructuring, cognitive defusion). Although this is a matter of personal style, I typically share my own thoughts about the ending of treatment, such as the gratification I experienced as I witnessed the client achieve personal growth and what I, myself, learned from working with the client. I also typically invite clients to share CBT "success stories" with me, or times in which they implemented what they had learned in treatment to resolve a problem that emerged in their lives or manage emotional distress.

Unless contraindicated clinically, I typically invite clients to return for sessions if they detect a relapse or recurrence. A return to treatment does not at all signify a "treatment failure;" in fact, cognitive behavioral therapists view the return to treatment in a positive light because it means that clients (a) recognized signs of relapse or recurrence; (b) they are doing something skillful to address the signs of relapse or recurrence; and (c) they valued their original course of CBT. Most clients find that they need not resume a full course of CBT; rather, that a few sessions that serve as a "tune-up" are all that are necessary.

Case Examples

In this section, I describe the way in which treatment ended with both of the cases followed in this volume. The actual clients that form the basis for these case descriptions continue to attend twice-yearly medication check-ups with their psychiatrist, is a close colleague of mine who practices in the same building, and gives me updates when she sees them. Moreover, as you will see in this section, Marilyn sometimes schedules booster sessions with me to check in when she is in the building to see my psychiatrist colleague.

Straightforward Case

Ashley attended a total of 22 CBT sessions. Her self-reported anxiety level was in the mild range for the last six sessions of treatment. As has been noted throughout the course of this volume, Ashley was diligent about completing her homework. Toward the end of the course of treatment, she had little to share for homework because her anxiety had decreased to such an extent that she had few instances to which she could apply CBT tools and strategies. On the basis of her mood ratings, the observation that she had much less "work" to bring to the agenda of each session, and the fact that she had met her treatment goals (perhaps save for a full resolution of her marital difficulties), we collaboratively decided to move toward the completion of treatment. The following dialogue is an excerpt of our conversation that occurred in our last session.

Dr. Amy: Could you take a moment to reflect on the course of our CBT work together, Ashley? I'm curious what you found the most helpful, as well as whether there was any aspect of our work that you would have liked to have been different.

Ashley: Sure, I've been thinking about this a lot. All of it was helpful, really. I know I have a tendency to catastrophize, so the reframing of my anxious thoughts is something that I do naturally now. And I would have never guessed I would have ever tried some of the things that I did through the exposures. They were hard, but they were worth it, because I'm living my life much differently now.

Dr. Amy: That's terrific to hear, Ashley.

Ashley: Oh, and I'm trying to make the commitment to do a mindful breathing exercise every morning before the kids wake up. Sometimes it doesn't happen, but I'm really trying to do this on a regular basis.

Dr. Amy: I like what you are saying, Ashley, that you're incorporating what you learned from CBT into the way in which you live your life.

Ashley: I think I have to. I don't want to live my life the way I was living it before.

Dr. Amy: Is there anything about therapy that you wish had been different?

Ashley: No, not at all. This was a perfect match for me. And you always checked in with me, so I know if I actually did have an issue, that you would have listened to me and not just dismissed it.

Dr. Amy: That's wonderful feedback, Ashley. I have to say that it has been so gratifying to work with you. You committed to your CBT homework in such an impressive way, and it is clear that you are reaping the benefits from it. It's great to hear you talk about the people from your mothers' group whom you now consider friends and the new experiences that you are pursuing. I'll certainly miss having our regular sessions. Please know that I truly enjoy hearing updates from my former clients describing the way in which they are using CBT in their lives, and that my door is always open if you need a refresher.

Ashley: That's reassuring to hear, actually. I was kind of nervous about ending treatment, but I know it is the right thing. I'm a lot stronger now. I've never quite had this feeling before—that nothing can stop me now!

Ashley sent me two email updates over the ensuing months, and in one of which, she indicated that one of her friends in her mothers' group disclosed having significant problems with anxiety to her, and Ashley not only educated her about CBT, but shared some of her tools and resources. The updates that I receive from my colleague, Ashley's psychiatrist, are that Ashley is on a low maintenance dose of a selective serotonin reuptake inhibitor and that she has reported no recurrence of symptoms for the past several years.

Difficult Case

Marilyn has seen me for a total of 30 CBT sessions, requesting that I leave her case "open" so that she can attend occasional booster sessions that are coordinated with her visit to my building to see her psychiatrist. Around the time of her 18th session (soon after I had implemented cognitive defusion with her, to which she responded quite well), many aspects of her life began to improve dramatically and all at once. Conflict with her co-workers seemed to decrease, and she was asked to play an important role in some special projects at the botanical garden at which she worked (e.g., the editing of a book of images of rare trees that were growing at the garden). Marilyn was gratified by these turns of events, perceiving that she was "finally" being recognized for all that she had dedicated to her job. In fact, obtaining her graphic design certificate was less important to her than it once was earlier in treatment because she was garnering much more gratification from her job. In addition, a new skating coach began to teach classes at the skating rink, and the two of them developed a budding romance. Unlike previous relationships, in which Marilyn claimed that she never knew what she had the "right" to say or think, she approached this relationship with openness, balance, and confidence. This man had three children, one in high school of whom he had custody, and Marilyn truly appreciated and handled well her emerging role as a "step-mother" of sorts.

As stated previously, I continue to see the client on whom Marilyn's case is based once or twice a year when she is in to visit her psychiatrist. We mainly focus on "tweeking" adaptive lifestyle changes she made throughout the course of CBT, such as making behavioral changes so that she can get more benefit out of her exercise routine, or negotiating minor conflicts that emerge now that she is living with her partner. However, her depression ratings have consistently remained in the range of "none" to "mild" for over three years, which has caused her to remark that she "never would have believed it" at the start of CBT. My colleague, her psychiatrist, has also commented that Marilyn seems like a much different person than she was when she scheduled her first psychiatric appointment—more centered, less bitter, and able to enjoy life and experience gratitude to a much greater degree.

Rather than ending my discussion of Marilyn with a dialogue, allow me to share one of the most touching moments of my career that emerged from my work with her. One afternoon, I walked into my waiting room and saw a package waiting for me. Inside the package was a signed copy of the book that Marilyn had edited for the botanical garden, along with a beautiful card. I have paraphrased her words in the card for the purpose of this volume, but it read something like this:

Dear Dr. Amy,

I knew how much you would appreciate this book, both because you are a prolific author and because you have been with me through thick and thin. You never gave up on me. I can't tell you what that means to me. My work with you has made such a difference. There is no way that I can thank you for the gifts you have given me.

Fondly, Marilyn

PS – I'M ENGAGED!

Your Own Growth as a Cognitive Behavioral Therapist: Past and Present

In Chapter 1 of this volume, I gave you a pre-test in which you assessed your "baseline" CBT knowledge and skill. Here, I would like you to retake this test and compare your results to the results of your pre-test.

Table 8.2 Post-Test: Self-Assessment of CBT Skills

Please use the following scale to rate your perceived ability to deliver aspects of CBT.
0 = Not At All (0%)
1 = A Little (25%)
2 = Somewhat (50%)
3 = A Good Deal (75%)
4 = Extremely (100%)

1.	I have a sound understanding of the fundamental tenets of CBT.	0 1 2 3 4
2.	I have a sound understanding of cognitive behavioral theory.	0 1 2 3 4
3.	I am confident in my ability to develop a case formulation and treatment plan with clients.	0 1 2 3 4
4.	I have a sound understanding of the fundamentals of the therapeutic relationship in CBT.	0 1 2 3 4
5.	I am confident that I can cultivate a strong therapeutic relationship while simultaneously implementing CBT structure and strategy.	0 1 2 3 4
6.	I have a sound understanding of CBT session structure.	0 1 2 3 4
7.	I am confident in my ability to implement CBT session structure.	0 1 2 3 4
8.	I have a sound understanding of ways to implement cognitive restructuring with clients.	0 1 2 3 4
9.	I am confident in my ability to implement cognitive restructuring with clients.	0 1 2 3 4
10.	I have a sound understanding of ways to implement behavioral activation with clients.	0 1 2 3 4
11.	I am confident in my ability to implement behavioral activation with clients.	0 1 2 3 4
12.	I have a sound understanding of ways to implement problem solving with clients.	0 1 2 3 4
13.	I am confident in my ability to implement problem solving with clients.	0 1 2 3 4
14.	I have a sound understanding of ways to implement exposure with clients.	0 1 2 3 4
15.	I am confident in my ability to implement exposure with clients.	0 1 2 3 4
16.	I have a sound understanding of ways to implement mindfulness and acceptance skills with clients.	0 1 2 3 4
17.	I am confident in my ability to implement mindfulness and acceptance skills with clients.	0 1 2 3 4
18.	I have a sound understanding of ways to implement relapse prevention with clients.	0 1 2 3 4
19.	I am confident that I can implement relapse prevention with clients.	0 1 2 3 4

What do you observe? In what areas have your understanding of the principles and confidence in your ability to implement interventions significantly increased? Were there any areas in which your ratings did not appreciably change from the pre-test to this post-test? If that is the case, it is okay. As I describe later in this chapter, all cognitive behavioral therapists—even the experts—are constantly learning and refining their clinical practice.

Just as it is important for our clients to commit to a lifelong practice of adaptive cognitive and behavioral tools, as demonstrated earlier in the section on relapse prevention, I encourage you to think about ways you can incorporate the principles and strategies described in this volume into your clinical practice and can continue to grow as a cognitive behavioral therapist. The emerging line of scholarship on the teaching and supervision of CBT suggests that the principles and strategies in CBT are best optimized and retained when a therapist participates in ongoing training and supervision, rather than reading a single book or taking a single workshop (Sudak et al., 2016). In the box below, I encourage you to reflect on the ways in which you have grown as a cognitive behavioral therapist by reading this book, applying the principles and tools in your own life, and practicing them with a client. Moreover, I encourage you to consider ways in which you will apply CBT to your clinical practice and commit to ongoing professional development.

BOX 1 REFLECTIONS ON YOUR GROWTH AS A COGNITIVE BEHAVIORAL THERAPIST

Here, I ask you to answer the same two questions that I posed in Chapter 1 of this volume. After reading this volume, what about CBT do you find attractive?

After reading this volume, what aspects of CBT concern you?

How have you grown as a cognitive behavioral therapist after reading this volume?

In what specific ways will you apply what you have learned by reading the volume to your clinical practice?

Please do not be discouraged if you view yourself as having much room for continued growth. I, myself, am constantly adjusting my CBT practice, as well as my thinking about CBT, on the basis of feedback from clients, new findings in the scientific literature, and intellectually stimulating and clinically meaningful conversations with colleagues. My lectures and trainings on CBT look very different today than they did even just three years ago. My clinical practice looks different today than it even did six months ago!

Licensed mental health professionals need a certain number of continuing education hours to maintain their licenses to practice. This means that therapists are expected to continue to educate themselves about new developments and current happenings in the field in order to give their clients the best care possible. There are many ways in which you can continue your training to grow as a cognitive behavioral therapist, including:

- Reading additional CBT books
- Viewing CBT video demonstrations
- Attending CBT workshops
- Seeking intensive supervision with a CBT trainer-supervisor
- Participating in peer supervision, in which CBT cases are discussed
- Joining a CBT professional society

What steps will you take to continue to grow as a cognitive behavioral therapist? In Table 8.3, list three courses of action you can take, including the specific nature of that course of action (e.g., the name of the book you will read next) and the time frame to which you will commit

Table 8.3 Your Growth as a Cognitive Behavioral Therapist

In the space below, please identify three ways you can continue to grow as a cognitive behavioral therapist. Specify the type of activity you will pursue, a specific target for that activity, and the time frame in which you will commit to completing the activity. Use the sample entry as a guide.

Take a CBT workshop.	*The Core I training on CBT for Depression and Suicidality offered by the Beck Institute for Cognitive Behavior Therapy*	*By the end of the year*
1.		
2.		
3.		

to pursuing this next step. Please note that you are not limited to the options I listed in this paragraph, as you very well might have other ideas, or access to unique training opportunities.

There are countless books and training opportunities to grow as a cognitive behavioral therapist. One source that deserves special mention is the Beck Institute for Cognitive Behavior Therapy, a non-profit institution in the Philadelphia suburbs that was founded by Drs. Aaron T. Beck and his daughter, Judith S. Beck. The Beck Institute offers numerous three-day intensive workshops on various topics related to the delivery of CBT, as well as online training, ten-week packages of individual supervision, and group consultation. For a complete listing of training and supervision opportunities, please visit https://beckinstitute.org/.

Final Thoughts

The beauty of CBT is that its fundamental principles and corresponding strategies have relevance to almost all manifestations of the human condition, as we all think about our worlds in a distinct way, and we all choose courses of behavior in order to navigate our environments. As the science underlying cognitive behavioral principles continues to be refined, so will our corresponding interventions. Thus, CBT is an example of a "living" approach to psychotherapy that continually is honed while, at the same time, retaining its fundamental principles.

I invite you to join me and thousands of other clinicians and researchers in the "CBT family" on this remarkable journey of disseminating CBT to people with mental health disorders who are in great need of quality mental health care. It is not an overstatement to say that every day you are in your office, you have the potential to witness and share in your clients' triumphs and transformations (a few of which you have read about in this volume!). The practice of CBT, as well as the corresponding understanding of its theory and eloquent research that is designed to provide empirical support, provides a great deal of gratification to those who identify with this approach. I wish you the best of luck on an enriching and meaningful journey in becoming a cognitive behavioral therapist and joining this close-knit "family."

How fitting is it, then, that I have typed the very last sentence of this volume on July 18, 2018, the 97th birthday of our "father" of CBT, Aaron T. Beck.

References

Abramowitz, J. S., & Arch, J. J. (2014). Strategies for improving long-term outcomes in cognitive behavioral therapy for obsessive-compulsive disorder: Insights from learning theory. *Cognitive and Behavioral Practice, 21*, 20–31.

Abramowitz, J. S., Deacon, B. J., & Whiteside, S. P. H. (2011). *Exposure therapy for anxiety: Principles and practice.* New York: Guilford Press.

Addis, M. E., & Martell, C. R. (2004). *Overcoming depression one step at a time: The new behavioral activation treatment to getting your life back.* Oakland, CA: New Harbinger.

Barlow, D. H., Gorman, J. M., Shear, M. K., & Woods, S. W. (2000). Cognitive-behavioral therapy, imipramine, or their combination for panic disorder: A randomized controlled trial. *JAMA, 283*, 2529–2536.

Beck, A. T., Rush, A. J., Shaw, B. F., & Emery, G. (1979). *Cognitive therapy of depression.* New York: Guilford Press.

Beck, A. T., Steer, R. A., & Brown, G. K. (1996). *Beck Depression Inventory-II: Manual.* San Antonio, TX: Pearson Clinical Assessments.

Beck, J. S. (2011). *Cognitive behavior therapy: Basics and beyond (2nd ed.).* New York: Guilford Press.

Blackledge, J. T. (2015). *Cognitive defusion in practice.* Oakland, CA: Context Press.

Bordin, E. S. (1979). The generalizability of the psychoanalytic concept of the working alliance. *Psychotherapy: Theory, Research, & Practice, 16*, 252–260.

Braun, J. D., Strunk, D. R., Sasso, K. E., & Cooper, A. A. (2015). Therapist use of Socratic questioning predicts session-to-session symptom change in cognitive therapy for depression. *Behaviour Research and Therapy, 70*, 32–37.

Bjork, R. A., & Bjork, E. L. (1992). A new theory of disuse and an old theory of stimulus fluctuation. In A. Healy, S. Kosslyn, & R. Shiffrin (Eds.), *From learning processes to cognitive processes: Essays in honor of William K. Estes* (pp. 35–67). Hillsdale, NJ: Lawrence Erlbaum and Associates.

Brown, K. W., Creswell, J. D., & Ryan, R. M. (Eds.) (2015). *Handbook of mindfulness: Theory, research, and practice.* New York: Guilford Press.

Burns, D. D., & Spangler, D. (2001). Do changes in dysfunctional attitudes mediate changes in depression and anxiety in cognitive behavioral therapy? *Behavior Therapy, 32*, 337–369.

Clore, G. L., & Palmer, J. (2009). Affective guidance of intelligent agents: How emotion controls cognition. *Cognitive Systems Research, 10*, 21–30.

Craske, M. G., Kircanski, K., Zelikowsky, M., Mystkowski, J., Chowdhury, N., & Baker, A. (2008). Optimizing inhibitory learning during exposure therapy. *Behaviour Research and Therapy, 46*, 5–27.

Craske, M. G., Treanor, M., Conway, C. C., & Zbozinek, T. (2014). Maximizing exposure therapy: An inhibitory learning approach. *Behaviour Research and Therapy, 58*, 10–23.

DeRubeis, R. J., Brotman, M. A., & Gibbons, C. J. (2005). A conceptual and methodological analysis of the nonspecific argument. *Clinical Psychology: Science and Practice, 12*, 174–183.

DeRubeis, R. J., Evans, M. D., Hollon, S. D., Garvey, M. J., Grove, W. M., & Tuason, V. B. (1990). How does cognitive therapy work? Cognitive change and symptom change in cognitive therapy and pharmacotherapy for depression. *Journal of Consulting and Clinical Psychology, 58*, 862–869.

DeRubeis, R. J., & Feeley, M. (1990). Determinants of change in cognitive therapy for depression. *Cognitive Therapy and Research, 14*, 469–482.

DeRubeis, R. J., Hollon, S. D., Amsterdam, J. D., Shelton, R. C., Young, P. R., . . ., & Gallop, R. (2005). Cognitive therapy vs medications in the treatment of moderate to severe depression. *Archives of General Psychiatry, 62*, 409–416.

Devilly, G. J., & Borkovec, T. D. (2000). Psychometric properties of the Credibility/Expectancy Questionnaire. *Journal of Behavior Therapy and Experimental Psychiatry, 31*, 73–86.

Dimidjian, S., Barrera Jr., M., Martell, C., Muñoz, R. F., & Lewinsohn, P. M. (2011). The origins and current status of behavioral activation treatments for depression. *Annual Review of Clinical Psychology, 7*, 1–38.

Dimidjian, S., Hollon, S. D., Dobson, K. S., Schmaling, K. B., Kohlenberg, R. J., . . ., & Jacobson, N. S. (2006). Randomized trial of behavioral activation, cognitive therapy, and antidepressant medication with the acute treatment of adults with major depression. *Journal of Consulting and Clinical Psychology, 74*, 658–670.

Dobson, D., & Dobson, K. S. (2009). *Evidence-based practice of cognitive-behavioral therapy.* New York: Guilford Press.

Dobson, K. S., Hollon, S. D., Dimidjian, S., Schmaling, K., Kohlenberg, R. J., . . ., & Jacobson, N. S. (2008). Randomized trial of behavioral activation, cognitive therapy, and antidepressant medication in the prevention of relapse and recurrence in major depression. *Journal of Consulting and Clinical Psychology, 76*, 468–477.

Doran, G. T. (1981). There's a S.M.A.R.T. way to write management's goals and objectives. *Management Review: AMA Forum, 70*, 35–36.

Dugas, M. J., & Robichaud, M. (2007). *Cognitive behavioral treatment for generalized anxiety disorder: From science to practice.* New York: Taylor and Francis.

Durvasula, R. (Academic). (2015). *The therapeutic relationship* [Streaming video]. Retrieved from SAGE Video.

Eells, T. D. (2007). History and current status of psychotherapy case formulation. In T. D. Eells (Ed.), *Handbook of psychotherapy case formulation (2nd ed.)* (pp. 3–32). New York: Guilford Press.

Elkin, I., Shea, M. T., Watkins, J. T., Imber, S. D., Sitsky, S. M., . . ., Parloff, M. B. (1989). NIMH Treatment of Depression Collaborative Research Program: General effectiveness of treatments. *Archives of General Psychiatry, 46*, 971–982.

Farmer, R. F., & Chapman, A. L. (2016). *Behavioral interventions in cognitive behavior therapy: Practical guidance for putting theory into action (2nd ed.)*. Washington, DC: APA Books.

Feeny, N., Hembree, E., & Zoellner, L. (2003). Myths regarding exposure for PTSD. *Cognitive and Behavioral Practice, 10,* 85–90.

Ferster, C. B. (1973). A functional analysis of depression. *American Psychologist, 28,* 857–870.

Foa, E. B., & Kozak, M. J. (1986). Emotional processing of fear: Exposure to corrective information. *Psychological Bulletin, 99,* 20–35.

Foa, E. B., Zoellner, L. A., Feeny, N. C., Hembree, E. A., & Alvarez-Conrad, J. (2002). Does imaginal exposure exacerbate PTSD symptoms? *Journal of Consulting and Clinical Psychology, 70,* 1022–1028.

Fresco, D. M., Mennin, D. S., Heimberg, R. G., & Ritter, M. (2013). Emotion regulation therapy for generalized anxiety disorder. *Cognitive and Behavioral Practice, 20,* 282–300.

Grayson, J. B., Foa, E. B., & Steketee, G. (1982). Habituation during exposure treatment: Distraction vs. attention focusing. *Behaviour Research and Therapy, 20,* 323–328.

Hayes, S. C., Luoma, J. B., Bond, F. W., Masudam, A., & Lillis, J. (2006). Acceptance and commitment therapy: Model, processes, and outcomes. *Behaviour Research and Therapy, 44,* 1–25.

Hayes, S. C., Strosahl, K. D., & Wilson, K. G. (2012). *Acceptance and commitment therapy: The process and practice of mindful change (2nd ed.)*. New York: Guilford Press.

Hembree, E. A., Foa, E. B., Dorfan, N. M., Street, G. P., Kowalski, J., & Tu, X., (2003). Do patients drop out prematurely from exposure therapy for PTSD? *Journal of Traumatic Stress, 16,* 552–562.

Hofmann, S. G. (2004). Cognitive mediation of treatment change in social phobia. *Journal of Consulting and Clinical Psychology, 72,* 392–399.

Hofmann, S. G., Meuret, A. E., Rosenfield, D., Suvak, M. K., Barlow, D. H. . . ., & Woods, S. W. (2007). Preliminary evidence for cognitive mediation during cognitive behavioral therapy of panic disorder. *Journal of Consulting and Clinical Psychology, 75,* 374–379.

Hollon, S. D., DeRubeis, R. J., Shelton, R. C., Amsterdam, J. D., Salomen, R. M., . . . Gallop, R. (2005). Prevention of relapse following cognitive therapy vs. medications in moderate to severe depression. *Archives of General Psychiatry, 62,* 417–422.

Greenberger, D., & Padesky, C. A. (2016). *Mind over mood: Change how you feel by changing the way you think (2nd ed.)*. New York: Guilford Press.

Jacobson, N. S., Dobson, K. S., Truax, P. A., Addis, M. E., Koerner, K., . . ., & Prince, S. E. (1996). A component analysis of cognitive– behavioral treatment for depression. *Journal of Consulting and Clinical Psychology, 64,* 295–304.

Joyce, A. S., & Piper, W. E. (1998). Expectancy, the therapeutic alliance, and treatment outcome in short-term individual psychotherapy. *The Journal of Psychotherapy Practice and Research, 7,* 236–248.

Kabat-Zinn, J. (1994). *Wherever you go, there you are: Mindfulness meditation in everyday life.* New York: Hyperion.

Kabat-Zinn, J. (2003). Mindfulness-based interventions in context: Past, present, and future. *Clinical Psychology: Science and Practice, 10,* 144–156.

Kazantzis, N., Brownfield, N. R., Mosely, L., Usatoff, A. S., & Flighty, S. I. (2017). Homework in cognitive behavioural therapy: A systematic review of adherence assessment in anxiety and depression (2011–2016). *Psychiatric Clinics of North America, 40,* 625–639.

Kazantzis, N., Luong, H. K., Usatoff, A. S., Impala, T., Yew, R. Y., & Hofmann, S. G. (2018). The processes of cognitive behavioral therapy: A meta-analysis. *Cognitive Therapy and Research.42*(4), 349–357.

Kazantzis, N., Whittington, C., & Dattilio, F. (2010). Meta-analysis of homework effects in cognitive and behavioral therapy: A replication and extension. *Clinical Psychology: Science and Practice, 17*, 144–156.

Kazantzis, N., Whittington, C., Zelenchich, L., Kyrios, M., Norton, P. J., & Hofmann, S. G. (2016). Quantity and quality of homework compliance: A meta-analysis of relations with outcome in cognitive behavior therapy. *Behavior Therapy, 47*, 755–772.

Kroenke, K., Spitzer, R. L., & Williams, J. B. (2001). The PHQ-9: Validity of a brief depression severity measure. *Journal of General Internal Medicine, 16*, 606–613.

Kuyken, W., Padesky, C. A., & Dudley, R. (2009). *Collaborative case conceptualization: Working effectively with clients in cognitive behavioral therapy*. New York: Guilford Press.

Lang, A. J., & Craske, M. G. (2000). Manipulations of exposure-based therapy to reduce return of fear: A replication. *Behaviour Research and Therapy, 38*, 1–12.

Lejuez, C. W., Hopko, D. R., Acierno, R., Daughters, S. B., & Pagoto, S. L. (2011). Ten year revision of the brief behavioral activation treatment for depression (BATD): Revised treatment manual (BATD-R). *Behavior Modification, 35*, 111–161.

Lejuez, C. W., Hopko, D. R., & Hopko, S. D. (2001). A brief behavioral activation treatment for depression. *Behavior Modification, 25*, 255–286.

Lench, H. C., Darbor, K. E., & Berg, L. A. (2013). Functional perspectives on emotion, behavior, and cognition. *Behavioral Sciences, 3*, 536–540.

Lench, H. C., & Levine, L. J. (2005). Effects of fear on risk and control judgments and memory: Implications for health promotion messages. *Cognition and Emotion, 19*, 1049–1069.

Lewinsohn, P. M. (1974). A behavioral approach to depression. In R. M. Friedman & M. M. Katz (Eds.), *The psychology of depression: Contemporary theory and research* (pp. 157–185). New York: Wiley.

Linehan, M. M. (1993). *Cognitive-behavioral treatment of borderline personality disorder*. New York: Guilford Press.

Linehan, M. M. (2015). *DBT skills training manual*. New York:Guilford Press.

MacPhillamy, D. J., & Lewinsohn, P. M. (1971). *The Pleasant Events Schedule*. Unpublished manuscript, University of Oregon, Eugene, OR.

Martell, C. R., Addis, M. E., & Jacobson, N. S. (2001). *Depression in context: Strategies for guided action*. New York: Norton.

Martell, C. R., Dimidjian, S., & Herman-Dunn, R. (2010). *Behavioral activation for depression: A clinician's guide*. New York: Guilford Press.

Martin, D. J., Garske, J. P., & Davis, M. K. (2000). Relation of the therapeutic alliance with outcome and other variables: A meta-analytic review. *Journal of Consulting and Clinical Psychology, 68*, 438–450.

Masley, S. A., Gillanders, D. T., Simpson, S. G., & Taylor, M. A. (2012). A systematic review of the evidence base for schema therapy. *Cognitive Behaviour Therapy, 41*, 185–202.

Miller, W. R., & Rollnick, S. (2013). *Motivational interviewing: Helping people change (3rd ed)*. New York: Guilford Press.

Morina, N., Ijntema, H., Meyerbröker, K., & Emmelkamp, P. M. G. (2015). Can virtual reality exposure therapy gains be generalized to real-life? A meta-analysis of studies applying behavioral assessments. *Behaviour Research and Therapy, 74*, 18–24.

Muñoz, R. F., Ippen, C. G., Rao, S., Le, H., & Dwyer, E. V. (2000). *Manual for group cognitive behavioral therapy of major depression: A reality management approach.* http://i4health.paloaltou.edu/downloads/CBT_Instructor_English.pdf.

Najavits, L. M. (2015). The problem of drop-out from "gold standard" PTSD therapies. *F1000 Prime Reports, 7,* 43.

National Collaborating Centre for Mental Health (2009). *Borderline personality disorder: The NICE guidelines for treatment and management.* London: The British Psychological Society and The Royal College of Psychiatrists.

Neff, K. (2011). *Self-compassion: The power of being kind to yourself.* New York: HarperCollins.

Newman, C. F. (2007). The therapeutic relationship in cognitive therapy with difficult-to-engage clients. In P. Gilbert & R. L. Leahy (Eds.), *The therapeutic relationship in the cognitive behavioral psychotherapies* (pp. 166–184). New York: Routledge.

Nezu, A. M., Nezu, C. M., & D'Zurilla, T. J. (2013). *Problem solving therapy: A treatment manual.* New York: Springer.

O'Donohue, W. T., & Cucciare, M. A. (Eds.) (2008). *Terminating psychotherapy: A clinician's guide.* New York: Routledge.

Olatunji, B. O., Deacon, B. J., & Abramowitz, J. S. (2009). The cruelest cure? Ethical issues in the implementation of exposure-based treatments. *Cognitive and Behavioral Practice, 16,* 172–180.

Opriş, D., Pintea, S., García-Palacios, C., Botella, C., Szamosközi, Ş., & David, D. (2012). Virtual reality exposure therapy in anxiety disorders: A quantitative meta-analysis. *Depression and Anxiety, 29,* 85–93.

Persons, J. B. (2008). *The case-formulation approach to cognitive-behavior therapy.* New York: Guilford Press.

Persons, J. B., & Hong, J. J. (2016). Case formulation and the outcome of cognitive behaviour therapy. In N. Tarrier & J. Johnson (Eds.), *Case formulation in cognitive behaviour therapy: The treatment of challenging and complex cases (2nd ed.)* (pp. 14–37). New York: Routledge.

Rowe, M. K., & Craske, M. G. (1998). Effects of varied-stimulus exposure training on fear reduction and return of fear. *Behaviour Research and Therapy, 36,* 719–734.

Safran, J. D., Crocker, P., McMain, S., & Murray, P. (1990). Therapeutic alliance rupture as a therapy event for empirical investigation. *Psychotherapy: Theory, Research, Practice, and Training, 27,* 154–165.

Safran, J. D., Muran, J. C., & Eubanks-Carter, C. (2011). Repairing alliance ruptures. *Psychotherapy: Theory, Research, Practice, and Training, 48,* 80–87.

Safren, S. A., Heimberg, R. G., & Juster, H. B. (1997). Clients' expectancies and their relationship to pretreatment symptomatology and outcome of cognitive-behavioral group treatment for social phobia. *Journal of Consulting and Clinical Psychology, 65,* 694–698.

Safren, S. A., O'Cleirish, C., Tan, J., Raminani, S., Reilly, L. C., . . ., & Mayer, K. H. (2009). A randomized controlled trial of cognitive behavioral therapy for adherence and depression (CBT-AD) in HIV-infected individuals. *Health Psychology, 28,* 1–10.

Schwarz, N., & Clore, G. L. (1983). Mood, misattribution, and judgments of well-being: Informative and directive functions of affective states. *Journal of Personality and Social Psychology, 45,* 513–523

Segal, Z. V., Williams, J. M. G., & Teasdale, T. D. (2013). *Mindfulness-based cognitive therapy for depression (2nd ed.).* New York: Guilford Press.

Shapiro, A. K., & Shapiro, E. (1997). *The powerful placebo: From ancient priest to modern physician*. Baltimore, MD: Johns Hopkins University Press.

Shelder, J. (2015) The therapy relationship in psychodynamic therapy versus CBT. *Psychology Today*. March 18. www.psychologytoday.com/blog/psychologically-minded/201503/the-therapy-relationship-in-psychodynamic-therapy-versus-cbt.

Sichel, D. A., & Driscoll, J. W. (1999). *Women's moods: What every woman must know about hormones, the brain, and emotional health*. New York: HarperCollins.

Siev, J., & Chambless, D. L. (2007). Specificity of treatment effects: Cognitive therapy and relaxation for generalized anxiety and panic disorders. *Journal of Consulting and Clinical Psychology, 75*, 513–522.

Sotsky, S. M., Glass, D. R., Shea, M. T., Pilkonis, P. A., Collins, J. F., Elkin, I., Watkins, J. T., et al. (1991). Patient predictors of response to psychotherapy and pharmacotherapy: Findings in the NIMH Treatment of Depression Collaborative Research Program. *American Journal of Psychiatry, 148*, 997–1008.

Stice, E., Rohde, P., Seeley, J. R., & Gau, J. M. (2010). Testing mediators of intervention effects in randomized controlled trials: An evaluation of three depression prevention programs. *Journal of Consulting and Clinical Psychology, 78*, 273–280.

Storberk, J., & Clore, G. L. (2007). On the interdependence of cognition and emotion. *Cognition and Emotion, 21*, 1212–1237.

Strauss, J. L., Hayes, A. M., Johnson, S. L., Newman, C. F., Brown, G. K., . . ., & Beck, A. T. (2006). Early alliance, alliance ruptures, and symptom change in a nonrandomized trial of cognitive therapy for avoidant and obsessive-compulsive personality disorders. *Journal of Consulting and Clinical Psychology, 74*, 337–345.

Sudak, D. M., Codd, R. T. III, Ludgate, J. W., Sokol, L., Fox, M. G., . . ., & Milne, D. (2016). *Teaching and supervising cognitive behavioral therapy*. Hoboken, NJ: John Wiley & Sons.

Webb, C. A., DeRubeis, R. J., Amsterdam, J. D., Shelton, R. C., Hollon, S. D., & Dimidjian, S. (2011). Two aspects of the therapeutic alliance: Differential relations with depressive symptom change. *Journal of Consulting and Clinical Psychology, 79*, 279–283.

Wenzel, A. (2012). Modification of core beliefs in cognitive therapy. In I. R. de Oliveira (Ed.), *Cognitive behavioral therapy* (pp. 17–34). Rijeka, Croatia: Intech (available online at www.intechopen.com)

Wenzel, A. (2013). *Strategic decision making in cognitive behavioral therapy*. Washington, DC: APA Books.

Wenzel, A. (2017). *Innovations in cognitive behavioral therapy: Creative interventions for strategic practice*. New York: Routledge.

Wenzel, A., Brown, G. K., & Karlin, B. E. (2011). *Cognitive behavioral therapy for depressed Veterans and Military servicemembers: Therapist manual*. Washington, DC: U.S. Department of Veterans Affairs.

Wenzel, A., Jeglic, E. L., Levy-Mack, H. J., Beck, A. T., & Brown, G. K. (2008). Treatment attitude and therapy outcome in patients with borderline personality disorder. *Journal of Cognitive Psychotherapy, 22*, 250–257.

Westra, H. A., Arkowitz, H., & Dozois, S. J. A. (2009). Adding a motivational interviewing pretreatment to cognitive behavioral therapy for generalized anxiety disorder: A preliminary randomized controlled trial. *Journal of Anxiety Disorders, 23*, 1106–1117.

Westra, H. A., Aviram, A., & Doell, F. K. (2011). Extending motivational interviewing to the treatment of major mental health problems: Current directions and evidence. *The Canadian Journal of Psychiatry, 56*, 643–650.

Wolpe, J. (Ed.) (1959). *Psychotherapy based on the principle of reciprocal inhibition.* Oxford: Prentice-Hall.

Young, J. E., & Beck, A. T. (1980). *Cognitive Therapy Scale rating manual.* Unpublished manuscript, University of Pennsylvania, Philadelphia, PA.

Young, J. E., Klosko, J. S., & Weishaar, M. E. (2003). *Schema therapy: A practitioner's guide.* New York: Guilford Press.

Zayfert, C., DeViva, J. C., Becker, C. B., Pile, J. L., Gillock, K. L., & Hayes, S. A. (2005). Exposure utilization and completion of cognitive behavioral therapy for PTSD in a "real world" clinical practice. *Journal of Traumatic Stress, 18*, 637–645.

Index

FSC
www.fsc.org
MIX
Papier | Fördert gute Waldnutzung
FSC® C083411

Kolibri 360 GmbH
Ferdinand-Jühlke-Straße 7
99095 Erfurt, Deutschland
produktsicherheit@kolibri360.de